Heathrow

From Tents to Terminal 5

Ian Anderson

BSc, CEng, MICE, MIStructE

First published 2014

Amberley Publishing
The Hill, Stroud
Gloucestershire, GL5 4EP

www.amberley-books.com

British Library Cataloguing in Publication Data.
A catalogue record for this book is available from the British Library.

ISBN 978 1 4456 3389 3
EBook ISBN 978 1 4456 3401 2

Typeset in 10pt on 12pt Sabon.
Typesetting and Origination by Amberley Publishing.
Printed in the UK.

Contents

Acknowledgements

I would like to thank the following for their invaluable assistance with piecing together the complicated history of Heathrow buildings and facilities, and providing photos in some cases. Some photographs are included for their rarity value because they illustrate specific subjects, but their origins are uncertain. While I have made every effort to contact the original owners of some of the photographs used, some proved impossible, so I apologise if names have been omitted. The excellent Air Britain Information Exchange (ABIX) has been an ever-interesting source of information and anecdotes about Heathrow. The Airfield Information Exchange (ARG-AIX) has also been helpful. I would like to single out a few for special praise, Geoff Ambrose for statistics and other snippets, Pete Bish (ex-CAA) for assistance with ATC matters, Peter W. Dance (AB) for information on dates, scans and 1953 Air Race, Mike Doyle (AB) for Heathrow Express photos and other snippets, Robert Heffernan and Carol Morgan (Institution of Civil Engineers) and Rob Thomas (Institution of Structural Engineers) who have sourced many of the technical papers, Iain Hill of Severfield-Watson Steel, for A380 hangar modifications, John McCrickard (AB) for Heathrow Express and early Ministry of Aviation publications, Phil Spencer (AB) for his help with the 1953 Air Race, Tony Szulc (AB) who has laboured taking many photographs of the hangars and provided other sources, Mick West (AB) for patiently providing any number of photos, links and general help with others and history, and Charles Woodley (AB) for his help with source material.

I would also like to thank the following who provided photos (even if in the end, regrettably there was insufficient space to include them), and/or information snippets: Neil Aird (AB), Geoff Ambrose (AB), Joe Barr (AB), Douglas Bastin (AB), Richard Biggins (Gibberd Architects), Graeme Bolton (AL), John Carter, Kevin Colbran (AB), Barry J. Collman (AB), David Cottam, Martyn Davies (geograph), Trevor Davics (AB), Mike Doyle, Tony Doyle (AB), Ken Ede (AB), Dave Fagan (AB), Richard Flagg (ARG), Paul Francis (ARG), John Hamlin (AB), Tony Hart (AB), Iain Hill (Severfield-Watson Steel), Paul Howard (AB), Frank Hudson (AB), Mike Hudson (AB), Allan Huse (AL), Paul Langfermann (AL), Bernard Martin (AB), Brendan McCartney (AB), Roger Mardon (fire stations), Carol Morgan (Institution of Civil Engineers), Geoffrey Negus (AB), Brian G. Nicholls (AB), Daniel Nicholson (AL), Peter Norris (AB), Thomas Nugent (geograph), Donna O'Brien (BAA), Malcolm Powles (Amey), Andres Ramirez (AL), Juan Rodriguez (AL), John Salmon (geograph), Ken Shadbolt, Philip Sherwood, Colin Smith (AB), John Tietjen (AB), Jody Webster (geograph), John Wegg (AB), Dave Welch (AB).

Abbreviations used above: (AB)=Air Britain, (ARG)=Airfield Research Group, (AL)=airliners.net, geograph=Geograph website.

Ian Anderson, 23 Jan 2014

Introduction

IATA Code: LHR, ICAO Code: EGLL
Elevation AMSL: 83ft/25m, Co-ordinates 51.4775 N, 0.46139 W
Runways: 09L/27R 3901m/12799ft asphalt, 09R/27L 3660m/12008ft asphalt
Aircraft movements 2012: 471,791, Passengers 2012: 70,037,417

Living in Hanworth, near Heathrow, from a young age, an early experience of Heathrow was in the mid-1950s as a youngster on horseback within the spectator area in the Central Area. Being a short cycle/bus ride away led to a lifelong interest in aircraft from about 1958, beginning at Heathrow with piston and turbine engined airliners and the early jetliners. A move to Sussex in 1960, a cycle ride away from the then new Gatwick, allowed the interest to continue. I became a Chartered Civil and Structural Engineer, working on the design of buildings and bridges, now retired, having latterly been Deputy Structures Manager in Suffolk County Council's Bridges team. I have had a growing interest in historic structures for most of my forty-odd years career, so it was opportune when someone at work suggested me to succeed the retiring East Anglian representative on the Institution of Civil Engineers (ICE) Panel for Historic Engineering Works (PHEW) in early 2002. In general the terms of reference of PHEW are to record those structures/works where they are rare in the region/country, unusual, the earliest, the largest. So it was inevitable that I was asked to become the Panel convenor on aircraft hangars, recording significant UK examples. Some of these were at Heathrow as the earliest of their type, including the three-bay alloy hangar as it became known, the first aluminium hangar in the world, the BEA complex using prestressed concrete, the BOAC headquarters hangar (now called TBA), BOAC's Wing Hangar, the BOAC 747 hangar and BEA's Cathedral hangar. Nearby Heston has the first reinforced concrete hangar in the UK, still used. Being a member of the Airfield Research Group (ARG), I had written up specific hangars across the UK for Airfield Review, the organ of ARG and, having done a series on the Heathrow hangars, I began a summary of Heathrow building history by way of background. The book grew way beyond an article, and having ascertained that quite a few aircraft enthusiasts would be interested in a book about Heathrow infrastructure including its hangars and buildings, I decided that a book was necessary, although it probably only scratches the surface of a lot of other upgrading operations, particularly recently as Heathrow Airports Ltd begins its next programme of £600 million per annum expenditure between 2014–19. With its familiar Star of David pattern of runways, only the two East–West runways are in use now, as the buildings have grown to fill every available building plot over the years. The current vision is of a toast rack array of parallel north-south terminals, allowing easier access to taxiways and runways. Currently, the talk is all about airport capacity and runways in the South East, but I feel sure that Heathrow will figure largely in the debate for some years to come.

Beginnings

1.1. THE FIRST ORDNANCE SURVEY LINE

The Ordnance Survey can trace its beginning to a triangulation survey carried out for King George III and The Royal Society between 1784 and 1790. This was to determine the relative positions of, and distance between the Greenwich Observatory and L'Observatoire de Paris. Major General William Roy FRS RE carried it out under the authority of the Master General of the Board of Ordnance. Roy's first action was to measure a survey base line across Hounslow Heath in the summer of 1784. He measured a 5.5 mile base line using glass rods as part of the very first triangulation survey. One end was at Kings Arbour in Heathrow, the other at Hampton Poor House. The third point of the triangle was at St Ann's Hill, Chertsey. He had come up with the idea of a triangulation survey of the country in 1763 to produce a complete map, laying the foundations for the Ordnance Survey, but his idea was not taken up until the Paris Observatory suggested to George III in 1783, that a triangulation network survey of south-east England to connect with the French network could determine the relative positions of the Greenwich and Paris observatories. The base line as measured by Roy was 27,404.01ft, and 27,406.19ft in 1858 (5.19 miles/8.35 km) by the Ordnance Survey geodesist Alexander Ross Clarke. A cannon replaced the original post at Heathrow in 1791, set with the muzzle upright in the ground. In 1926 on the 200th birthday of this 'Father of the Ordnance Survey' (which was 4 May 1726) a commemorative plaque was placed on the cannon. Both cannon and plaque were removed for the construction of the new airport in 1944. They were returned later to near the site a few feet north of the North Perimeter Road adjacent to Nene Road, 200 metres east of the tunnel, next to a taxi rank, in 1968. The south-east-terminal, appropriately at Roy Grove, Hampton-upon-Thames, is also marked by a cannon and plaque.

1.2. EXISTING LAND USE

Originally the Heathrow area, whose brick earth overlay gravel and was therefore well drained, was regarded as Grade 1 land by the Ministry of Agriculture, and was used for orchards and cereal crops, but mainly market gardening. The brick earth was also suitable for bricks. The Great West Road from Chiswick to Bath Road was opened by King George V in 1925, and was reputedly the UK's first dual carriageway; 3 miles from Heathrow, it allowed fruit and vegetables from the area to be more speedily transported to Covent Garden market. One year later the extension of the Great South West Road, the start of the A30, bypassed Hounslow Heath to join up with the Great West Road east of Heathrow, creating the familiar two sides of the triangle of roads surrounding the airport.

1.3. PERRY OAKS SLUDGE DISPOSAL WORKS

Between 1931 and 1935, the West Middlesex Drainage Scheme was constructed to replace twenty-eight old district sewage works with 70 miles of new sewers, leading to a large new works at Mogden, Isleworth; it served an area of 160 sq. miles, and an eventual planned population of 2 million. The scheme was opened on 23 October 1936 by Sir Kingsley Wood, the Minister of Health. Perry Oaks sludge disposal works was an important part of the scheme. The original site, occupying 220 acres, was bought by Middlesex County Council on 12 June 1931 for £33,000 from W. Whittington, who also occupied Perry Oaks Farm on the opposite side of Tithe Barn Lane. The eventual site of 250 acres on the west edge took sludge, separated from the main sewage works at Mogden, in a pumped pipeline 7 miles to Perry Oaks in twin twelve-inch cast-iron pipes with an 18-inch cast-iron pipe draining back to the Bath Road sewer. At Perry Oaks there were settling lagoons to reduce the water content of the sludge; the dried sludge was like a cake after water removal and was taken by tanker to be used as fertiliser on agricultural land. In 1952 the pipes were diverted, in a subway for maintenance, so as to run south under the west end of the north runway, which was being reconstructed at the time.

1.4. NEARBY AIRFIELDS

Near to Heathrow were other pioneering airfields. Hounslow Heath was used in the First World War for training and Zeppelin defence. After the First World War, Hounslow Heath reopened as London's first airport, and pioneered the first international civil passenger flight to Paris, before opening up the Empire route to Australia in 1919. The aerodrome closed in March 1920, all services transferring to Croydon. The original buildings burnt down in 1929, by which time Croydon had become London's main airport. By the end of the Second World War it was obvious that Croydon, with no hard runways and being surrounded by developments, was not suitable as London's airport. Similarly, Hanworth (opened in 1917 as the Whitehead factory test and delivery airfield, closed in 1918, then reopened in 1928) and Heston (opened in 1929) were not capable of expansion for modern airliners after the Second World War.

1.5. FAIREY'S GREAT WEST AERODROME

1.5.1. Fairey's were testing aircraft at RAF Northolt, but were told to quit by the end of 1929. When Richard Fairey bought the first few acres of market gardening land from the vicar of Harmondsworth in December 1928 to build what became Fairey's Great West Aerodrome (eventually occupying 240 acres), he could not have foreseen the growth of what is now the UK's largest airport and the world's busiest international airport, carrying over 67 million passengers and 1.3 million tons of cargo over 450,000 aircraft movements each year; over ninety airlines, including British Airways, bmi and Virgin Atlantic, use Heathrow as their main hub. Of the 67 million passengers, 11 per cent are for internal flights, 43 per cent short-haul international and 46 per cent long-haul.

1.5.2. Fairey's bought 71 acres on 31 January 1929 from Revd R. Ross, the vicar of Harmondsworth; a further three plots, totalling 78 acres, were added in 1929, followed by 29 acres in 1930, 12 acres in 1939, 38 acres in 1942 and 10 in 1943, making 240 acres in all by 1943. Fairey's built their main hangar in the north-east corner (size given as 87 feet x 270 feet in 1937 *Air Pilot*) with FAIREY in capitals emblazoned on the roof, as well as a concrete apron and surround by spring 1930. The main grass surface was prepared by Hunters of Chester, who performed similar work on many pre-war aerodromes. The airfield was formally opened on 28 June 1930, the same day as the 11th RAF Pageant at Hendon. Within the month the first aircraft had been rigged and flight-tested: a Firefly II biplane. The second hangar was built in 1937. In all, some 1,500 aircraft, built at their nearby factory at Hayes, were finally assembled and tested at Fairey's Great West Aerodrome. Heathrow was also the scene for a series of Royal Aeronautical Society garden parties in 1935, 1936, 1937 and 1939. Wartime production at the main Hayes factory initially went to Heathrow, but by 1943 the first steps were being taken to acquire the land for the future airport. Fairey's finally quit Heathrow in July 1945, moving to Heston, then White Waltham. The first Fairey's hangar on the north-east corner, the last remaining vestige, was visible for many years until 1964 on the east side of the Central Area, housing the London Airport firefighting unit; it was only removed after compensation had been agreed with Fairey's over the eviction from the Great West Aerodrome.

Heathrow Confidential

The Air Ministry requisitioned land in and around the village of Heath Row, including the aerodrome, and work on construction started in May 1944, the official explanation being to develop it into a major transport base for the RAF to be used to carry troops to the Far East. However, the government always intended it to be a civil airport, and the RAF base was a ruse to circumvent a public inquiry. Harold Balfour in his autobiography, *Wings over Westminster*, admitted that when he was Parliamentary Undersecretary of State from 1938 to 1944 he deceived the cabinet committee over the requisitioning of land for post-war needs, by claiming it was needed for a bomber base. This allowed the requisitioning of land under emergency powers to circumvent usual peacetime procedures and prevented any appeal. The end of the Second World War saw the RAF 'plans' change to a large expansion of civil aviation instead. By then an RAF control tower had been built on the north side, close to the present police station.

2.1. LONDON AIRPORT OFFICIALLY

2.1.1. After the Second World War the airfield was operated by the RAF for a few months, but Donald Bennett of Pathfinder fame had by this time founded British South American Airways and wanted to use Heathrow for international services. He got permission to land the first civil aircraft – G-AGWG *Starlight*, a Lancastrian – at the proposed airport on 6 December 1945. Heathrow was officially handed over to the Air Ministry on 1 January 1946, and BSAA claimed another first when the same Lancastrian took off for Lisbon on the same day on a proving flight to Buenos Aires, South America. The last RAF personnel were withdrawn on 25 January 1946. On 13 March it was announced that Heston would close as it was just over a mile from the end of runway No. 1 and too close to be safe. On 25 March 1946 the airport was officially named London Airport by the Minister of Aviation, Lord Winster, with a selection of aircraft expected to use it. These included BSAA Lancastrian G-AGPV, RAF Avro York MW128, Avro Tudor 1 prototype G-AGRC, Bristol 170 prototype G-AGPV, RAF HP Halifax C.VIII PP280, BOAC Dakota G-AGNC, Auster J/1 G-AGTY, Avro 19 G-AGPG, BOAC Avro York G-AGNX, Miles Aerovan 2 G-AGWO, Miles M28 G-AGVX, Percival Proctor V G-AGTC and Vickers Viking G-AGOM.

2.1.2. On 10 April in the House of Lords, the Minister for Civil Aviation, Lord Winster, was asked about the development of the London Airport at Heathrow by his predecessor Viscount Swinton. Lord Winster summarised the current position in regard to the immediate and long-

Above right: Heathrow, original 1945 three-storey brick RAF control tower with room on top, on the north side plus spectators enclosure and ubiquitous chestnut paling fence, with notice for 'Airport Tours Start Here'. (John Carter)

Right: Heathrow aerial photo from NE, late 1940s, with full Star of David runway layout complete, the initial eight B1 hangars lower left, Fairey hangar in the centre, Perry Oaks Sludge Disposal Works at top and north side terminal buildings on right. Note the old and newer Runway 6 at the top, moved out to allow Central Area buildings. (via Doug Bastin)

Heathrow north side buildings 6 July 1953, from spectators enclosure, with SAS DC6 plus DC4. Note the array of hats. (John Carter)

Heathrow, North side, BOAC Lancastrian loading passengers on what looks a windy wet day. (via Philip Sherwood)

term futures. He also referred to a plan showing the three-runway extension to the north of Bath Road. *Flight* for 25 April 1946 reported the statement almost verbatim, as follows:

The site is only about 12 miles from the centre of London and, being on the west side of the capital, it is comparatively free from industrial haze and has a favourable meteorological record. It has good road access, and this will be better still when certain plans, which the Minister of Transport has under consideration, have been carried out. The land is remarkably level, both on the site and in the surrounding area, and the gravel subsoil has excellent bearing and drainage qualities. To meet the need for a major air terminal to serve London, fifty-two sites were surveyed, and no better site for the purpose could be found than the one at Heathrow.

One of the runways, 9,000 feet long, is now completed and is in use. Two subsidiary runways 6,000 feet long are in an advanced state of construction and will be ready in July. Until permanent buildings are erected, passenger-handling facilities will be provided in temporary hutted accommodation between the main runway and the Bath Road.

As regards further development, the total area of land which, subject to Parliamentary approval, will be acquired is something over 4,000 acres. It extends both north and south of the Bath Road. The ultimate airfield layout will consist of three sets of parallel runways – nine in all – with the terminal area in a central position. The runways will vary in length between 9,200 and 5,300 feet, but one can be extended, if necessary to 15,000 feet and another to 12,000 feet. Three runways will be capable of use at a time, and the maximum capacity of the airport when entirely completed (in accordance with the accompanying diagram), will be 160 aircraft movements an hour in good weather and 120 aircraft movements in bad weather. One take-off or one landing each counts as one aircraft movement.

Many different runway designs, including the much-debated tangential pattern, have been considered. In order to have the best possible advice, consideration of the runway layout was referred to a committee on which outside experts as well as Ministry staff served.

Although nine runways are to be available when the airport is fully developed, the plan actually shows ten. The explanation is that one of the runways – marked 3 on the plan – will, in due course cease to be as such, but all except a small portion of it will be used for other purposes. If this runway had been retained as such in the final plan, a greatly inferior layout would have resulted, and the terminal area, which must be centrally situated, would have been badly cramped.

The Buildings: The terminal building is intended to be worthy of London's main airport and all necessary steps will be taken to ensure this result. In addition to bays for aircraft loading, traffic handling, accommodation, rooms for aircraft employees and for operators staff, there will also be all the amenities which a passenger would expect to find at a first-class airport. The total area of land required is extensive, but not when considered in relation to the capacity of the airport. The main reasons for so large a tract of land are the need for long runways for safe operation in all weather conditions by large modern aircraft, the wide separation between runways essential for safety reasons, particularly in bad visibility, the large terminal area required for passenger handling and related activities, and the generous space which must be allowed for hangarage. The area south of the Bath Road will be fully developed as rapidly as circumstances allow, so as to provide six runways in all. Development of the area north of the present Bath Road, which will have to be diverted to the north of the new boundary, will not start for at least five years.

This phasing of the work will fit in with the need to minimise demolitions while the present housing shortage continues, and to keep the maximum amount of agricultural land in cultivation for the next few years. The Government is aware of the anxiety which has been felt, and expressed, by residents in the area, and will endeavour to mitigate hardship, and in the event of a continuance of housing shortage in this area in five years time, the Government will arrange with the local authorities concerned to provide houses in place of any which have to be demolished. One of the reasons which led to the siting of the London Airport in this district was that it could be done with the minimum disturbance of householders. Compensation will, of course, be payable for houses and other buildings demolished, on the basis prescribed in the relevant statutes. Steps will be taken to mitigate the loss of agricultural land, and to make as good use as possible of available land during the conduct of the operations.

The area contains some buildings of archaeological or historic interest, and the plans for the development of the airport have been so framed that there will be the minimum disturbance of such buildings.

The airport at Heston has become completely out of date and, owing to its proximity to the new London Airport, will have to go out of use as an airfield. The land thus made available will do much to compensate for the loss of the building and agricultural land which will be absorbed by the new airport. The buildings at Heston will prove to be of great value to the British airline operators for various non-flying purposes, such as the accommodation of stores and motor transport.

Following the Minister's statement, further questions were asked about access to the airport, to which he replied that he and the Minister of Transport were alive to the road access as well as rail transport in conjunction with the main railways and London Passenger Transport Board. Finality on the matter could not be reached until there was a decision on the ultimate location of a terminal building for our airlines. For airport employees access would probably be by extending the Underground from Hounslow West to the airport.

The Minister added that Commonwealth and transatlantic services would be able to use Heathrow this summer, as soon as the first three runways were completed.

Viscount Swinton stated that he had no doubt that Heathrow was the one and only possible site for a great London airport. It had been considered by the RAF really as a civil aviation problem before the Ministry of Civil Aviation had been created. He said that when he went into office he considered it his duty to go into the matter afresh with an entirely open mind and to view all possible sites. He continued: 'Not only did it appear to me quite conclusively that Heathrow was the best site, but I say it without the least hesitation that it was the only possible site on which a great airport for London could be built.'

2.1.3. The first foreign aircraft to use Heathrow was PP-PCF, a Lockheed L-049

Constellation of Panair Do Brasil, after a proving flight from Rio on 16 April 1946. The first BOAC aircraft away was a Lancastrian, G-AGLS, on 28 May to Australia. The airport was officially opened on 31 May 1946 by Lord Winster. Also on that date the first Pan American and American Overseas Airlines Constellations arrived from New York. In July 1946, BOAC transferred transatlantic and Empire services from Hurn to Heathrow, while short-haul services by other airlines used Northolt until facilities at Heathrow were ready. By September 1946, the original caravans and marquees for passengers were being replaced with prefabricated buildings, mainly single storey, to remain in use until the Central Area buildings were complete from 1955, or 1962 in the case of the intercontinental airlines.

2.2. RUNWAY LAYOUT DECIDED

In late January 1947 the *Report of the London Airport Advisory Layout Panel* was published, recommending a triple parallel pattern of runway system by superimposing a second triangle on the original RAF triangle, and the laying down of a third triangle north of the Bath Road. They confirmed retention of two of the three RAF runways, but the third runway would be built further west, making room for the Central Area terminals and tower in the middle of the double triangle. The stages of development were:

    Stage I, completion of the RAF scheme.
    Stage II, the dual runway system south of the A4 Bath Road, with most of the Central Area
    aprons and parts of the terminals completed.
    Stage III, extending runways westwards and the three runways north of the Bath Road.

The last stage was later modified to two divergent runways, but eventually dropped completely, to resurface as the third runway issue in the 2000s. The final area was 2,705 acres. The extra runways involved the excavation of 10 million cu. yds of earth, and filling in 80 acres of old gravel pits. So the familiar Star of David pattern of runways was begun. The twin runway system allowed one to be used for take-offs and one for landing simultaneously, avoiding collisions and increasing capacity. The double triangle arrangement allowed aircraft to use the subsidiary runways as taxiways and as run-up areas before take-off. Also the twin runways would allow maintenance on one, while using the other.

2.3. RIVER DIVERSIONS AND RAINWATER DISPOSAL

The original development involved diversion of two rivers, the Longford River, said to have been cut on the orders of Charles II to feed the Hampton Court fountains, and the Duke of Northumberland's River, which was from the Napoleonic era for the said duke, so that barges could reach his gunpowder mill on Hounslow Heath. Both rivers emanated from the same source, the River Colne. Construction squared off the south-west corner by running the two rivers in artificial channels for over a mile, not the last time they would need alteration. Rainfall on the 2 million sq. yds of concrete runways and taxiways could not be easily drained to the existing Longford and Duke's Rivers as they would flood, so large balancing reservoirs were built south of the A30 Great South West Road and south-east of the airport, each side of the A312, to hold rainwater temporarily and release gradually into the River Crane 1 mile to the east. These reservoirs are still visible and used today, albeit supplemented by other rainfall disposal measures.

2.4. EARLY TERMINALS NORTH SIDE

The early terminals were ex-military marquees forming a tented village along Bath Road, the A4, on the north side, known as London Airport North, until new buildings were completed in the 1950s. To reach the aircraft, duckboards had to be placed to miss the mud, and the tents were cold in winter and hot in summer. By the end of the year, 63,000 passengers had passed through the new airport, the number rising to 796,000 by 1951. The tents were replaced by prefabricated buildings, which were used by intercontinental passengers through to 1961, when Terminal 3 in the Central Area was opened. London Airport North also handled freight through to the 1960s, until a new cargo area was built on the south side.

2.5. FIRST NEW RUNWAYS CONSTRUCTED

By 1947, three runways had been completed, and work on the other three to form the now-familiar double triangle had begun, although most of these were later abandoned as unnecessary. The initial three comprised the main east–west No. 1 runway (10L/28R), which was 9,300 feet long, on the north side; No. 2 Runway (05R/23L); and No. 6 runway (33L) – the latter two were both 6,000 feet long, and all three runways were 300 feet wide. The pavements were laid over 3 feet of brick earth on 12–20 feet of Taplow gravel, overlying London clay. The original RAF pavements were designed for wheel loads of 81,000 pounds, but the panel recommended designing the pavements for 360,000 pounds' wheel load, akin to the Brabazon main wheels. The runways were laid with 12-inch-thick concrete in 20-foot-wide strips, with transverse and longitudinal expansion joints at 60-foot intervals (later increased to 120 feet), on compacted gravel from on site to replace the brick earth, but the centre strip was laid on 8 inches of 1:12 mix concrete. The terminal aprons comprised an 8-inch-thick slab including one taxiway where a 12-inch thick prestressed concrete slab was trialled. This first phase of work, as well as the perimeter taxi-strip and the arrival/departure area on the north side, was carried out by George Wimpey & Co. Ltd. [Ref: *Concrete Quarterly* 2, February 1948. See also 'Heathrow Airport 1946–1956', Paul Francis, *Airfield Review* 60, August 1992, for more on the runway layout, history and construction plus aircraft ground control facilities.]

2.6. SIR JOHN H. D'ALBIAC APPOINTED FIRST COMMANDANT

In 1946 Air Marshal Sir John Henry d'Albiac was appointed as the first Commandant of London Airport. His military way of doing things did not please everybody but he did get things moving at the airport. In particular he was remembered for his shooting parties among the runways, pheasant, partridge and hare apparently being plentiful.

2.7. AIRCRAFT MAINTENANCE AREAS

2.7.1. Early on in its development, Heathrow had planned three maintenance areas. No. 1 maintenance area covered 240 acres east of the runway system, with eight 'temporary' B1 hangars with lattice truss roof of 100-foot span, used by BOAC and erected 1947–50; it was positioned in a roughly triangular array south of the Runway 1 (28R) threshold. Hangars 2, 3 and 4 were oriented south-west of Runway 2 (05R/23L). These were used by BOAC pending construction of their large headquarters complex with four hangar pens on the east side. Hangars 2, 3 and 4 were used by Eagle Airways after BOAC moved in to their new complex. At least two of the original B1 hangars, Nos 3 and 4, were still extant in 1990. The new BOAC headquarters complex opened in 1955, and comprised two pairs of hangar pens, between which was an engineering hall 800 feet long by 90 feet wide, with offices attached. Each hangar pen was 330 feet wide by 45 feet high. Also in No. 1 Maintenance Area was the first phase of the BEA hangar complex built 1952–3 in a U-shape with two long hangars split by engineering accommodation, all 1,000 feet long, to be added to from 1957 as part of Phase 2. The BOAC HQ was added to later by the addition of the wing hangar on the south side close to the A30.

Heathrow, Pan American hangar with door cut-out, plus PanAm DC7C N755PA in original colour scheme. (Frank Hudson)

Heathrow, Pan American hangar with door cut-out, plus B25 Mitchell N9089Z, later to become famous on film shoots, still extant at Booker. (Mick West)

2.7.2. No. 2 maintenance area covered 72 acres south-south-east of the runways, and contained the Pan American hangar, the first on site. It was 160 feet wide by 122 feet long, with doors approximately 140 feet wide x 25 feet high with a special door tailgate 12 feet wide by 12 feet high to accommodate Boeing Stratocruisers. Also in the No. 2 Maintenance Area was the three-bay aluminium hangar used for the early BOAC Comet fleet. No. 3 maintenance area covered 91 acres south-south-west of the runways and eventually became the cargo area.

2.8. AIRLINE DEVELOPMENTS IN THE 1940s

All the British airlines except BOAC and BEA operated as charter airlines, operating indigenous types like the Vickers Viking, DH Dove and Dragon Rapide, Airspeed Consul, Avro Anson, Bristol Freighter, Miles Aerovan, and HP Halifax on short-haul services, plus Lancastrians, Yorks and Tudors for longer haul, as well as American types like DC3s, DC4s, L049 and L749 Constellations. BOAC, as one of the two British airlines operating regular services out of Heathrow, were operating Yorks and Dakotas to Africa, the Middle East and India, and Liberators and L749 Constellations across the Atlantic to New York and Montreal, with Lancastrian freighters as far as Australia. British South American Airways, the other British airline, operated a fleet of Lancastrians and Yorks on services to Central and South America. See Appendix D for airline types operated in the 1940s.

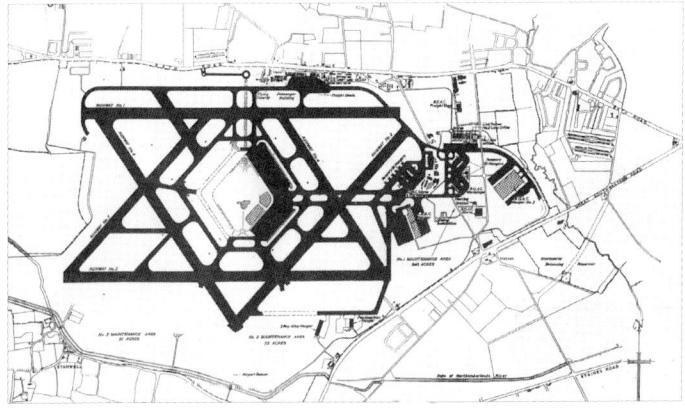

Heathrow overall plan, showing runway numbering, north side facilities, maintenance areas and Central proposals, from a September 1953 Ministry of Civil Aviation report on Central Area. (via Author)

Heathrow, north side entry to Central Area tunnel 1955, with Aer Lingus Viscount heading to north side terminal. (via Philip Sherwood)

3

Central Area Development

3.0.1. In 1950 Frederick Gibberd was appointed architect to design new permanent buildings in the 158-acre diamond-shaped Central Area with access through a new tunnel under the northern East–West runway, the original Runway No. 1.

3.0.2. The 158-acre Central Area's estimated cost when the plans were published in September 1953 was £6.75 million, comprising £1.5 million land cost, £1.33 million services and £3.5 million on the three buildings. Consulting engineers were Sir William Halcrow & Ptnrs, Westminster; Ewbank & Ptnrs, Grosvenor Place, SW1; and G. H. Buckle & Ptnrs, Harrington Gdns, SW7. Principal contractors were Redpath, Brown & Co., Edinburgh, for steelwork and Taylor Woodrow Construction Ltd, Southall, for foundations and general building work. All the buildings were designed on a 12-foot grid, with steel frames clad in brick, stone or glass. The floors and roofs were mostly precast concrete units, the rest being reinforced concrete.

Heathrow Central Area, Control Tower model from a September 1953 Ministry of Civil Aviation report on Central Area. (via Author)

Heathrow Central Area, Control Tower from the north-east with BEA one and a half decker buses used to transport BEA passengers from West London Air Terminal. (via Philip Sherwood)

Heathrow, Control Tower, ground radar display. (Richard E. Flagg)

Heathrow, Control Tower, penthouse controllers. (via Peter Dance)

Heathrow Central Area, Passenger Building model, airside view showing extensive Roof Gardens, entered from the Queens Building, from a September 1953 Ministry of Civil Aviation report on Central Area. (via Author)

False ceilings were provided throughout to accommodate services. Essential communication between operational and controlling authorities was achieved by a pneumatic tube system. A ventilated subway system below and between the buildings contained all necessary services.

3.0.3. The Central Area was provided with two aprons, north-east and south-east, with a total of thirty-four stands, split inner and outer with tunnels at the north and south ends for coaches etc. to convey passengers/luggage etc. to the outer stands, although their use did not last long, as the airside vehicles could travel reasonably safely without the tunnels.

3.1. MAIN CENTRAL AREA ACCESS TUNNEL AND UNDERGROUND WORKS

A tunnel was needed to give access from the north for the building of the Central Area. Only after the second east–west runway, No. 5, on the south side had been completed and become operational could the main north east–west runway, No. 1, be closed, along with its three flanking taxiways, to allow tunnel construction. Due to the high ground-water level in the underlying gravels, the new tunnel was built by the cut and cover method. The overall width of 86 feet comprised two parallel vehicular tunnels 26 feet 1 inch wide by 17 feet 1 inch high with 20-foot-wide two-lane roads and an elevated walkway for firefighting in each. In addition, on each side were 13-foot-9-inch-wide pedestrian/cycleway tunnels, with reduced clearance to allow ventilation ducts underneath. All in reinforced concrete, the tunnel walls were 14-inch-thick except the external walls at 18 inches, while the roof was 28-inch-thick and the floors 15 inches under the road and 30 inches under the walls. Total cover over the tunnel was about 10 feet. The tunnel excavation was 2,060 feet x 86 feet wide and about 30 feet deep through topsoil, 4 feet of brick earth, 7–8 feet of water-bearing gravel and into the underlying blue clay. The sides were sloped at 1:1.5. The tunnel was waterproofed with two layers of bituminous sheeting around its perimeter. Total length of the tunnel was 2,041 feet long excluding approaches, and constructed in 50-foot lengths weekly with joints between each. Excavation began on 23 October 1950 and was complete by the end of 1952. It consumed 750,000 cu. yds of excavation, 100,000 cu. yds of concrete and 3,000 tons of reinforcement. Designed by the Air Ministry Works Directorate for the Ministry of Civil Aviation, the contractors were Taylor Woodrow Construction Ltd and the cost was £1 million. Part of the tunnel came into use at Easter 1953 to allow access to the public enclosure at the centre. In addition, vehicle subways at the new Central Area aprons were constructed to allow access to the outer aircraft stands, plus 85 miles of storm-water drainage leading to the balancing reservoirs to the south-east for holding, before release to rivers.

3.2. CENTRAL AREA TOWER BUILDING

3.2.1. The central building was the nine-storey, 122-foot-6-inch (some quote 127 feet) -high control tower, south of the centre of the inner terminal area facing the south end of the main tunnel, with a public car park between it and the tunnel. On a T-shaped plan, it had commanding views over the dual runways, approaches and taxiways. The tower building controlled all movements of aircraft using the airport, as well as all motor vehicles, and also contained the headquarters of airport management, aeronautical telecommunications, the medical centre, restaurants and welfare facilities for all staff within the area. Air traffic control occupied the upper floors and the glazed penthouse on the ninth floor. The Approach Control Room, the nerve centre of the building, occupied the sixth and seventh floors, the penthouse taking over the last moments of approach and the departure of aircraft from the Approach Control Room. The eighth floor contained ventilating plant and lift motors. All movement of aircraft on the ground and vehicles was controlled from the ground movement room, which was on the fourth and fifth floors. The second and third floors had a conference room, administration offices and the offices of the General Manager and the Airport Commandant.

3.2.2. The building was steel-framed, encased in concrete with 11-inch cavity brick walls, on a column grid of 12-foot multiples and beams of 12-, 18- and 24-foot modules. The tower itself consisted of two intersecting trapeziums, approximately 82 feet east–west and 68 feet north–south, with staircases between them and a central services core. The wider trapezium faced east and contained the approach and ground control rooms with windows on three sides. The narrower trapezium faced west and contained smaller rooms for the control organisation. The penthouse had headroom of 15 feet to allow for a control information panel. The two-storey T-shaped base building comprised a trapezium-shaped south wing 168 feet north–south and 220 feet max./85 feet min. east–west with restaurants, while the medical centre and administration offices were in the 168-foot-long by 50-foot-wide west wing, and the main telecommunications services in the 132-foot-long by 80-foot-wide east wing. Management offices occupied the lower part of the tower and part of the wings. The tower came into operation on 17 April 1955.

3.3. PASSENGER TERMINAL (EUROPA BUILDING)

The first of the passenger buildings, opposite the south-east terminal apron, the No. 1 Europa Building, besides providing passenger handling, also held bonded spare parts, baggage stores and workshops for minor aircraft maintenance. The Europa Building was originally designed to handle 1.2 million passengers annually. The drawings were completed in 1950, with the foundations and steelwork contract being ready by 1951, and the main building contract following between December 1953 and April 1955. The main parts were steel-framed, concrete encased, on a 12-foot structural grid with beam spans in multiples of 12, 18 and 24 feet, with external 11-inch cavity brick walls. The Customs Hall comprised a series of multi-span welded steel portal frames. The floors and roofs were mostly precast concrete units. At 620 feet long by 250 feet wide, it was opened on 17 April 1955 for domestic/European

Heathrow Central Area, Passenger Building model, landside view with Queens Building behind, from a September 1953 Ministry of Civil Aviation report on Central Area. (via Author)

Heathrow Central Area, Britannic Building, the domestic end of the Passenger Building, c.1956, with BEA one-and-a-half decker plus drop-off/parking area in front. (via Philip Sherwood)

Heathrow, No.1 Building Europa Terminal 1956, the European end of the Passenger Building, opposite end to Britannic Building. (via Philip Sherwood)

Heathrow, Passenger Building airside (later to become Terminal 2) with Air France Viscount F-BGNT. White building in middle was the restaurant, giving the sole access to the Waving Base on the right. (via Charles Woodley)

Heathrow, Passenger Building plus Control Tower behind, early 1960s, with BEA and Air France Viscounts. The full extent of the Waving Base may be seen. (via Philip Sherwood)

Heathrow Central Area, Apex Building model, later renamed the Queens Building, airside view, from a September 1953 Ministry of Civil Aviation report on Central Area. (via Author)

services. The ground floor entrance hall had airline check-ins with escalators up to the main concourse, which was 500 feet long by 50 feet wide, widening to 150 feet in the centre. The Continental section with customs facilities was on the first floor, in the form of a series of transverse bands containing the main concourse, customs, immigration, health and waiting rooms. Ten parallel passenger channels cut across these bands at right angles between land and air sides, each channel having its own baggage conveyor belt below first floor, except where needed for customs. Each conveyor was reversible for inward/outward passengers. Initially, in April 1955, six channels were operational, and the rest were open by October 1955. Domestic passengers would be handled at the southern end of the building, called the No. 2 Britannic Building, while passengers in transit would remain behind customs in a special suite with restaurant, buffet and shops. An airside gallery ran the full length of the building, connecting all the channels with footbridges and ramps down to the apron to take coaches to the aircraft. The whole of the ground floor was for baggage handling, the accommodation of technical staff and equipment, and food preparation, while the second floor had offices for airlines, the balcony extension of the concourse leading to a restaurant overlooking the apron. The large roof area had a series of gardens and terraces at different levels for spectators, accessed from the third building, the Queens Building, for a small fee.

3.4. QUEENS BUILDING

The Queens Building was the eastern apex block, sited midway between the two terminal aprons on the east side, forming a link between the Europa Building on the south and a

Heathrow Central Area, Queens Building landside view, *c.* 1956, with crowds of spectators plus coaches outside, and early B1 and BEA hangars behind. (via Philip Sherwood)

Heathrow Central Area aerial view, late 1950s, showing Queens Building, Passenger Building plus Control Tower, plus SAS DC6 and BEA Elizabethan. (via Philip Sherwood)

similar proposed terminal to the north. The shape was dictated by the two buildings north and south and the curve of the eastern apron at that point. The roughly pentagonal shape was 490 feet max. north–south by 320 feet east–west, the whole being steel-framed with brick cladding like the other buildings. The main entrance on the land-side facing west gave access to the first floor, but was isolated from the operational side of the building. The first floor had an exhibition hall, news cinema and post office for the airport, and gave access to the public roof gardens and a restaurant with a curved face cantilevered from the building so as to allow users a good view over the eastern aprons. The roof gardens extended across the roof of the south-east Europa Building, linked to the Queens Building by an 87-foot-span tubular steel footbridge at roof level. The Queens Building also accommodated aircraft handling and crews, their briefing rooms and Customs examination, meteorological forecasting and flight planning. Two separate entrances, one each side, gave access to a central corridor with flight planning and briefing rooms, companies' operations rooms and crew customs. The crew dining and rest rooms were on the first floor, reached by stairs. Airline offices were on the first floor and the second floor of the central block. Her Majesty Queen Elizabeth officially opened the Central Area, including the new Queens Building and the Europa Building, for European passengers on 16 December 1955, along with the tunnel into the Central Area.

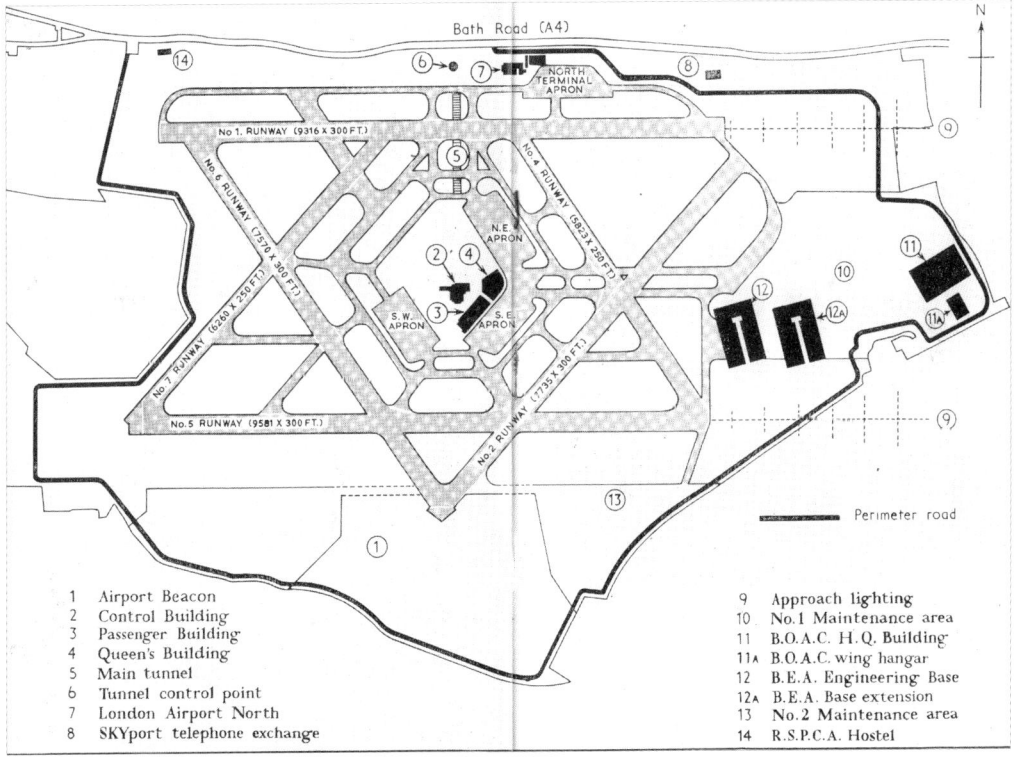

Heathrow 1959 plan, showing runway numbering and principal buildings, the south west apron to become Oceanic Building/Terminal 3. (via Author)

1950s Developments

4.1 HEATHROW'S FIRST NEW (ALUMINIUM) HANGAR

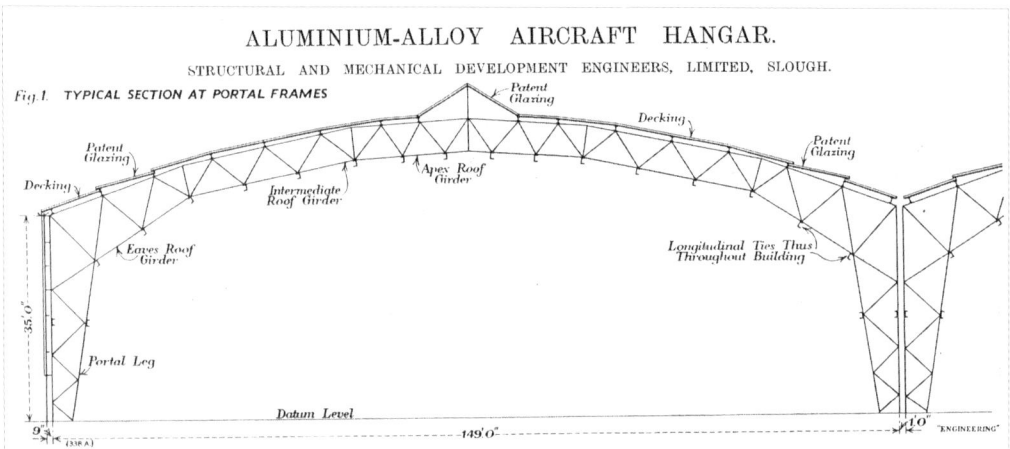

Heathrow, Three Bay Alloy Hangar, by SMD, showing typical lattice frame 125ft span. (via Author)

4.1.1. In May 1950 the Ministry of Civil Aviation invited tenders for the speedy design and erection of a three-bay hangar for BOAC, of clear span, 125 foot by 110 foot depth with a clear door height of 30 feet to be located in No. 2 Maintenance Area beside the A30 Great South West Road. In order to keep maintenance costs to a minimum the roof was to be in aluminium but the columns could be either steel or aluminium. It was to be designed to accommodate a snow load of 15 lb/ft² and a wind load of 25 lb/ft². Three weeks were allowed for the design, and the chosen arrangement was in aluminium by the designers Structural and Mechanical Development Engineers (SMD) of 2 Buckingham Ave., Slough. SMD was the construction company for the parent Associated Light Metal Industries Group, or Almin Ltd, of Farnham Royal. The hangar was claimed to be the first aluminium hangar in the world, with overall dimensions of 450 feet 6 inches along the front by 123 feet 2 inches in depth. The main aluminium alloy used in sections was HE10WP.

4.1.2. Two-pinned lattice portal frames with hinge pins at 145-foot-6-inch centres were chosen, each of the three bays being structurally independent. Overall span was 149 feet to the outer legs of the columns to allow door stacking each side. Each bay comprised six

Heathrow, Three Bay Alloy Hangar, during construction, 1951. (via Author)

Heathrow, Bristol Brabazon G-AGPW visit 15 August 1950. (Tony Hart via Mick West)

Heathrow, DH Comet 1 G-ALYP in No.1 Maintenance Area, July 1953, later to be lost over Elba on 10 January 1954, the first of the tragic Comet losses. (John Carter)

frames at 22-foot centres, with braced joist purlins at 9-foot-3-inch average centres spanning between. Each portal comprised double channel and bulb joist sections battened together 6.5 inches apart as main boom sections with diagonal members between. The columns tapered from approximately 3 feet 6 inches deep at base to approximately 8 feet at eaves, and the rafter from approximately 9 feet 6 inches at eaves to approximately 6 feet at ridge. The roof had a generally curved appearance made up of a 19° slope at eaves then 11° and 3.5° at the ridge. Overall eaves height was 35 feet and maximum internal clearance at ridge was 60 feet. The hinge at the base of the columns was a high-tensile steel pin passing through an aluminium gusset at the column, and a special aluminium casting set into the foundation. The rear wall of each bay was supported by five lattice columns 5 feet deep at 25-foot centres. Glazing comprised strips 10 feet wide front to back in the roof next to the eaves, with a 17-foot width at the ridge, plus a 10-foot-wide strip parallel and behind the doors, and a 10-foot-deep strip along the walls. Roof cladding was 18 SWG corrugated aluminium sheet with insulation and roofing felt. The walls comprised 8-foot-high brickwork, with 10-foot-high glazing above that, and 20 SWG corrugated aluminium sheeting with a 4-inch gap to the foil-backed asbestos-cement insulating board lining for the walls. Sheeting rails to the walls were at 4-foot centres to fit the standard insulating boards. The foundations were designed primarily to hold the hangar down rather than up, the larger foundations being designed for an uplift of 75 tons with a 3-foot-thick slab, 23 feet by 14 feet, set 2 feet below floor level. The aluminium base casting for the pin was cast into the concrete base with four holding-down bolts acting in tension. The first bay to be completed was nearest the airport and was fitted with Esavian sliding folding doors. The other two bays had L-shaped sliding doors by SMD. All doors were insulated and electrically operated. Aluminium allowed rapid erection by constructing pairs of half portal frames at ground level from prefabricated riveted lattice sections joined with bolts, with purlins and bracing attached, and hoisting them up to be joined at the ridge with bolts. Four half frames took five days by six men, plus two men on winches. The horizontal wind girder between the first and second frames behind the top door guides was similarly fabricated at ground level and hoisted in one. The total weight of the complete building was 312 tons, comprising 95 tons structure, 7 tons sheeting, 11 tons insulation, 48 tons doors, 52 tons glazing, and 100 tons roof decking.

4.1.3. The first bay was officially opened in May 1951 by Sir Miles Thomas, Chairman of BOAC, with a BOAC Hermes stationed partly inside. It was complete by August 1951. The hangar was used as BOAC's first hangar at Heathrow including for Comet 1s, the main (much larger) four-bay reinforced concrete hangar taking over when completed later.

4.1.4. In 1954 Hunting Air Travel moved to Heathrow from Bovingdon, together with the servicing division of Fields, also part of the Hunting Group. At that time Hunting Clan was formed, the result of an association with British and Commonwealth Shipping (comprising Clan Line and Union Castle) and the Cayzer family. Hunting Clan flew Vikings, Yorks and later Viscounts, Britannias and DC6s on cargo, African and trooping services. The Hunting Clan name was emblazoned on the hangar rear, visible from Heathrow Central for years until 1960 when it was forced into a merger with Airwork under government pressure to form British United Airways, based at Gatwick. The story goes that, when permission from the authorities was sought for the name to be painted on the hangar, someone misread feet for inches, and it was approved on that basis, thus 12-foot-high letters. After the demise of Hunting Clan, 400 staff were dismissed at Heathrow.

4.1.5. For a brief period the hangar was used as a freight shed by Seaboard World, an American freight airline operating Constellations, CL44s and DC8s, their name being painted above the three sets of doors in 1968 at least.

4.1.6. The year 1962 saw the arrival of Shell Aircraft Ltd under the director Douglas Bader, basing its fleet in the Hunting hangar, serviced by Fields and forming the nucleus of the Executive Jet Centre. Introduction of the DH125 the same year put it on an even firmer footing. The name Hunting could remain on the rear wall for twenty more years, by just removing the word Clan. The head offices, administration, sales and laboratories of Fields were in prefabricated buildings on the south side, and threatened by Terminal 4, as was the hangar, resulting in a new Fields HQ with workshops and offices in Longford village north-west of Heathrow, opened by HRH The Duke of Edinburgh on 14 December 1981. A new Executive Jet Centre comprising a custom-built hangar, workshops and administration complex on the south side of Heathrow was opened in May 1983, costing £3.6 million, servicing Gulfstreams, Learjets, Falcons, Citations, HS125s and other corporate jets. The original aluminium hangar was demolished to make way for British Airways Terminal 4, which was constructed in 1983–6. In 1995 the renamed Hunting Business Aviation was taken over by Mohammed Al Fayed and renamed Harrods Aviation Ltd, but by then Fields had been forced out of Heathrow to set up new operations at Stansted and Biggin Hill.

4.1.7. Structural designers and Main Contractor: Structural and Mechanical Development Engineers (SMD) of 2 Buckingham Ave, Slough (parent company Almin Ltd).
Foundation consultant: Mr J. Bak, BSc, MIStructE.
Aluminium extrusions: Southern Forge Ltd (parent company Almin Ltd).
Aluminium castings: Renfrew Foundries Ltd (parent company Almin Ltd).
Aluminium plate: TI Aluminium Ltd.
Aluminium sheet: British Aluminium Co. Ltd.
Roof decking contractor: Wm Briggs & Sons Ltd.
Glazing contractor: Williams & Williams.
Door contractor: Esavian Ltd (first bay only).
Foundation contractor: Geo. Wimpey & Co. Ltd.

4.2 BRABAZON VISIT

The Bristol Brabazon G-AGPW visited Heathrow briefly on 15 June 1950. Intended for the BOAC North Atlantic service, it was the largest land-based aircraft at the time, with wingspan of 230 feet, length 177 feet and tail height 50 feet. The prototype was powered by eight Bristol Centaurus radial engines driving contra-rotating propellers, arranged in pairs enclosed within the wings to allow in-flight inspection. Capacity was 120 seats and a range of 5,500 miles, with a take-off weight of 131 tons.

4.3 COMET AND VISCOUNT ENTER SERVICE

On 2 April 1951, Comet 1 G-ALZK landed at Heathrow on loan from De Havilland to BOAC for crew conversion. On 2 May 1952, BOAC Comet 1 G-ALYP, with a standard thirty-six-passenger capacity, departed for Johannesburg via Rome, Beirut, Khartoum, Entebbe and Livingstone, on the world's first jet passenger service. The first service with Comets to Singapore began on 14 October 1952 after proving flights from 15 May. The service went via Rome, Beirut, Bahrain, Karachi, Calcutta, Rangoon and Bangkok, with Delhi added on the return trip, the journey taking 27 hours 30 minutes out and 34 hours

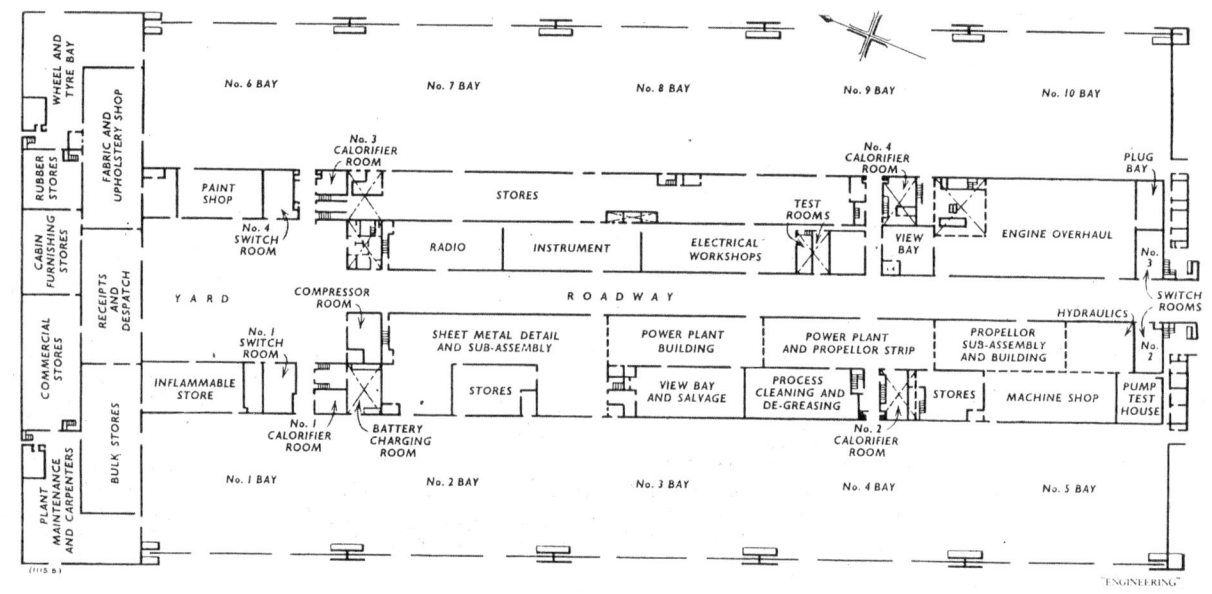

Heathrow, BEA Engineering Base Phase 1, plan showing ten aircraft bays 150ft clear door width x 30ft clear height x 110ft deep plus workshops. (via Author)

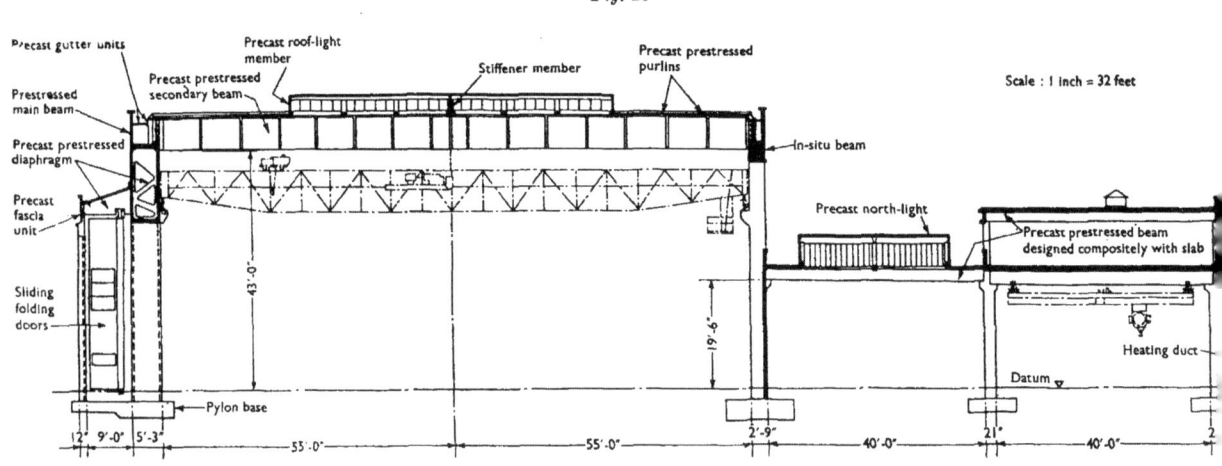

Heathrow, BEA Engineering Base Phase 1, cross-section showing 110ft clear span prestressed concrete roof beams over west side aircraft bays, plus central workshop. (Institution of Civil Engineers)

back. Unfortunately several accidents to Comet 1s, including the loss of G-ALYP off Elba on 10 January 1954, to be followed on 8 April 1954 by the loss of G-ALYY off Naples, saw the Comet 1 fleet grounded for good. Several months were spent searching for the Elba crash remains in deep water. Exhaustive investigation was undertaken including testing another Comet in a specially built water tank at RAE Farnborough, which culminated in an explosive split of the fuselage. The investigation concluded that both Comets had suffered explosive cabin decompression and break-up because of fatigue. On 18 April 1953 BEA Viscount G-AMNY departed to Nicosia via Rome and Athens on the world's first turboprop scheduled passenger service.

4.4. BEA HANGARS PHASES 1 AND 2

4.4.1. BEA Phase 1

4.4.1.1. At the time of construction in the early 1950s the British European Airways Engineering Base was believed to be the largest example of prestressed concrete in the country. The most visible hangar complex from Heathrow Central, it was built to maintain the two fleets of Airspeed Ambassadors (BEA fleet name Elizabethan Class) and Vickers Viscounts (BEA fleet name Discovery Class). The Ambassador/Elizabethan had a span of 115 feet, a length of 81 feet and tail height 18 feet 4 inches. It was in BEA service from March 1952 to 1958. The Viscount 700 had a span of 93 feet 9 inches, length of 81 feet 10 inches and tail height 276 feet 9 inches. It entered service from April 1953, with BEA ordering twenty-seven, followed by twenty-four of the 802 and nineteen of the 806 series, which were longer, at 85 feet 8 inches. The Viscounts continued in service with British Airways until 1985.

4.4.1.2. Planning began in 1948, and in 1950 the Ministry of Civil Aviation asked twenty contractors in competition to submit tenders to plans and specifications by the Ministry, including ten selected specialist contractors in concrete plus additional structural steel specialists. Only three months were allowed for preparation of the scheme including design, quantities and pricing. BEA took over responsibility and appointed Scott and Wilson as Principal Consulting Engineers. It had a 1,000-foot x 465-foot footprint, a North–South U-shaped plan, comprising two large hangars, each facing outwards, 900 feet wide by 110 feet deep, with workshops behind, back to back with a 30-foot access road between, ending in a square courtyard and a stores block to close the U on the north side. Each hangar was divided into five 180-foot bays (with no division between them), with five doors giving 150 feet x 30 feet clear height access, roof clear 43 feet to allow the crane hook to be not less than 30 feet clear height, and an apron 900 feet x 300 feet wide. The workshop annexes behind each hangar comprised two 40-foot spans the full 900 feet behind each hangar, with offices over the span nearest the internal road.

4.4.1.3. Work began on site on 10 August 1950 with 4-foot depth of excavation to remove soft topsoil and brick earth, to be filled with gravel in 8-inch layers. The RC foundations extended 4–7 feet to the underlying gravel. Excavations for the column bases were 8 feet deep, and comprised 4-foot-deep mass concrete footings with 2-foot-deep RC bases on top. The floor slabs and aprons comprised 8 inches of concrete. The whole structure was concrete, prestressed concrete being used in the roof. The main beams over the doors were post-tensioned box girders 150-foot span, 14 feet deep x 5 feet wide with 4-inch walls, 5.5 inches bottom slab and 8 inches top slab. Fins projected out 9 feet from the outer face to carry Bison prestressed floor units with roofing felt as a door canopy. The front elevation had ribbed precast concrete fascia units above the canopy. There were precast prestressed

Heathrow, BEA Engineering Base Phase 1, showing special lattice beam to erect prestressed concrete roof beams. (Institution of Civil Engineers)

Heathrow, BEA Engineering Base Phase 1, completed aircraft bays with Elizabethan inside, completed 1953. (Institution of Structural Engineers via Author)

Heathrow, BEA Engineering Base Phase 1, west side still extant, 17 December 2009 internal view. (Tony Szulc)

concrete diaphragms at 15-foot centres with crane rail brackets projecting inwards. The main beams were cast *in situ* at high level on falsework and were stressed with 41 x 5 mm diameter twelve-wire cables on the Freyssinet system, two layers of six and four each side arranged parabolically in the walls, with the remaining twenty-one in the bottom.

4.4.1.4. The main beam support pylons at 180 feet c/c were 30 feet wide, comprising two columns 5 feet 3 inches x 2 feet 6 inches joined by two 4-inch-thick RC walls with a load-bearing 12-inch-thick vertical rib midway between. Further RC walls formed recesses 9 feet wide x 14 feet 9 inches long to house the folding doors. The load from the main beams was transmitted to the two pylons, one rigidly fixed to the 4-inch walls, the other separated by a construction joint and free to flex about the base to allow beam expansion.

4.4.1.5. The rear wall of each hangar had RC columns 2 feet 9 inches x 2 feet at 30-foot centres with intermediate 15-inch x 12-inch columns supporting the workshop annex roof. The main columns supported RC eaves beams 3 feet 6 inches x 2 feet 9 inches, which in turn carried the secondary beams, with wall infilling of 6-inch-thick RC panels up to 24 feet 9 inches with glazing above. The columns also carried the steel crane girders on concrete brackets. The south end wall was 5-inch-thick RC with 1-inch wood wool permanent formwork and 21 per cent glass. The 6-inch-thick north wall formed part of the North Stores Block.

4.4.1.6. Spanning 110 feet between the main front beams and the rear eaves beam were the knife-sharp T-section beams at 15-foot centres, with top flange 3 feet wide, web 5 feet 10 inches deep, both 4 inches thick. They were precast by Girling Ferro Concrete Ltd, Glasgow, in sixteen stiffened sections 7 feet long, assembled on the ground and the eight twelve-wire 5 mm Freyssinet cables threaded through and post-tensioned. Weighing 26–27 tons, they were then lifted into position 43 feet above floor level. Precast prestressed purlins cast on a longline system in Concrete Development Co.'s factory spanned between, and were bolted down to the secondary beams from 25 feet each end of the secondary beams, and carried pressed aluminium decking with insulation and felt. The middle 45 per cent of the secondary beams carried triangular-shaped precast beams supporting the

Heathrow, BEA Engineering Base Phase 1, completed west side external view. (Institution of Structural Engineers via Author)

lantern roof lights.

4.4.1.7. The hangar doors were Esavian electrically powered folding sliding doors, retracting into recesses in the six pylons, to give a clear door opening 150 feet x 30 feet.

4.4.1.8. The workshop annexes had site-cast precast columns 15 inches x 12 inches and factory-made precast beams. The 80-foot width of each workshop was divided into two 40-foot-wide sections by a central row of columns at 15-foot centres, which had brackets to carry the 40-foot span prestressed roof and floor beams. The floor and roof beams were largely composite T-beams with precast prestressed webs 34 inches x 12 inches and 21 inches x 12 inches at 8.5 and 5 tons respectively.

   The outer walls to the workshops were 5-inch-thick RC with wood wool panels as permanent formwork. The internal 40-foot span had offices over, which had Triad floor units in the first (west) wing as flooring, resting on the edges of beams with concrete pots between and *in situ* concrete topping to create composite T-beams. Owing to an acute steel shortage in the winter of 1951/2 the floors and roofs of the east wing had Pierhead prestressed X-joists with pot slabs and *in situ* concrete as before.

4.4.1.9. The 465-foot-long x 100-foot-wide Stores Block at the north end, forming the base of the U, used prestressed roof beams on RC columns. A row of columns 24 inches x 18 inches at 42-foot centres down the centre (which carried the temporary floor and crane girders on brackets) divided the 100-foot width into two 50-foot spans. The central columns supported precast prestressed I-beams 45 inches x 12 inches wide as spine beams, which in turn carried 50-foot span prestressed roof I-beams 27 inches x 12 inches (web 5 inches) at 14-foot centres spanning between the spine beam and external columns. Rectangular precast prestressed roof purlins 9 inches x 4 inches spanned between the secondary roof beams, and carried light metal decking, roof lights and small water tanks. Walls were 5 inches RC with 1 inch wood wool except the south wall at 6-inch-thick RC. The whole block was single storey except one area with a temporary floor using Bison precast units.

4.4.1.10. Each hangar had full-length 110-foot-span overhead cranes of 5-ton capacity by Vaughan Crane Co. Ltd, West Gorton, Manchester, running on rails on brackets off the front beams and rear columns. Originally two cranes of 55-foot span were envisaged, spanning from front to back to a central triangulated spine beam picked up at the bottom of the secondary beams as a central point load. The secondary beams were to be prestressed I-beams with few diaphragms. However, when the crane specification became one of 100-foot span, eliminating the need for a central spine beam, it was too late to radically alter the secondary beams, so the bottom flange was deleted making them T-beams braced laterally by the lantern roof light beams, and by uniting web and flange with frequent diaphragms. The workshop annexes had two 35-foot-span, 5-ton cranes and the North Stores Block had a 47-foot-span, 5-ton crane.

4.4.1.11. Heating for the hangars was by a combination of radiant and convection heating with heating coils in the floor and hot air blowers over the doors.

4.4.1.12. By September 1952 the west wing hangar and workshops were complete and in use for minor maintenance, the east wing being used for major maintenance on aircraft; the whole was complete by 1953. BEA had by this time moved their maintenance facilities from Northolt to Heathrow. The design was carried out by the winning main contractor,

Heathrow, BEA Engineering Base Phase 1, *c.* 1954, showing the five bays each side, complete with BEA Viscounts, recently withdrawn BEA Vikings, plus the eight BOAC B1 hangars behind. (via Philip Sherwood)

Heathrow, BEA Engineering Base Phase 1, behind Eagle Britannia G-AOVR. Note BEA Vanguard with tail protruding as too tall. Phase 2 behind would allow for Vanguard tails. (Paul Howard)

Heathrow, BEA Engineering Base Phase 1, 10 August 1980, plus Cathedral Hangar behind Lufthansa A300 D-AIAA, with Trident visible in hangar plus tail dock assembly on one bay to allow for larger tails.

Heathrow, BEA Engineering Base Phase 1, 20 March 2010, showing door opening instead of tail dock for one aircraft, and two bays now vehicles only.

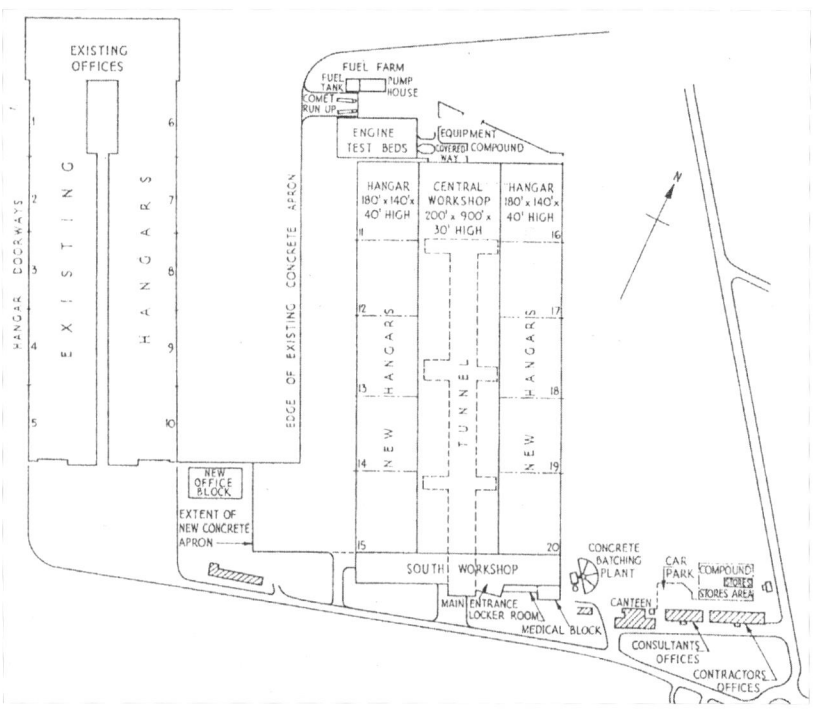

Heathrow, BEA Engineering Base Phases 1 and 2 plan, showing much larger workshops for Phase 2 plus 40ft clear height hangars, to accommodate Vanguards. (Institution of Structural Engineers via Author)

Holland, Hannen and Cubitts, with A. E. Beer retained as Consulting Structural Engineer in collaboration with Alan J. Harris of the Prestressed Concrete Co. Ltd (main and secondary beams), subcontractor Girlings Ferro Concrete Co. Ltd (for the precast segments of the hangar secondary beams), Concrete Development Co. Ltd (pre-tensioned purlins), and PSC Equipment Ltd (Freyssinet anchorages and jacks). Crane rails and temporary floor frames were by Lindsay's Paddington Ironworks. BEA's Consulting Engineers were Scott & Wilson, with Mr A. W. C. Villiers as Resident Engineer, the Architect being Keith Murray of Ramsey, Murray & White.

4.4.2. BEA Hangars Phase 2

4.4.2.1. To meet the maintenance requirements for the new Vickers Vanguard and Comet 4 fleets, BEA decided in November 1956 that it was necessary to add a further block of ten hangars approximately similar to Phase 1 but larger, with workshops giving direct access to all hangars. The Vanguard had a span of 118 feet 7 inches, length 122 feet 10 inches and tail height 34 feet 11 inches. BEA ordered twenty Vanguards, which entered service in late 1960 and continued until June 1974 as passenger aircraft on high-density European and UKL trunk routes, nine being converted to Merchantmen freighters for service 1969–1979. The initial seven Comet 4Bs had a span of 107 feet 10 inches, length 118 feet and tail height 29 feet 6 inches, and were designed for shorter-range routes, doing the work of three Viscount 701s, entering service April 1960. BEA eventually had fourteen Comets until the last service in October 1971, when they were passed on to BEA Airtours at Gatwick between 1970 and 1973. To have unobstructed workshops, it was decided to create a basement to house plant rooms, services, substations, locker rooms and toilets. The new complex was sited to the east of Phase 1.

4.4.2.2. The programme for construction was related to delivery of the Vanguard and called for two bays to be ready approximately twenty-one months from the date of start on site, the last to be complete forty months from start of contract. From the beginning, the contractor looked to precast concrete extensively. Oversite excavation removed 4 feet of brick earth and sandy clay to reach the top of the underlying gravel, the whole being backfilled with hoggin in 9-inch layers. The basement was formed by three separate cofferdams, with two 70-foot-long sheet pile division walls to allow excavation to proceed. Larssen No. 2 sheet piles 28 feet long were used, 10 feet into the blue clay underlying the gravel approximately 18 feet below existing ground level. The piles were tied back to anchor piles 50 feet back, up to thirty piles being driven per day. Floors and walls were of concrete, columns were *in situ*, precast beams to the underside of the floor which were precast prestressed units with tile infill and *in situ* topping. Columns were taken through at 60-foot centres for the workshop roof.

   The pavement of the hangars and aprons had to take the individual wheel load of 66,000 lb of the new Vanguard, which required a 10-inch-thick slab to the aprons. The hangar floors were 10.5 inches thick with heating coils, perforated extensively by precast service ducts.

4.4.2.3. Each hangar bay was 180 feet long x 141 feet 3 inches wide clear, with main doors 168 feet x 40 feet clear and 3-ton overhead cranes spanning the width of the hangar. The main beam over the doors was 14 feet deep by 6 feet 6 inches wide, cast *in situ* at high level, with precast diaphragms at 10-foot centres (every alternate one taking the door head/canopy and the secondary beams) and precast end anchorages. The top slab was 8.5 inches thick, the bottom slab 5.5 inches, and the walls 5 inches thick. The beams were post-tensioned with thirty-eight twelve-wire 0.276-inch Freyssinet cables, the wall strands being arranged parabolically towards each end. Triangular tubular steel space-frame secondary beams 7 feet 6 inches deep at 20-foot centres spanning 133 feet (weight 6 tons) were used over the hangars for lightness compared to Phase 1's concrete beams, with aluminium decking, insulation and roofing felt. These secondary beams were welded together on site and metal sprayed to save painting cost.

4.4.2.4. The main beam was supported on 6-foot-6-inch x 3 foot *in situ* columns, one stiffened by 9-inch walls each face, with the other column free to flex about the base to allow beam expansion. The canopies and fascias were precast in 20-foot lengths. The rear walls comprised columns at 20-foot centres with 9-inch-thick infill brickwork up to 33 feet above floor level with glazing up to 50 feet to the underside of the 30-inch square capping beam. To allow for likely future aircraft's longer noses, a rear door opening was provided 40 feet wide x 20 feet high. This was achieved by carrying two columns of the 20-foot module on a beam 48 inches x 30 inches at 26 feet above the floor, 42-foot span on two extra columns. All columns were braced by beams at the underside of the glazing and at the top. Columns 60 feet 9.5 inches high were cast with hollow cores, 30 inches x 24 inches up to the 51 feet above the base, reducing to 11 inches x 15 inches upper to allow for precast fascia panels, plus corbels for the crane rail. Foundation bases for these columns also took the 24-inch square workshop columns.

4.4.2.5. The north and south walls of the hangar were glazed above 22-foot-high, 6-inch-thick walls, with precast columns at 14-foot-4.5-inch centres, 36 inches x 20 inches hollow at base reducing twice to 24 inches x 20 inches at the capping beam.

4.4.2.6. The central 200-foot-wide full-length workshop roof (30 feet clear height)

Heathrow, BEA Engineering Base Phases 1 and 2 newly completed, aerial view from east, 1 November 1961. Note PanAm and 3-Bay Alloy Hangar far left and original Fairey hangar far left in Central Area. (via Philip Sherwood)

Heathrow BEA Phase 2 hangars on left, February 1973, with two of the last B1 hangars behind and two BEA Vanguards, one tailless plus a Northeast Viscount. In the distance the Ariel Hotel, one of the first at Heathrow, can be seen on the Bath Rd. (Mick West)

comprised a north light tubular steel roof on a 20-foot module spanning between the edge columns and the central columns at 60-foot centres. Each 20 feet comprised a north and south tubular lattice girder with a common top boom with three north lights per 60-foot module. Cranes provided included two lanes of crane track in each 100-foot width with 3-ton and 1-ton cranes. The columns adjacent to the hangar walls were 24 inches square precast, with the central columns 3 feet x 2 feet 6 inches, reducing to 12 inches x 2 feet 6 inches at mid height. The north wall of the workshop comprised precast columns at 16-foot-8-inch centres with precast purlins 9 inches x 9 inches at 5-foot-5-inch centres supporting aluminium sheeting. The workshop floor slab was 6 inches thick below the top layer of 4 inches containing services.

4.4.2.7. The south workshop was 100 feet wide by 500 feet long abutting the two hangars and workshop, and utilised a tubular steel framework and precast columns. On the north side, abutting hangars/workshop were 24-inch square precast columns at 50-foot centres with a 33-inch x 24-inch capping beam. The outer faces utilised 18-inch x 15-inch precast columns at 16-foot-8-inch centres with a 24-inch square capping beam. The east end had a 50-foot x 25-foot-high sliding door. The roof was a series of monitors on a 16-foot-8-inch module on main lattice girders 9 feet deep with hipped ends with tubular steel purlins and decking. The sides of the girders were glazed.

4.4.2.8. Phase 2 cost £5.5 million over 3.5 years, October 1956 to May 1960. Main Contractor was Holland, Hannen & Cubitts; BEA's Consulting Engineers were Scott & Wilson and Kirkpatrick & Partners.

4.4.2.9. In addition to the Vickers Vanguard and Comet 4 fleets, another aircraft serviced in the Phase 2 hangars was the Hawker Siddeley Trident. BEA originally ordered twenty-four Trident 1s with seventy-nine-seat capacity in 1959, entering service in March 1964, the longer-range Trident 2 following in 1968. The Trident 2 had a span of 98 feet, length of 114 feet 9 inches and tail height of 27 feet. The Trident 3 was chosen to replace the Vanguard and Comet Fleets. Having a 98-foot span, length 131 feet 2 inches and tail height 28 feet 3 inches, with 180-seat capacity, the Trident 3 entered service in 1970. The first aircraft to have a blind landing ability, the Trident was finally retired in 1986. The east wing of Phase 1 was demolished in 2000, with the whole of Phase 2 following, to be replaced by a parking area.

4.5. BOAC OWEN WILLIAMS HANGARS

4.5.1. The British Overseas Airways Corporation HQ building at Heathrow was one of Sir Owen Williams' iconic designs and, although heavily modified externally, still remains in use today. From 1948 BOAC looked at aircraft suitable for the North Atlantic route. The Boeing Stratocruiser was regarded as the best aircraft for the job, as it had 50 per cent more capacity than the L749 Constellation and the operating cost per seat-mile was similar. As Scandinavian Airlines System (SAS) and Aer Lingus were unable to take up their options on the Stratocruiser, BOAC took them over, acquiring ten. For the Empire routes to Australia, Africa and the Far East, L049 and L749 Constellations were acquired, and to make up numbers for the required capacity twenty-two Canadair Argonauts (a licence-built DC4 with Rolls-Royce Merlin engines) were bought. Between them the Argonauts and Constellations would form the backbone of the BOAC fleet on Empire routes until Comet 1s and Britannias entered service. New aircraft were required from 1950 to replace the older types, i.e. Avro Yorks and Short Solent flying boats. At that time the BOAC boardroom and top management were in Stratton House, Piccadilly. The main aircraft staff and supplies department were in a building in Brentford on the Great West Road called

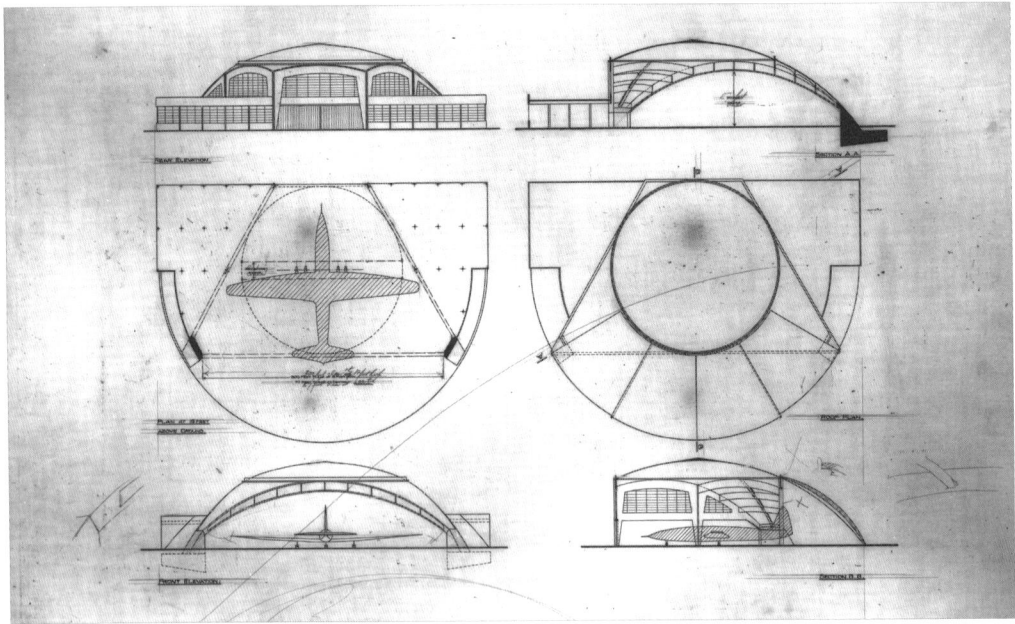

Heathrow, BOAC HQ hangars, original Owen Williams' proposal for concrete dome hangar to accommodate the then proposed Brabazon (shown). (Owen Williams Archive-Amey)

Heathrow, model of Owen Williams' proposed BOAC HQ hangars, six concrete domes grouped together with Brabazon alongside. (Owen Williams Archive-Amey)

Airways House, along with staff from Filton and other places of war evacuation, with sales staff and reservations at the Airways Terminal, Victoria. In late 1947 the Government decided to transfer BOAC Atlantic Division from Dorval, Montreal, to Filton and the west bay of the new Brabazon Hangar was allotted to them. Additional workshops and offices were constructed on the west side of the Brabazon Hangar in reinforced concrete, with work beginning in April 1948 and BOAC beginning the move seven months later. The BOAC aircraft fleet was split among several sites also; the No. 3 fleet of Stratocruisers was based at Filton, while the Argonaut and Constellation fleets were at Heathrow in the eight B1 hangars there. By 1950 Head Office had moved from Piccadilly to Brentford, but the boardroom was maintained at Stratton House, Piccadilly.

4.5.2. The only buildings at Heathrow being the Argonaut and Constellation facilities, special hangars would be needed for the Stratocruisers with their high tails (38 feet 3 inches) and broad wingspan (141 feet 3 inches). By the end of 1952 all the aircraft fleets, including one based at Hurn, had moved to Heathrow except the Stratocruisers which remained at Filton for two more years. In 1953 BOAC's Chairman Miles Thomas, and Basil Smallpeice, BOAC's financial comptroller, convinced the rest of the board that the new hangar block nearing completion should have office accommodation at both ends and in the transepts to allow transfer of the HQ from Brentford and to sell the latter. Thus the new BOAC building at Heathrow, apart from the four hangar pens, was designed to accommodate the corporation's complete HQ staff of 4,000, nearly a quarter of the total at home and abroad, and would handle the majority of the corporation's major aircraft maintenance as well as repair and overhaul of components including radio and instruments. Fully centralised maintenance became available when the new Heathrow hangar block became ready for the Statocruisers in 1955.

4.5.3. The building, of reinforced concrete throughout, was laid out with the hangars arranged in pairs back to back with the main workshops between. The four hangar pens

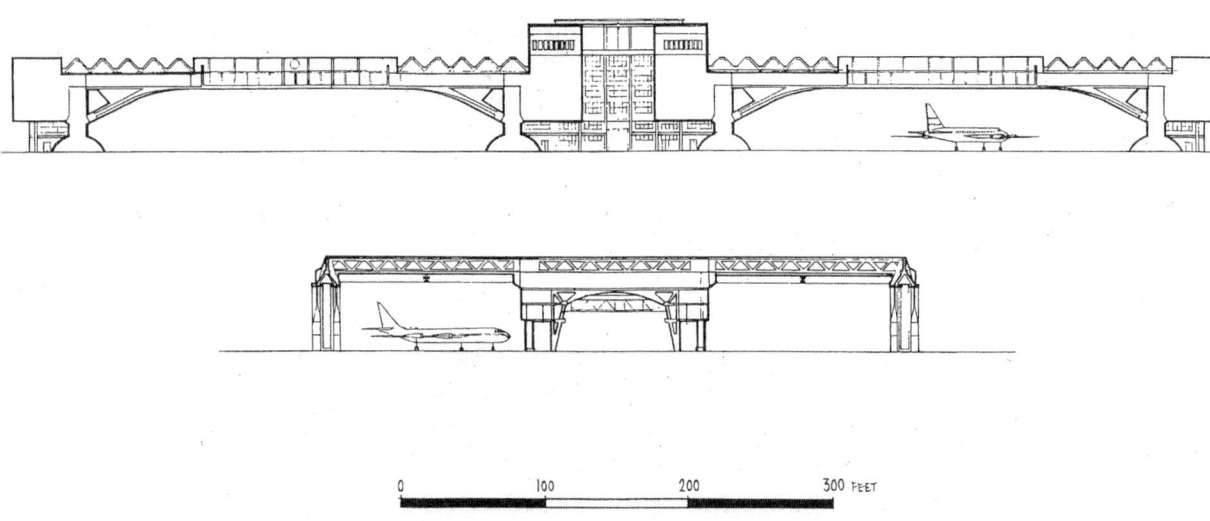

0   100   200   300 FEET

Heathrow, Owen Williams' revised more conventional BOAC HQ hangars, designed for the Stratocruiser originally. (David Cottam)

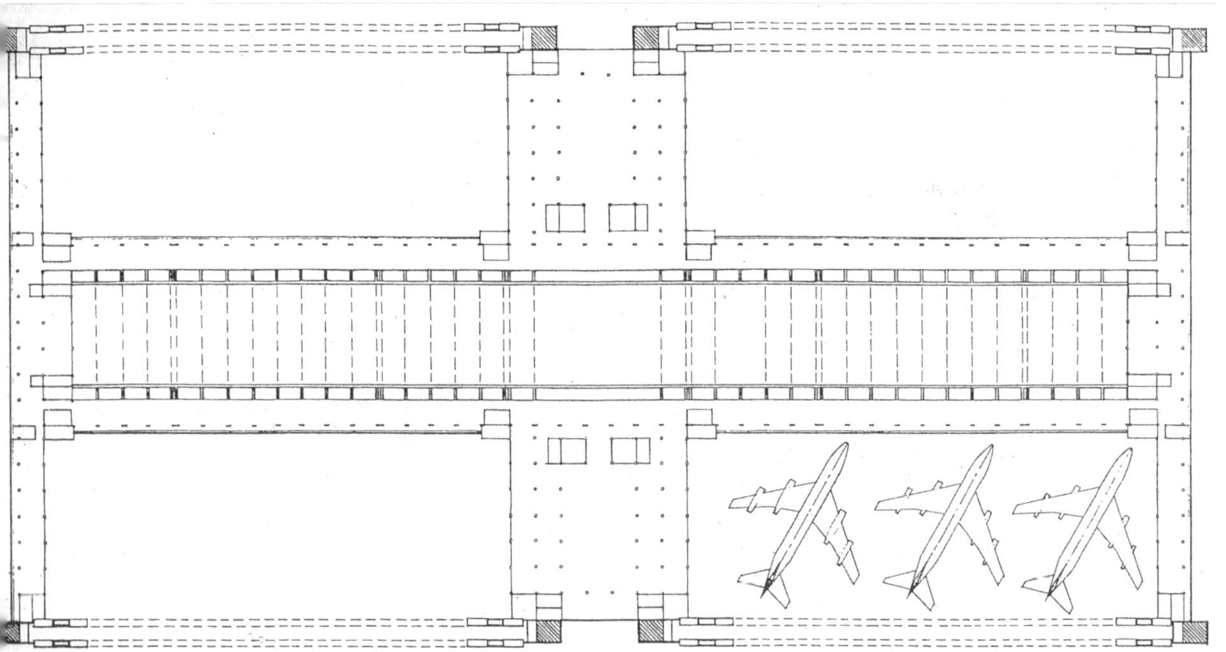

Heathrow, Owen Williams' BOAC HQ hangars, proposed plan view with four so-called hangar pens around a central workshop. (David Cottam)

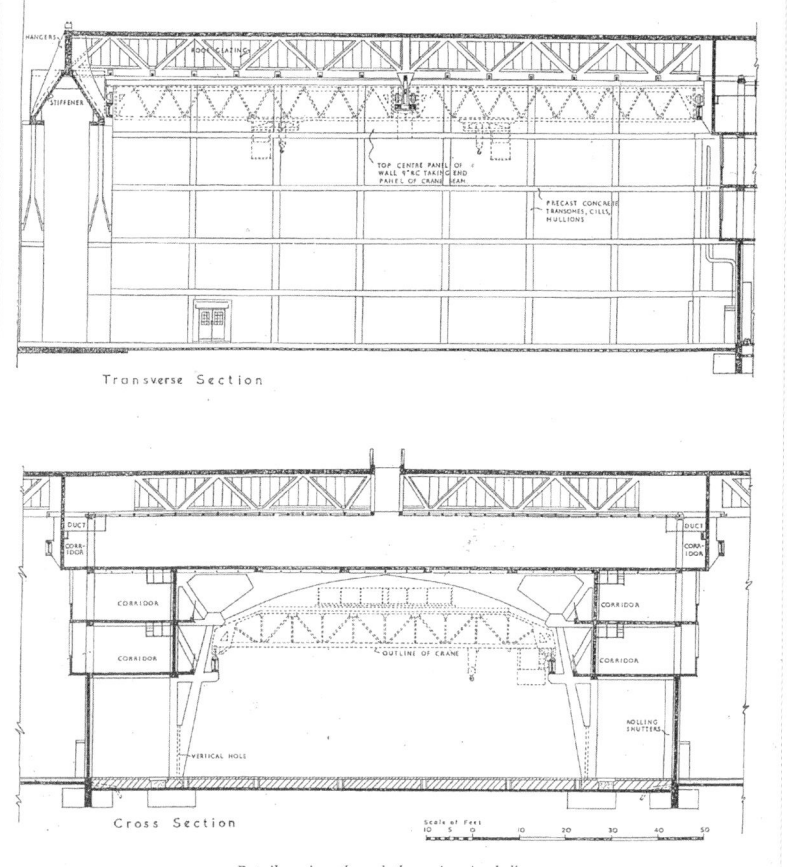

Right: Heathrow, Owen Williams' BOAC HQ hangars, Central Engineering Hall cross sections. (via Author)

Below: Heathrow, Owen Williams' BOAC HQ hangars, final plan view with the four hangar pens around a central workshop, plus offices between pens and at south-west end. (via Author)

Transverse Section

Cross Section

Detail sections through the engineering hall.

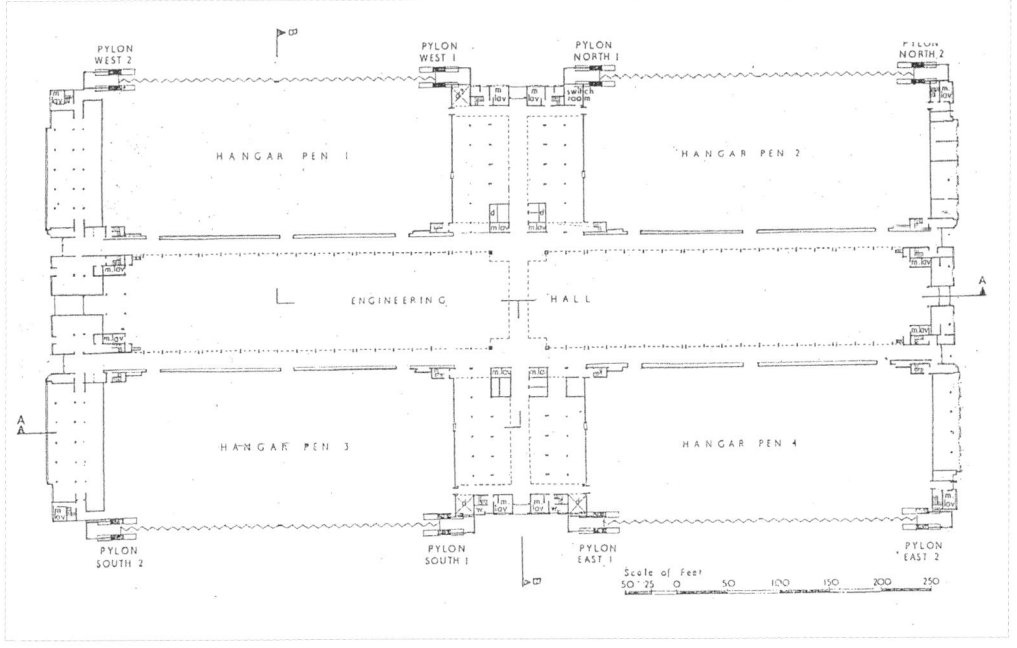

Heathrow, Owen Williams' BOAC HQ hangars, with Britannia 102s inside. Door width 300ft x 46ft clear height. Large BOAC and Speedbird symbols positioned on the 1,000 ton concrete counterweight boxes. (Owen Williams Archive – Amey)

Heathrow, Owen Williams' BOAC HQ hangars, showing the end office block, with BOAC and QANTAS Constellations. (Richard Flagg)

Heathrow, Owen Williams' BOAC HQ hangars, aerial view, showing Stratocruisers, plus DC7Cs and Britannias outside/inside the Owen Williams-designed Wing Hangar behind. The road in the foreground allowed through traffic from the Great South West Rd on the south side to the Bath Road on the north side. (Geoffrey Negus)

Heathrow, Owen Williams' BOAC HQ hangars, internal with three Boeing Stratocruisers fitted in including G-ALSC. The middle one has to leave before the others can. (Owen Williams Archive – Amey)

Heathrow, Owen Williams' BOAC HQ, Central Engineering Hall, which dealt with engines and propellers amongst other components. (Owen Williams Archive – Amey)

provided a total hangar floor space of 188,000 sq. ft. An aircrew training school was included, as well as supplies and operational staff, administrative offices and four canteens capable of accommodating more than 800 people at once. The building footprint was 420 feet wide by 867 feet long, occupying a ground area of 8.5 acres, with a total floor area of approximately 1 million sq. ft.

4.5.4. Each of the hangars was 336 feet wide x 140 feet deep and was designed to hold two 150-foot-span aircraft with 12 feet of space beyond the wings. It was intended for Britannias (310 series tail height 37 feet 6 inches, span 142 feet 3 inches, length 124 feet 3 inches) to be on the south side, and Comets, Stratocruisers and Constellations (L749 tail height 23 feet 8 inches, span 123 feet, length 97 feet 4 inches) on the north side. Three four-engined aircraft could be accommodated by reversing a third aircraft between two aircraft previously positioned in the rear corners. The entrances were 46 feet high and 300 feet wide. The main door opening was spanned by two 75-foot-span double cantilevers supported on pylons, balanced by rectangular box counterweights of 1,000 tons each. The pylons carry 4,000 tons each on 72 foot x 36 foot bases. The ends of the cantilevers support a central V-shaped infill beam of 150-foot span. The counterweight boxes were filled incrementally with ballast as the roof progressed. The hangar doors were aluminium folding leaf electrically operated doors by Head Wrightson Aluminium, the doors folding into pylon support recesses each side to provide a 300-foot clear opening. The hangar roof comprised 10-foot-deep reinforced concrete V-shaped lattice beams at 18-foot centres, each sloping face being fully glazed. The roof beams span 140 feet over the hangars each side and over the central workshop. The hangars were heated by radiant heat from heating coils set within the floor.

4.5.5. Both hangars and main central workshop have overhead travelling cranes of 5-ton capacity, all running parallel to the hangar doors. Between the hangars is the central cross-shaped workshop separating the four hangars. The longer part runs between the north and south hangar pairs and is 867 feet long x 140 feet wide, but the main floor is restricted to 90 feet wide. The short arms between each of the hangar pairs have stores and offices up to six storeys high. The main central workshop has a reinforced concrete structure with frames at 18-foot centres comprising raked columns supporting 76-foot-span arches and supporting the overhead travelling crane rail each side as well as the upper floors each side. Between the rear walls of each hangar and the main workshop frames was a full length 15-foot-wide roadway each side to enable goods transport within and directly from outside. The ends of the hangars comprise five-storey offices, to complement additional office space along the short arms (transepts) of the workshops.

4.5.6. Total cost was £3 million.
Architect and Engineer was Sir Owen Williams & Partners.
Construction by main contractor W. & C. French began in October 1950 and was complete by 1955, all staff then transferring from Airways House at Brentford in July 1955.

4.5.7. Also built nearby was a four-storey office complex further south, closer to the A30, for administration, which became Comet House for catering. The office complex at the west end of the hangar pen complex was unpopular and a further six-storey office complex called Speedbird House (known as Birdseed House), was built between Comet House and the main hangar, with a footbridge to the hangar. Both were demolished after British Airways staff moved to new headquarters at Waterside, Harmondsworth, close to the M4 in June 1998.

4.5.8. In late 1980 the last of three steel-framed extensions to cater for larger tail heights of modern aircraft were provided to the west, north and east hangar pens, hiding Sir Owen Williams' curved façades on all but the remaining south pen. The south pen was not modified due to the restricted aircraft manoeuvring space between it and the adjacent (but now demolished) Wing hangar to the south. Now known as Technical Block A or TBA, the hangars and part of the workshops and stores are still in use but the offices are now disused. The Owen Williams hangar pen complex acquired the nickname The Kremlin, believed to be because of its massive construction. See also modifications for the A380 in Section 14.13.

4.6. PUBLIC VIEWING AREAS

Apart from the small viewing area on the north side adjacent to the original control tower (from 1948 until the 1960s), a short-term summer 1953 area on the closed runway 28R/

Heathrow, Comet House, eventually the Catering Dept. (via Charles Woodley)

Heathrow, BOAC Maintenance Area February 1973, inc. Comet House (Aircraft Catering), Speedbird House behind, with Owen Williams' BOAC HQ right and multi-storey car park and offices behind 747 hangar on left, with BOAC 707, Comet and 747 visible. (Mick West)

adjacent grass south of northern taxiway (accessible only by escorted walk), and another short-term enclosure near the Fairey hangar south of the incomplete Queens Building for the October London–NZ Air Race, there was a 350-foot-long public viewing area in the north-eastern corner of the Central Area, over the tunnel, from 1954 to 1958. In the early days, Rapide flights were available, plus horse rides for children. The advent of the Queens Building Roof Gardens from 1955 brought considerable improvements for the general public, gradually reduced and closed for security reasons several times in the latter part of twentieth century, finally closing in 2003 with the second Iraq War.

4.7. RSPCA ANIMAL HOSTEL

The RSPCA Animal Hostel opened on the extreme north-west corner on 20 November 1952, with facilities for animals, birds and sea creatures to remain for short periods, either before departure, after arrival or in transit.

4.8. LONDON TO CHRISTCHURCH, NEW ZEALAND AIR RACE

To commemorate the centenary of the city of Christchurch, New Zealand, an air race was organised; the New Zealand Air Race from Heathrow. Starting on 8 October 1953 from Heathrow, the 12,270-mile London to Christchurch, New Zealand Air Race had two

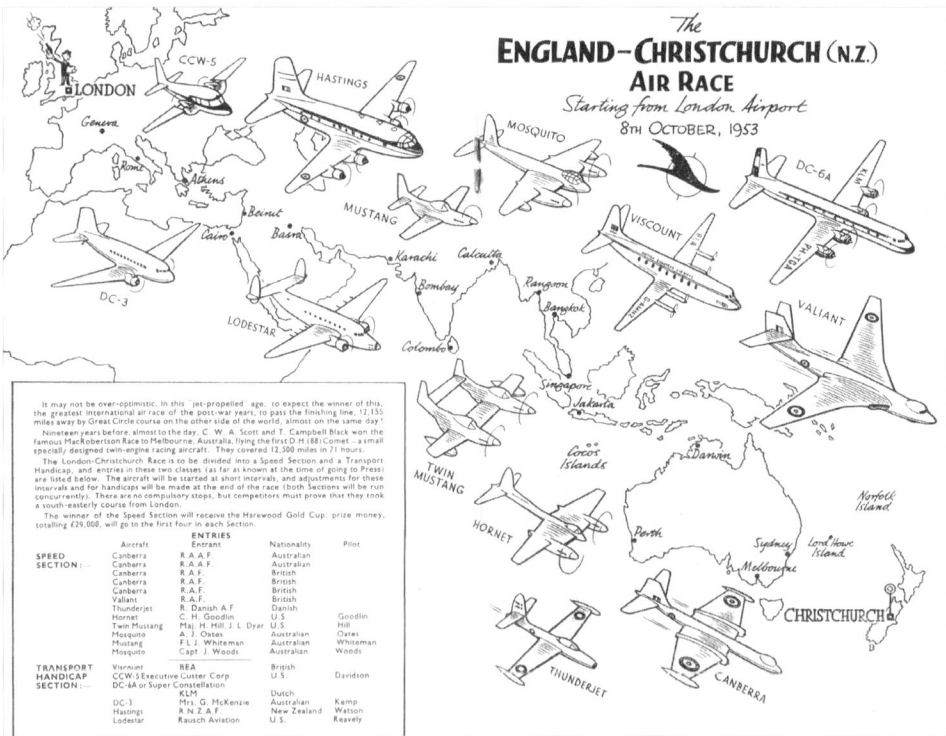

Heathrow, England to Christchurch (NZ) Air Race 1953 cartoon with entries by Wren. The race was to commemorate the centenary of the City of Christchurch, New Zealand. Not all the entries portrayed started and/or finished. (*The Airport Visitor* 1953 via Author)

categories, a Speed Section for the fastest and a Handicap Section for transport aircraft. The general public were able to use the new Central Area tunnel for the first time; it opened on Monday 5 October, to allow three days of public viewing of the participants. Out of nineteen original entries, twelve aircraft were due to take part, most having some significance, race numbers in brackets. Four aircraft were in the Transport Section: a KLM DC6A PH-TGA (21); an RNZAF Hastings NZ5804 (22); the V700 Viscount prototype G-AMAV (23) in BEA colours; and a Lockheed 18-56 Hudstar (Hudson/Lodestar) (24). The other category, the Speed Section, had eight aircraft: two Mosquito 41s (6 and 8); two RAF Canberra PR3s WE139 (2) and WE142 (3), and a PR7 WH773 (1); two RAAF Canberra Mk 20s A84-201 (5) and A84-202 (4); and the second prototype Vickers Valiant WB215 (10). By the start date, just eight aircraft were left. The Lockheed Hudstar was withdrawn, reportedly due to Russian refusal to use the northern Great Circle route, the Valiant (due to lack of time for long-range testing), and the two Mosquitoes, one due to lack of financial backing, the other, VH-KLG (No. 6), due to a forced landing on the Burmese coast while flying from Perth to take part. The race was started by the Duke of Gloucester and the eight aircraft departed at five-minute intervals from 16.30 on 8 October. The KLM DC6A was away first at 16.30, then the RNZAF Hastings at 16.35, and the Viscount at 16.40. The Canberras departed in race number order: WH773 (1) at 17.35, WE142 (2) at 17.40, WE139 (3) at 17.45, A84-202 (4) at 17.50, and finally A84-201 (5) at 17.55. All aircraft took off from Runway 6 westwards (15R/33L), which was possibly one of the few times it was used. The first aircraft to arrive at Christchurch and so win the speed section was one of the Canberra PR3s, WE139 (No. 3), in a time of 23 hours 51 minutes with four stops en route; the average speed of 494.5 mph was a new point-to-point record. Second was one of the RAAF Canberras, A84-201 (5), in 24 hours 32 minutes. The first to arrive in the transport section was the Viscount with four stops en route in 40 hours 41 minutes, including long stages London–Bahrain 3,218 miles and Cocos Islands–Melbourne 3,600 miles. The KLM DC6A with seven stops en route took 49 hours 57 minutes, but when handicap adjustments were made came in as winner. The RNZAF Hastings withdrew at Negombo, Ceylon, with engine problems, no replacements being allowed.

4.9. PASSENGER FIGURES REACH 1 MILLION

The end of 1953 signalled the first year with 1 million passengers per annum.

4.10. NORTHOLT CLOSES TO AIRLINE TRAFFIC

Croydon, with no hard runways and surrounded by housing, was not considered suitable as the main airport for London so, after the Second World War, Northolt, 6 miles north of Heathrow, was used for civil services until Heathrow was ready. Up to its transfer, Northolt was handling 1,531 air transport movements in March 1954, for instance, compared to 3,959 at Heathrow. In particular BEA was eager to transfer services to Heathrow and their first scheduled departure from Heathrow was a Viking to Paris on 16 April 1950. Northolt was finally handed back to the RAF on 30 October 1954, when the last civil services transferred to Heathrow.

Heathrow, KLM DC6A PH-TGA 7 October 1953, entry in the England to Christchurch (NZ) Air Race. Winner in the Transport category (of two that finished) after handicaps accounted for. (Tony Clarke Collection – David Whitworth – Flickr)

Heathrow, Viscount 700 prototype G-AMAV in BEA colours, entry in the England to Christchurch (NZ) Air Race. Fastest in the Transport category, but second after handicaps accounted for. (Tony Clarke Collection – David Whitworth – Flickr)

Heathrow, Royal Australian Air Force Canberra A84-202, entry in the Speed section of the England to Christchurch (NZ) Air Race. Note the Passenger Building steel frame behind with Scotch Derrick cranes. (Tony Clarke Collection – David Whitworth – Flickr)

4.11. BATTLE OF BRITAIN STATIC DISPLAYS AND OTHER UNUSUAL MILITARY VISITS

4.11.1. Battle of Britain static displays were held in September 1951, 1953, 1954, 1956, 1957 and 1958, some lasting for weeks. The 1951 line-up included Chipmunk WB656/L-13, Meteor F8 WA924/R (56 Sqn), Prentice VR307 (FAIP South Cerney), Spitfire PK622/39M and Washington WF553 (15 Sqn). The 1953 line-up included Canberra B2 WH711 (149 Sqn), Devon VP975 (HQ Coastal Command), Valetta C1 VL267 (167 Sqn), Vampire FB5 WA187/RS-O, and F86E Sabre 19190 (439 Sqn RCAF). The RCAF Sabre was part of a flight of three to Heathrow. The 1954 line-up included Canberra B2 WH731 (15 Sqn), Hastings C2 WD497 (1312 Flt), Meteor F8 WK693/T (111 Sqn), Meteor NF11 WD593/A (151 Sqn), Hastings C2 WD497, and Vampire FB5 VZ126 (233 OCU). The 1956 line-up included Canberra PR3 WE151, Hastings WJ333/GAL, Hunter F6 XE603, Meteor NF14 WS785/C and Venom WX906/H. The 1957 line-up included Canberra WH959, Hastings C1 TG604/H, Hunter F4 XF990/16, Meteor NF14 WS786/F, Valetta T3 WJ462/B and valiant XD870. The 1958 line-up included Beverley C1 XL151/L, Comet C2 XK670/670, Hunter F6 XE597/A, Javelin F7 XH718/X, Victor B1 XA937 and Vulcan B2 XH498.

4.11.2. In addition in May 1957, six F100C Super Sabres were present at Heathrow, 54.1753/1754/1765/1786/1813/1829, apparently on a transatlantic record flight

4.12. LAST ROYAL AERONAUTICAL SOCIETY SUMMER GARDEN PARTY

On 13 June 1954 the Royal Aeronautical Society held a summer garden party at Heathrow, the first since the old pre-war Fairey gatherings. This was to be the last RAeS garden party. Squeezed in at the south end of the new Central Area Terminal Building, and having to fit in with the normal scheduled arrivals and departures, they still managed to have a BEA Ambassador, BOAC Stratocruiser, Trans Canada Airlines Super Constellation, a BEA Bristol 171 helicopter plus an example of the new BEA Vickers Viscount, destined to become the mainstay of BEA and other European airlines at Heathrow for some decades to come.

Heathrow, RAF Beverley XL151, 21 September 1958, at the last of six Battle of Britain static displays at Heathrow. (Tony Clarke Collection – David Whitworth – Flickr)

Heathrow, Alcock and Brown statue in its original position at the west end of the North side ramp, with RAF Britannia XN398, plus Bristol Sycamore overhead. (via Charles Woodley)

4.13. ALCOCK AND BROWN MEMORIAL

The Sir John Alcock and Sir Arthur Whitten Brown memorial, designed by William MacMillan, RA, was unveiled at the west end of London Airport north apron by the spectators enclosure on 15 June 1954, the thirty-fifth anniversary of the first transatlantic flight, pending construction of the Central Area. It was proposed to place it opposite the Queens Building main entrance, but after being positioned near Terminal 3 by 15 June 1966, it was moved again to the west end of the tower building on 25 April 1974 to enable construction of new subways to the underground station.

4.14 BEA HELICOPTER SERVICE

4.14.1. On 1 June 1951, proving flights by S51s G-AJOV and G-AJHW were undertaken for an intended Birmingham helicopter service from Heathrow via Northolt. Services proper began on 4 June, although flights were to Birmingham Haymills Rotor Station rather than Elmdon Airport, continuing until 9 April 1952. The service continued from 10 April but cargo only until 15 January 1954. From 13 July 1953 the new Bristol 171 Sycamore G-AMWH was introduced, replacing the S51s eventually. The passenger numbers and the amount of freight carried were not large, but BEA was able to prove that there was a demand, albeit small.

4.14.2. On 16 June 1954 a new service Heathrow–Northolt–Southampton/Eastleigh began with Bristol m1717 Sycamore G-AMWH until 16 April 1955. On 30 October 1954 the BEA base at Northolt closed and services then ran direct Heathrow–Eastleigh. From 22 December 1954 WS55s were introduced, the first being G-ANPH, able to carry eight passengers compared to the three-four on previous helicopters. In addition, the opportunity to carry passengers was used on the positioning flights of helicopters from the BEA helicopter base at Gatwick to Heathrow between 1 November 1954 until the end on 16 April 1955.

4.14.3. On 24 July 1955 BEA began a helicopter service between Heathrow and the South Bank Heliport, Waterloo with Westland Whirlwind G-ANUK, with a fare of £1.15 s. By the end of operations on 31 May 1956, 3,833 passengers had been carried.

4.15 SOUTHERN AIR TRAFFIC CONTROL

4.15.1. The new Southern Air Traffic Control Centre (SATCC) began operations from a single-storey building (with air-conditioned basement for radar servicing and electric equipment racks) on the north-west corner of Heathrow in April 1955, having previously been bases at nearby Uxbridge. Details of aircraft leaving Heathrow were handed over to SATCC from the Heathrow control tower, and inbound aircraft are handed over by SATCC to Heathrow approach controllers and radar directors who direct them on to final approach or act as approach control for Northolt or Bovingdon. One of three main ATC centres covering the three Flight Information Regions, the others being at Prestwick

Heathrow, Southern Air Traffic Control Centre Ops room, August 1959. (CAA Archives via Pete Bish)

Heathrow, Southern Air Traffic Control Centre, Sector radar controllers, July 1963. (CAA Archives via Pete Bish)

(Scottish Area) and Preston (northern England, North Wales and Northern Ireland), SATCC was the largest and busiest, and was divided into six sectors. Sector 1 covered traffic east of London on Green One and Red One airways to and from Brussels, Amsterdam, and Scandinavia, as well as south-east of London covering Amber Two from Paris and Rome. Sectors 2 and 3 covered inbound traffic in the vicinity of the London Control Zone, either bound for aerodromes in the zone or overflying to Manchester, for example. Sector 4 covered outbound traffic from aerodromes in the London Central Zone. Sector 5 covered traffic on Amber One south of London to Paris and Rome, and Red One west of London to the Channel Islands, Spain, Portugal and western France. Sector 6 covered traffic on Green One west of London serving transatlantic flights via Shannon, Amber One and Amber Two north of London to Dublin, Belfast, Prestwick, Manchester and Birmingham.

4.15.2. The main operations room was 25 feet by 30 feet with the Sector Controllers, their assistants, radar operators, teleprinters, meteorological officers, and RAF liaison. Each sector had its own controller and assistant communicating with aircraft over the whole route, with their own radar controllers watching aircraft within the sector. Radar types included long-range surveillance, short-range (zone control) and height-finding, enabling aircraft to be monitored from take-off to 130 miles out. The Meteorological Section provided controllers with forecasts and up-to-date wind and weather conditions, and an RAF Liaison Unit in direct contact with RAF Air Traffic Control at Uxbridge. The SATCC would continue at Heathrow until the first staff moved to new premises at West Drayton north of Heathrow from late 1966 to early 1971, from when the controllers also covered the Preston FIR, the whole being renamed London Air Traffic Control Centre (LATCC) and with radar coverage from 5,000 to 25,000 feet, where it would enjoy much-enhanced facilities including computers. SATCC at Heathrow was closed then and eventually demolished.

4.16 MILLBOURN REPORT, LONG-HAUL TERMINAL PROPOSED, NEW FINGERS

4.16.1. Passenger throughput was up to 3 million per annum by 1956. The escalating passenger figures were beginning to cause alarm, so a committee was set up under Sir Eric Millbourn and the Millbourn Report was published on 1 August 1957, producing a list of serious recommendations. First they recommended the expansion of Gatwick to take some of the pressure off Heathrow. They confirmed the original Layout Panel's view that all the Heathrow terminals should be in the Central Area. They recommended immediate construction of a new long-haul terminal on the south-west face of the Central Area (which would become Terminal 3), plus a new short-haul terminal on the north-east face exclusively for BEA (which would become Terminal 1), and to complete the Central Area, a new cargo area and freight building on the north-west side. BOAC and BEA had cargo sheds on the north-west quadrant, before they moved their main bases to the Cargo Area on the south-west of the airport in 1968, see below. The Millbourn Committee also pushed for the 'finger and gate' system of piers, which allowed passengers to walk under cover directly to their aircraft rather than be coached, the aircraft being nose-on to the pier. There was much agonising at the time about the effect of jet blast on passengers, which would eventually be resolved by leaving passengers at the gates until ready to embark, and pushback techniques of manoeuvring aircraft.

4.16.2. A boiler house to provide central heating via an underground network of pipes to the various buildings was also proposed. Sited between the Control Tower and the proposed long-haul terminal (later Terminal 3), it was designed with an ultimate 100,000-BThU/hr capacity, and is still visible.

4.16.3. To enable all this building work in the Central Area, which was now becoming cramped, the committee reluctantly agreed that it was necessary to close Runway Nos 4 (15L/33R) and 6 (15R/33L) running parallel approximately north-west to south-east. It was also going to be necessary to provide a fire station on the north side, which would become the main one, the Central Area one to be a satellite.

4.16.4. By 1958 there were fifty-two aircraft stands at Central Area (eighteen on the north side), with the need to increase Central Area's total to 100.

4.17. BOAC WING HANGAR

4.17.1. The Wing Hangar at Heathrow was built for BOAC in 1954–56, opening in 1957. It was designed around the Bristol Britannia, the primary requirement being maintenance access to the wing. The original Britannia 102 entered BOAC service in February 1957 and

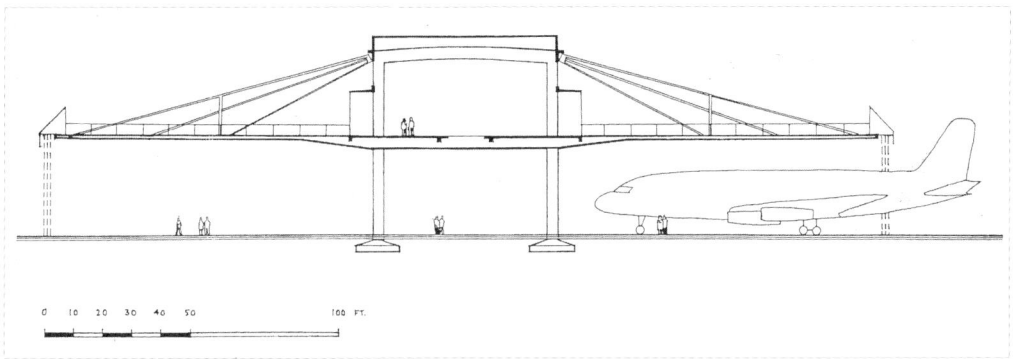

Heathrow, Owen Williams' BOAC Wing Hangar cross-section. (David Cottam)

Heathrow, Owen Williams' BOAC Wing Hangar external with Britannia tails. (Owen Williams Archive – Amey)

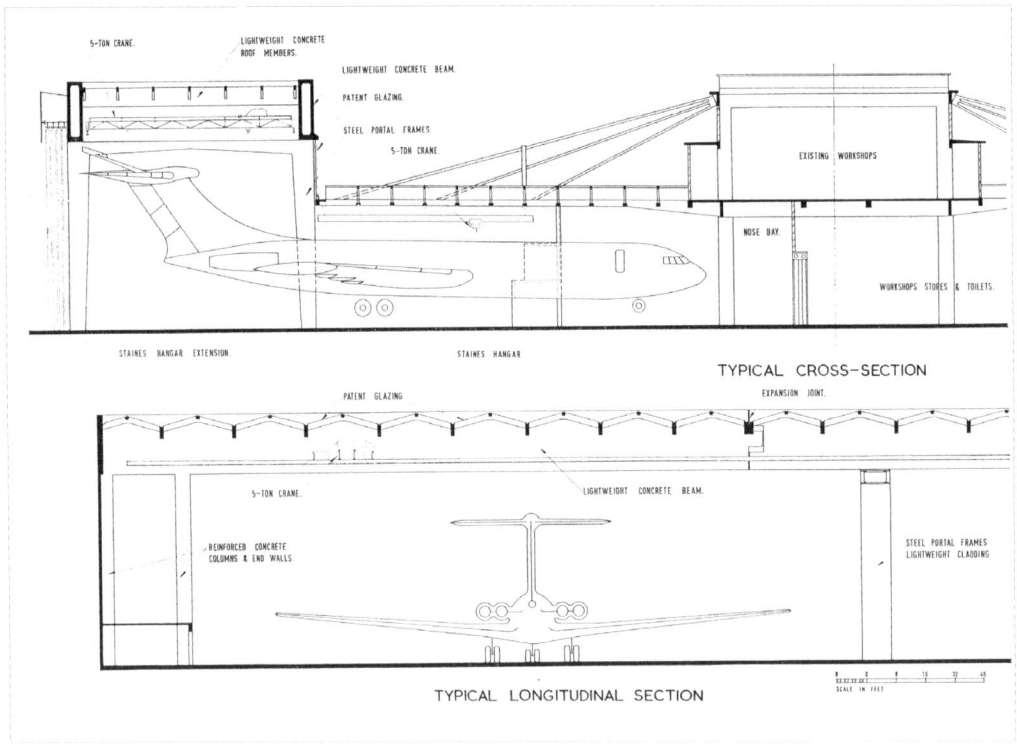

Heathrow, BOAC Wing Hangar modifications for VC10 tails, cross-section. (Ken Shadbolt)

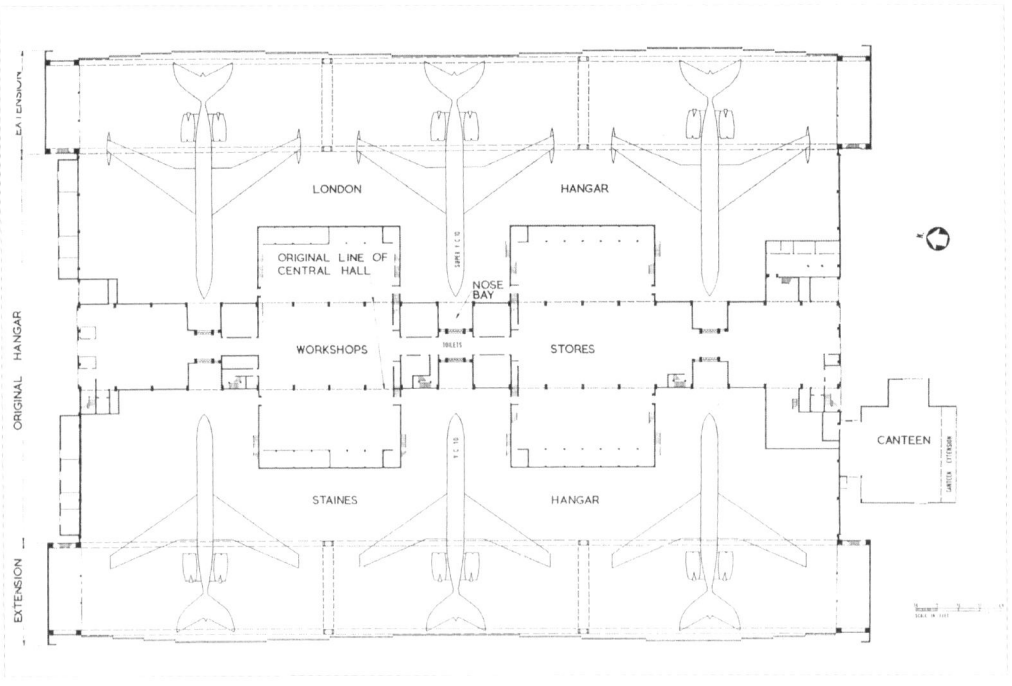

Heathrow, BOAC Wing Hangar modifications for VC10s, plan showing three VC10s each side. (Ken Shadbolt)

Heathrow, BOAC Wing Hangar modifications for VC10s, completed with Comets. (Ken Shadbolt)

had a wingspan of 142 feet 3 inches, length of 114 feet and tail height 36 feet 8 inches. The longer 312 series had a similar span, length of 124 feet 3 inches and tail height 37 feet 6 inches. In all, BOAC had thirty-three Britannias, withdrawing the fourteen No. 102s in 1962, and the rest by 1965, the VC10 having entered service in April 1964. The hangar was shortened for economy by allowing the tail and rear fuselage to be outside, the doors being shaped to wrap round the fuselage allowing the tail to project outside, saving the cost of building and heating a high hangar. This became the Wing hangar with a double cantilever roof designed by Sir Owen Williams and Partners. Of overall size 565 feet by 280 feet, it had ten double cantilever frames with 111-foot cantilevers each side with 30-foot clear height. The simplicity of design allowed one frame to be completed every five weeks. The roof is all glazing on concrete purlins on concrete booms tied to the two-storey central spine by steel ties cased in concrete, providing large open areas with no columns.

4.17.2. In September 1960 BOAC appointed Sir Frederick Snow & Partners to prepare a design for extensions to the Wing hangar to accommodate the new Vickers VC10 coming into service, with its high tail and four engines mounted at the rear, as the four hangar pens in the existing Owen Williams BOAC HQ building were committed to servicing Boeing 707s and Comets. This required a 68-foot deepening of the bays with a clear height of 50 feet. The twelve initial VC10s had a span of 146 feet 2 inches, length of 158 feet 9 inches, and tail height of 39 feet 6 inches. The seventeen Super VC10s had a similar span and tail height with a length of 171 feet 8 inches. The original VC10 entered service in April 1964, the Super VC10 following in April 1965, all being retired/sold by 1984. Due to the existing double cantilever construction it was not possible to extend without rebuilding the central core. The existing overall width was ideal to accommodate three VC10s side by side, which with a wingspan of 146 feet would allow for the introduction of internal columns at third points for the extensions. The solution chosen for each side, therefore, was to construct two beams each 618 feet long at high level, supported by columns at the ends and by portal frames at the third points. The portal frames were capable of being moved to accommodate more aircraft of smaller wingspan if needed.

4.17.3. The portal frames were of steel, but the two main beams were constructed as prestressed concrete beams, using the then new lightweight concrete, after considering other forms including steel truss and ordinary prestressed and reinforced concrete beams. This was the first major structure in the UK to use lightweight concrete, and no code of practice existed at the time, so much investigative work had to be carried out on the properties. The two ends of the extensions projected beyond the existing building width by 24 feet 6 inches to accommodate the four leaves of the doors each end and provide more workshop space. Nose bays were provided in the central hall walls to accommodate the then future Super VC10. The main beams were 16 feet deep by 4 feet wide hollow box section with 12-inch-thick flanges and 9-inch-thick walls generally thickening to 12 inches at supports and ends, with crosswalls at 10-foot centres, the beams being solid at supports present and future. The beam soffites were positioned at 50 feet in height, the depth of the beam allowing the overhead travelling cranes to be positioned above the internal portal frames. The roof comprised main rectangular cross beams 40 inches by 15 inches at 20-foot centres with seven pitched rafters 15 inches by 7.5 inches at 10-foot centres on top and a purlin 12 inches by 6.5 inches at the rafter apex, all in lightweight concrete. The use of lightweight concrete at 2/3 the density of normal concrete significantly reduced the roof dead weight. The portal frames were twin I-frames built up from 1/2 inch to 5/8 inch web plates and 20-inch x 1-inch flanges braced together. Web depth was 5 feet 6 inches at columns tapering to 3 feet at the centre of the 64-foot span. The end columns, four at each end, were 4 feet square in normal reinforced concrete, carrying 643 tons on the inner columns and 330 tons uplift on the outer ones. Three 5-ton cranes were provide on the Staines side and two of 5 tons on the London side. The existing 2-ton cranes under the cantilevers were re-erected one bay out to cover the wings. The original hangar doors were extended from 32 feet 6 inches clear height to 50 feet by extending the Corten weathering steel frame and re-sheeting with aluminium sheet, filling in the original Britannia cut-outs. The new doors were on four tracks to allow over half the elevation to be clear or for all bays to be open at once. Construction began in the Staines hangar in November 1961, allowing maintenance to continue on the London side, being complete by November 1962, when construction work switched to the London side. This was handed over in November 1963. The total cost was £1.5 million. The overall design and construction for the extensions contract was under the control of BOAC Properties Branch, headed by Kenneth J. Joyner.

Extensions Contract:

Main Contractor: W. & C. French.

Steel Subcontractor: Robert Watson & Co.

Hangar Door Subcontractor: HBR Metal Industries Ltd.

4.17.4. In September 1990 work was begun to protect the cable stays, which had cracks appearing in the bitumen coating and to the underlying concrete encasement, with rust showing through. The hangar was demolished reputedly by explosives in the 1990s and is now a car park.

4.18. SIR JOHN D'ALBIAC RETIRES, REPLACED BY JAMES JEFFS

In 1957, Sir John d'Albiac retired after ten years as Commandant of London Airport. He has been remembered by D'Albiac House, a three-storey office block with single-storey rear annexe behind (the ex-BOAC Cargo Shed), built to house the new British Airports Authority from 1966, on Cromer Road, on the north side of the Central Area, west of the main access tunnel. He was replaced by Group Captain James Jeffs, who had previously been Commandant at Prestwick from 1950 to 1957. He had been involved with Air Traffic Control development at Croydon in the 1920s, and had been instrumental in the installation of ATC at most of the UK principal airports. He was in charge of ATC at Heston, supervising the RAeS garden parties there, and was in the tower when Chamberlain returned from Germany in September 1938. During the war Jeffs set up the transatlantic control centre at Prestwick. In 1945 he was put in charge of ATC for the London area, including Heathrow, and was present at Don Bennett's first departure. He was Commandant for only three years.

4.19. FUEL DEPOTS

4.19.1. The main fuel farm at Perry Oaks was erected early on, sited close to the Perry Oaks sludge works, between the two western diagonal Runways 6 (15R/33L) and 7 (05L/23R).

A satellite fuel depot had been built west of the site of the Central Area Boiler House by 1958, fed by underground pipes from the main Perry Oaks fuel farm. From here tankers refuelled from hydrants and left to refuel aircraft out on the surrounding stands. This first Central Area fuel depot was a joint Shell and Esso depot, to be joined by another smaller one run by the Hydrant Servicing Co. (Chevron Petrofina and Gulf) on the north side just west of the main tunnel by 1967. A third fuel depot was also built in No. 1 Maintenance Area near Hatton Cross. A new pipeline was opened in July 1960, feeding Shell-Mex and BP fuel from Walton-on-Thames to Heathrow. Comprising two 6-inch-diameter pipes, it was the first such pipeline into any British Airport, although fuel continued to be supplied by tankers as well.

4.19.2. In the early days tankers were only having to refuel smaller aircraft, but as larger aircraft came into use, so tanker sizes grew. The DC7C had 6,500-gallon capacity, and the Britannia 8,600 gallons. Hydrants at aircraft stands would eventually supplant much of the tankers' work, but the Millbourn Committee had not felt able to commit to stand size or hydrant capacity in 1957 before the advent of the intercontinental jets from 1958 on, like the Boeing 707-320 or DC8, which had fuel capacities of the order 20,000 gallons. By 1968 Esso were operating six Python six-axle tankers at 12,000 gallons, ten Struvers at 9,000 gallons and sixteen Super Plutos at 6,000 gallons, plus eight smaller units. Esso's storage tanks at the time stored 1 million gallons at Perry Oaks, plus half a million more at the Central Area depot.

4.20. VISUAL APPROACH-SLOPE INDICATOR SYSTEM

4.20.1. Approach lighting for night-time or poor visibility landings at Heathrow's two main east–west runways comprises 'line-and-bar' lighting to help guide the pilot on the approach to the runway. Developed by Mr E. S. Calvert of RAE Farnborough, and initially installed on trial there in 1948, the Calvert system, adopted worldwide, comprises a straight line of lights 3,000 feet long leading to the end of the runway, with crossbars of lights at right angles at intervals of 500 feet. The crossbars become progressively shorter nearer to the end of the runway, so the appearance is of a funnel, with the narrow end at the runway end. The crossbars help the pilot to maintain the aircraft horizontally. The centre line lights provide additional guidance in that the first 1,000 feet has triple lights, the next 1,000 feet double lights and the last 1,000 feet nearest the runway, single lights. In poor visibility the intensity of the lights can be increased. It is believed to have been installed at Heathrow soon after 1948 trials at Farnborough.

4.20.2. The Royal Aircraft Establishment had been researching the causes of accidents, and undershooting runways in particular. Using a landing simulator at Farnborough it was proved that, under certain weather or terrain conditions, pilots would not be able to recognise an imminent undershoot until very low. Previously, angle-of-attack indicators used single lamps with red, green and orange segments, but they were not considered to give sufficient glide path guidance. Two new methods of visual glide-slope indication were under investigation by RAE by late 1958, the Australian Cumming/Lane system using two wing-bars of lights, one close to the ground, the other elevated on poles. Their relative heights were such that the correct glide slope was when they were in line. The other system being tested was the RAE Calvert visual glide-path indicator. This consisted of two bars about 30 feet wide, spaced about 50 feet from the runway edge at the fore-and-aft limits of the prescribed touchdown area, approximately 500 feet from the threshold and 500–1,000 feet apart. Each bar comprised a powerful lamp with the upper half covered by a red filter. The lamps and lenses were set in shallow boxes with both red and white rays coming through slits in the box ends. Each box was then inclined such that the centre was at the correct 3° slope. If the aircraft is too low, both bars show red; if too high, both would be white. The correct glide slope is shown when the nearer bar shows red and the further one white. A battery of three is used each side of the runway for safety. Highly accurate guidance on glide slope is given right down to touchdown, and the system also gives the pilot some idea of bank. The Calvert system was initially installed at Blackbushe, then Aberdeen, Prestwick, Belfast and Liverpool, before Heathrow in July 1959. Eventually the Calvert system was adopted by ICAO as a world standard in 1961. The British preferred the term visual glide-path indicator, or v.g.p.i, but ICAO referred to it as VASI, visual approach-slope indicator.

4.21. THE FIRST AIRPORT HOTELS

In 1959, plans were announced for the Skyways Hotel on the Bath Road near the North Terminal, with 200 rooms plus a further 83 planned later. Eventually the Skyways Hotel was built with 160 rooms and a further 100 added later. A second hotel, the Ariel, was begun in 1959 and opened in January 1960, at Harlington Corner on the north side of Bath Road. This was an unusual addition to the local landscape as it was circular with a central courtyard, and it stands today as the Holiday Inn Ariel with four floors and 184 rooms.

4.22. AIRLINE DEVELOPMENTS IN THE 1950s

4.22.1. In March 1950 BOAC took delivery of the first of twenty-five Handley Page Hermes. They first entered service to Accra in August, replacing Solents and Yorks on the African services by the end of the year. On 16 April 1950 BEA operated its first scheduled service from Heathrow with Vickers Vikings to Paris. On 2 May 1950 BOAC made history with the first pure jet passenger service, introducing the DH Comet 1 on the Johannesburg service. By September BOAC had nine Comets in service. Comets replaced Argonauts on the Tokyo service slashing 50 hours off the trip. The first scheduled BEA Airspeed Elizabethan service was operated on 13 March 1952 to Paris, but a more important first occurred on 18 April 1953 when V701 Viscount G-AMNY operated BEA's first turboprop service to Nicosia. The BOAC Hermes fleet was retired in 1953. However events were to take a nasty turn on 10 January 1954 when BOAC Comet G-ALYP broke up in mid-air off Elba in the Mediterranean, having taken off from Rome's Ciampino Airport 20 min earlier. All Comets were grounded and an intensive investigation undertaken, but no obvious cause was concluded although modifications to the fleet were carried out. Services restarted on 23 March, but on 8 April a second Comet G-ALYY crashed near Naples and the aircraft's Certificate of Airworthiness was withdrawn for good. In their place some of their Hermes were reintroduced, twelve L749 Constellations and seven Stratocruisers were bought and remained in service until the first Britannia 102 arrived at the end of 1955. 30 October 1954 saw the last scheduled BEA service leave Northolt, all services now operating from Heathrow. The first operational service from Heathrow Central was a BEA Viscount G-ALWE on 17 April 1955 to Amsterdam. Problems with the introduction of BOAC Britannias, including the longer range 312, caused BOAC to order ten Douglas DC7C, which were used on the New York service from 6 January 1957, and extended to San Francisco by March.

4.22.2. Tu-104 CCCP-L5400 arrived at Heathrow on 22 March 1956, the first visit of the type, to be followed on 25 April 1956 by three Tu-104s (CCCP-L5400, 5412 and 5413) on

Heathrow, first visit of Tupolev Tu104, 22 March 1956, CCCP-L5400 carrying Comrade Serov of the Soviet Secret Police. (Frank Hudson)

Heathrow B1 hangar with BOACD Comet 2 G-AMXD. (The late Ian MacFarlane)

proving flights. On 1 October 1957 TWA L-1649 Starliner N7307C departed on the longest ever non-stop scheduled commercial flight to San Francisco, taking 23 hours 21 minutes. The first Boeing 707 to be seen at Heathrow landed on 8 September 1958, being Pan American N709PA. On 4 October 1958 BOAC Comet 4 G-APDC departed for New York on the first transatlantic jet passenger service. Another Comet 4 G-APDB left New York at the same time bound for London. Pan American were not able to compete with their 707-120 New York–Heathrow service until 16 November 1958, and then only with an intermediate stop at either Gander or Shannon because of insufficient range. On 31 March 1959 BOAC inaugurated a round-the-world service by Britannia via Atlantic/Pacific and Comet 4 Tokyo to London. Pan American introduced the intercontinental version of the Boeing 707-321 on 10 October 1959, able to serve Heathrow–New York without a refuelling stop. Then on 18 October 1959 Pan American Boeing 707 N719PA inaugurated the first all-jet round-the-world service. TWA followed Pan Am with a Boeing 707-320 service to New York on 23 November 1959. Long range, higher capacity Boeing 707s were introduced by BOAC on the New York service on 27 May 1960, retiring the Comet from this route.

4.22.3. The war surplus aircraft or derivatives like the DC3 and DC4 were being replaced by British products like the Viscount and Britannia, or less successful types like the Ambassador and Hermes, although the DC3 would still be a common sight until the early 1960s with BEA, Cambrian, KLM and Sabena. Avro Yorks could be seen with Skyways and Trans Mediterranean up to the end of the 1950s. When the BEA Vikings were retired, they were stored at Heathrow until sold to other newer operators. The top-selling British Viscounts were operated by thirteen airlines. The Americans had products from the Boeing, Convair, Douglas and Lockheed stables like the Stratocruiser (BOAC and PanAm), Convair 240/340/440 series, DC6 and DC7C, the Super Constellation and the Electra (although the latter would only be seen in KLM colours at Heathrow from 1959). The Convair 240/340/440 series, competing with the Viscount, were operated by ten airlines. The first Aeroflot Il-18 appeared in 1959. Long-haul types were dominated by the Douglas DC6 and DC7 series and Constellations. See Appendix D for airline types operated in the 1950s.

Heathrow, BOAC Comet 4 G-APDJ with BEA Vanguard & Fairey Hangar behind with BEA Maintenance Base in the distance, 21 August 1962. (John Hamlin)

5

Oceanic Terminal

Heathrow, Terminal 3 external soon after opening, *c.* 1961. (via Philip Sherwood)

Heathrow, Terminal 3, internal soon after opening, *c.* 1961. (via Philip Sherwood)

5.1 Frederick Gibberd & Ptnrs designed the new long-haul terminal on the south-west side of the Central Area close to the fuel bowser filling area, but built outside the original Central Area diamond shape in order to accommodate car parks. It was larger and a much simpler terminal compared to the Europa Building with large airy space internally and much more glass externally. The project got underway soon after the Millbourn Committee had reported, to become the No. 3 Oceanic Building. Costing £3 million, with an overall size of 430 feet by 280 feet, the main building comprised uncased steel columns on a 60-foot by 30-foot grid with 7-foot-6-inch-deep roof trusses used for services. The interior height was 28 feet 6 inches. The Oceanic Building was restricted to two storeys in height so as not to obstruct taxiway views from the tower, compared to the three storeys of the Europa Building. Also because of the high ground water table, it would have been expensive to build underground. The planning led to a U-shape with the main terminal flanked by north and south office blocks, each comprising 411-foot-long reinforced concrete frames with 25-foot transverse central span and 15-foot side cantilevers making 55-foot width.

5.2. The Oceanic Terminal opened on 16 November 1961 for all BOAC flights, eventually to handle all long-haul flights, previously handled from London Airport North. By 28 March 1962, when the latter closed except for the royal suite and freight operations, all the other airlines had moved in from the north side. Runway 4 (15L/33R) closed, and large areas of concrete were laid south-west and north-east of the centre for new aprons. Departing passengers arriving by coach, already checked in at the London terminal, their luggage weighed beforehand, would go direct to the first-floor concourse, either by the main staircase or from the south office block. Independent travellers would check in on the ground floor, hand in their luggage, go upstairs to immigration control and customs, then through to the departures lounge and along the airside gallery to the aircraft via two ramps. There were further ramps from the two office blocks with additional piers proposed. Arrivals came in via the airside gallery to an arrivals lounge, then immigration control, then down to the customs hall. There was a quick-service restaurant and bar on the first floor plus a main restaurant and another bar in the south office block. Initially there were no escalators, as foreigners apparently disliked them, leading to complaints about those in the Europa Building. They were therefore dispensed with as the floor level difference was only 13 feet with a wide staircase, but allowance made for installation of escalators later. There was a VIP suite in the north office block. Eventually a multi-storey car park (to be known as Multi-Storey Car-park No. 3) was built to the Terminal's north-west, between the Shell/Esso Fuel Depot and Terminal 3.

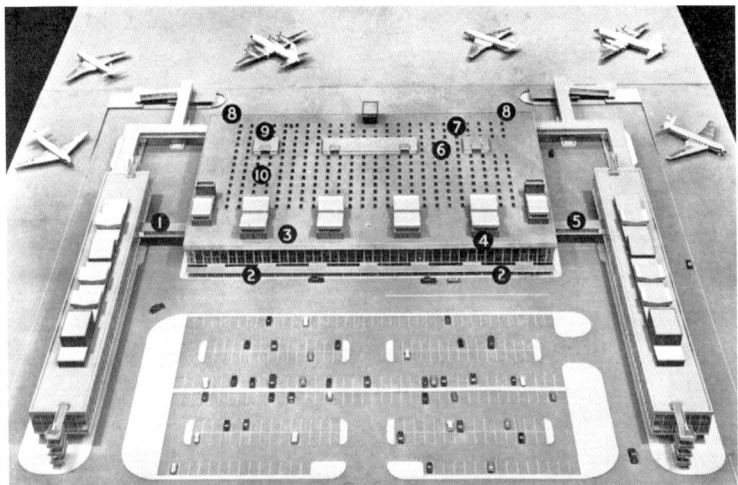

Heathrow, Oceanic Terminal 3 model in London Airport – Pitkin Pictorial book, showing the two office wings and car parking in front. The terminal opened in 1961. (via author)

1960s Developments

6.1 EARLY B1 HANGAR MODIFICATIONS

The three early Type B1 hangars, most visible from the Central Area facing the diagonal Runway 2 (23L/05R), were used by a succession of airlines after BOAC, including Skyways and Eagle, later Cunard Eagle/British Eagle. The middle hangar of the Cunard Eagle hangars was enlarged frontwards by Taylor Woodrow Construction in 1962, by widening from 120 feet to 168 feet, involving jacking up the two existing 120-foot-span trusses on to new 24-foot-span cantilever frames. The front was then brought forward by 20 feet to accommodate a Britannia tail fin. The last remaining of the B1s were two of the three facing 23L/05R, Hangars 3 and 4, demolished in around 1990.

Heathrow, Lloyd International Britannia G-AOVP landing on Runway 28R, 1968, with B1 hangars behind, including (middle) Eagle hangar modifications to fit Britannia tail. (Paul Howard)

6.2. AUTOLAND TRIALS AND IN SERVICE

6.2.1. The RAE Bedford Blind Landing Experimental Unit had been trying for some time to arrange a demonstration of their autoland system, for use with the ILS system at Heathrow if ever it was enveloped in fog with nothing else able to fly, when the opportunity occurred on 4 December 1962. One of the Vickers Varsities fitted with the equipment lacked a piece of test equipment that would have given directional guidance after autopilot

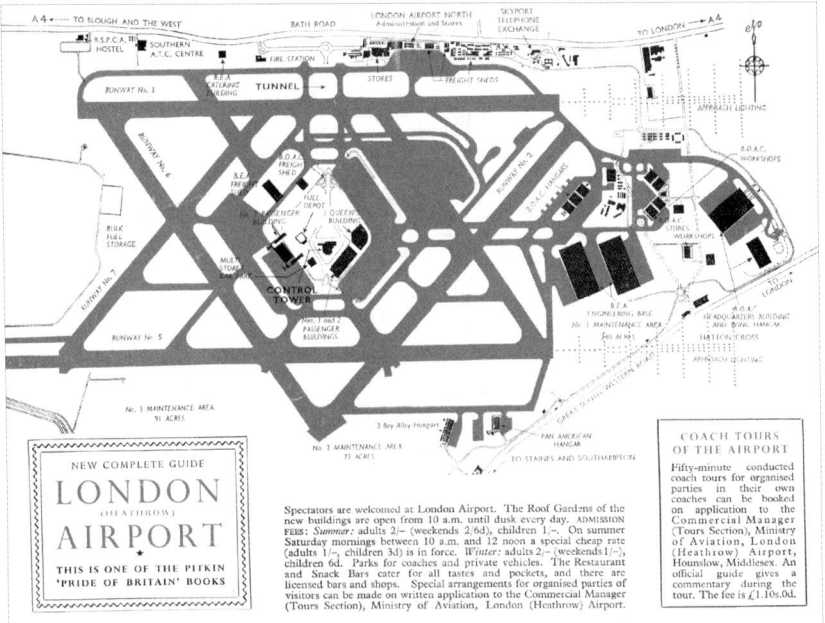

Heathrow plan, showing runway layout, and principal buildings inc. RSPCA Hostel and Southern Air Traffic Control Centre on NW side, London Airport North, Central Area and two Maintenance Areas, in *London Airport* – Pitkin Pictorial book 1964. (via Author)

disengagement after landing, and so was only able to carry out touch-and-go landings. The following night, 5 December 1962, another attempt was made with the Varsity, but this time was able to land. The fog was so thick, with a Runway Visual Range of 45 feet, that only one runway light at a time could be seen (at 100-foot centres) and assistance from Airfield Radar was needed to turn 180° back to the take-off point. They were supposed to pick up some VIPs, but they were unable to make Heathrow because of the fog. They did manage to pick up the BEA training pilot from a van, only navigable by the Ground Radar. In all four, circuits and landings were made, before returning to Bedford.

6.2.2. BEA wanted the Smith's Industries all-weather flight control system, developed with the Blind Landing Experimental Unit, installed in their Trident fleet. The Air Registration Board allowed the use of the Trident's duplex system for autoflare on a commercial flight in good weather on 3 June 1965. One week later, on 10 June 1965, BEA Trident 1 G-ARPR carried out the first autoflare landing on a commercial flight with passengers, namely BE343 from Paris Le Bourget to Heathrow. An autoflare landing is not fully automatic but only in the sense that the pilot has to line the aircraft up on the runway approach. The rate of descent, speed and touchdown are all governed by the automatic landing system.

6.2.3. Further development saw one Trident fitted with a triplex system, with three autopilots operating separately, such that if one failed the other two would override it. If another one failed, the system would cut out and trim the aircraft to allow the pilot to take over manual control. Trident G-ARPB was fitted with the same full system as in the Varsity trials, and by early September 1966 had made about 1,500 automatic landings, but none in the type of weather it was intended for. Just such an occasion came up on 4 November 1966 when Trident G-ARPB landed at Heathrow in Category 3B conditions, i.e. runway visual range 50 m. For much of November, the country was covered in thick fog and G-ARPB made good use of it with a series of automatic landings, many at Heathrow. On 25 November 1966, it collected BEA Chief Executive Henry Marking from Manchester and flew him to Heathrow for such a landing. The Chief Executive's flight had been diverted to Manchester because of the fog, and the Trident was the only aircraft to land at Heathrow that day. Shortly after that, in December 1966, BEA announced that all its Tridents would be fitted with the autoland system.

6.2.4. The world's first fully automatic landing by an aircraft on a scheduled passenger service was performed by BEA Trident 1 G-ARPP at Heathrow on 16 May 1967, returning from Nice. It would be several more years of development and testing before permission was gained to use it commercially in Category 3B conditions. The Americans were not that interested in the system as they suffered very few fog days compared to Europe, which resulted in the Boeing 757s, ordered by British Airways as a launch customer, having inferior all-weather ops capability compared to those aircraft leaving service.

6.3. PASSENGER THROUGHPUT EXCEEDS 1 MILLION PER MONTH

By 31 July 1963, Heathrow's peak monthly throughput of passengers had reached more than 1 million.

6.4. FIRST MULTI-STOREY CAR PARKS

On 20 August 1963 the first multi-storey car park was opened, occupying five floors and with space for 1,150 cars and 20 coaches. With a reinforced concrete frame, it was 300 feet by 200 feet by 50 feet high, and was built over an existing 260-space surface car park opposite the Europa Building. Later to be known as Multi Storey Car-park No. 2, it was demolished in March 2010. The Architect was Frederick Gibberd, Consulting Engineers L. G. Mouchel and Contractors Taylor Woodrow. Multi-storey Car-parks 5 and 6 opened on the north-east side on 19 April 1966, for airport employees, occupying six floors with 2,129 spaces, the largest in Europe, now known as Short Term Car-park No. 1a.

6.5. FIRE STATION

Fairey's first hangar on the east side of the Central Area east apron housed the London Airport firefighting unit until 1964, when the hangar was removed, after compensation had been agreed with Fairey's over the eviction from the Great West Aerodrome. The new fire station in use by 1967 on the north side, west of the main tunnel, became the main one. A satellite would remain at the Central Area, to deal with the then frequent fuel spillages during apron refuelling, latterly on the end of Pier 1 at the south end of Terminal 2.

6.6. M4 OPENS WITH HEATHROW SPUR

The M4 was opened on 23 March 1965, beginning at Chiswick through to Osterley Park on elevated viaduct, and continuing through the old Heston Airport westwards. It had a Heathrow Spur, Junction 4, passing under the old Bath Road to the Central Area tunnel, providing much quicker journey times to Heathrow.

6.7. BRITISH AIRPORTS AUTHORITY FORMED

The airlines had been complaining about the inefficiency in the handling of London Airport by Whitehall civil servants. In addition, the London airports were losing money. Peter Thorneycroft , the Minister of Aviation, announced in January 1961 that, from 1 April, London Airport would be known as London (Heathrow) Airport and Gatwick would be London (Gatwick) Airport. In 1961 a Parliamentary Select Committee issued a critical report and revived the idea for a new independent authority to manage the London airports. Roy Jenkins, the Labour Minister of Aviation, introduced the Airports Authority Bill in 1965, and it received royal assent on 2 June. The first chairman was Peter Masefield, who had started work in the Great West Aerodrome drawing office in the 1930s. He moved on to serve as Secretary to the War Cabinet Committee on Post-War Civil Air Transport from 1943–45, then spent two years at the new Civil Aviation Ministry in charge of long-term planning, followed by six years as Chief Executive of BEA in the formative years of 1949–55, before becoming Managing Director of Bristol Aircraft. On 1 April 1966 the British Airports Authority took over the three London airports – Heathrow, Gatwick and Stansted – as well as Prestwick. Gatwick was London's second airport but, with only one runway and a location 26 miles from London, it was shunned by the scheduled airlines, especially BEA and Air France. Stansted was even more remote, at 35 miles from London, with few direct transport links, being used mainly for training and general aviation. Stansted's role would be very much in the future. Prestwick had been busy during the war for the transatlantic traffic, but being 30 miles from Glasgow was too remote.

6.8. GENERAL ROY PLAQUE ERECTED

A slate plaque was unveiled on the south wall of the Nene Road police station some 100 m north of the cannon, on the north side on 17 November 1967, commemorating General Roy's first Ordnance Survey Base Line from Heathrow to Hampton in 1784. The plaque reads:

> 109 yards to the south of this tablet is THE NORTH OF THE TRIANGULATION OF GREAT BRITAIN. The base was measured in 1784 by MAJOR-GENERAL WILLIAM ROY FRS 'the Father of the Ordnance Survey'.

The original cannon marking the Heathrow end of the 27,406.19-foot survey line was restored to a site on the north side in 1968.

6.9. ST GEORGE'S CHAPEL

A new chapel was proposed in 1965, to be squeezed into an underground site between the west and south wings of the Control Building opposite the Europa Terminal. Designed by Architect Frederick Gibberd & Ptnrs, with structural consultant Lowe & Rodin, the new St George's chapel comprised an underground concrete structure away from noise, with a circular nave approximately 45 feet in diameter and three apses with altars with 120° between each, the whole structure occupying an 85-foot by 55-foot approximate footprint, plus a quiet paved garden area at ground level. Constructed by Dove Bros for £80,000, it was constructed inside a bored pile cofferdam perimeter. The new interdenominational St George's chapel was dedicated on 11 October 1968, serving the 42,000 staff at Heathrow. This quiet area of Heathrow can still be found.

Heathrow, north side Fire Station, 1972. (Mick West)

6.10. SHEILA SCOTT ROUND-THE-WORLD FLIGHTS AND SOUTH AFRICA

Sheila Scott started her round-the-world flight at Heathrow on 18 May 1966 in Piper Comanche G-ATOY *Myth Too*, returning on 20 June in a record thirty-three days total (189 net flying hours). She left Heathrow on 29 June 1967 for South Africa in the same aircraft. Still in *Myth Too*, she took part in the Daily Mail Transatlantic Race from Heathrow. Her second round-the-world flight began on 12 December 1969, again in *Myth Too*, from Heathrow, as part of a London–Australia Air Race, but no records were broken after she got lost, returning in January 1970. Her third and last round-the-world flight, this time in Piper Aztec D G-AYTO *Mythre*, officially began at Nairobi, with four crossings of the Equator but flying from Heathrow as one of the intermediate stops via Bodo over the North Pole to Alaska, finishing at Heathrow on 4 August 1970, having broken Amy Johnson's 1937 Darwin–London speed record. The flight was the first light aircraft Equator–Equator over the Pole. NASA used the flight to test the Nimbus satellite to track her.

6.11. CARGO TERMINAL

6.11.1. Cargo throughput at Heathrow had increased from 136,000 tons in 1962 to 276,000 tons in 1967, with the prospect of a 15 per cent increase annually. It was clear that the original Millbourn recommendation for a cargo area on the north-west corner of the Central Area would not be adequate. BEA and BOAC occupied temporary cargo buildings on the north-west corner of Central Area, while Air India had a freight shed within the No. 2 Maintenance Area south of runway 10R/28L, and west of the three-bay aluminium hangar. The requirement for more cargo space led to the new cargo terminal on a 155-acre site on the south-west corner, with Runway 5 (10R/28L) to the north, connected to the Central Area by a new tunnel. Subsequent extensions to the terminal were added 1970–72.

6.11.2. Sir William Halcrow & Ptnrs were commissioned in 1963 to report on the tunnel options, a single tunnel with two-lane road being cheaper than two individual tunnels. As Runway 5 (10R/28L) was in constant use, it was obviously not suitable to construct the new tunnel by the cut and cover method as the original Central Area tunnel had been. The new tunnel would run from the south end of the Britannic Building/Terminal 2, under Runways 5 (10R/28L) and 6 (15R/33L) with minimum covers of 6.5 m approximately, to the east end of the cargo area. It was shield-driven underground with precast concrete boltless linings. Claimed at the time to be the largest-diameter shield-driven tunnel through soft ground in the British Isles, the 10.9-m bore was 625 m long with reinforced concrete box approaches built in cut and cover at each end, 100 m at the south end and 110 m at the north, plus ventilation buildings at each end. There were short retaining wall approaches before the tunnel at each end. The overall approaches were 412 feet long at the south end and 445 feet at the north, giving an overall tunnel length of 885 m, approximately 0.5 miles. The £2.4-million tunnel was opened on 9 December 1968, using some 28,000 12-inch-thick precast segments, twenty-seven to each 2-foot-long ring. All the segments were cast on site at the south end, 120 per day. Driving of the hydraulic shield began in September 1967. Progress was up to 30 m per week. The two 12-foot-wide roadways within the tunnel were being constructed within the tunnel behind the segment placing. The roads were designed to handle 500 vehicles per hour in each direction, with 16 feet 6 inches clearance throughout. Consulting engineers for the tunnel were Sir William Halcrow & Ptnrs, and the Contractors were Taylor Woodrow Construction Ltd.

6.11.3. Fifteen airlines had space in the new cargo terminal in five building groups. The Air Freight Working party recommended the basic provision required in 1963. BOAC/BEA and the other independent airlines then formed two groups to finalise arrangements. Construction began on 3 October 1966, to be completed at the end of 1968. The first stage included buildings with a total floor area of 611,000-foot^2 floor area, expanding to 825,000 feet^2, able to handle 560,000 tons of cargo p.a. out of an estimated 1-million-ton capacity required by 1973. The independent airlines occupied the three westerly buildings oriented north–south. The extreme west building, approximately 750 foot by 175 foot footprint, was used from north to south by Aer Lingus, El Al, Air India, MEA, PIA, British Eagle and Alitalia. The two middle buildings, oriented north–south and approximately 1,300 feet by 210 feet footprints, were split Seeboard World, KLM, Air France and Lufthansa in the west one, the east one having Air Canada, TWA, Trans Mediterranean and Pan American. The £11-million BOAC/BEA building on the east side ran east–west and was opened by the Duke of Edinburgh in May 1970. A total of twenty-nine aircraft stands up to 747 size were provided for within the Cargo Area. BOAC/BEA had fourteen at 160 feet by 180 feet, the three other buildings five stands each of size 180 feet by 215 feet. Refuelling was from two hydrants on each stand, the first at Heathrow, fed from a fuel installation on the west side, in turn fed from the main installation at Perry Oaks. A boiler house to serve this area was built south of the Cargo Terminal. Total cost of the cargo terminal was £25 million, shared between BAA £8–9 million on infrastructure, and BEA/BOAC approximately £11 million, and the other airlines about £4 million on the buildings and cargo handling equipment.

6.11.4. After the merger of BEA and BOAC freight operations, the new British Airways Cargo Centre was inaugurated in late April 1974. Handling more than 25,000 tons per annum, the old BEA section became the import unit, while the BOAC section became the export unit, the whole occupying 33.5 acres.

6.11.5. The growing size of passenger aircraft, the ability to carry more freight in the holds, and the option to use convertible Combi wide bodies led to a decline in the use of exclusively cargo aircraft, much freight being delivered through the Cargo Terminal and tunnel to aircraft at Central Area.

Heathrow, Air India Boeing 747 VT-EBE in the Air India freight compound, 1971, on the south side near the Three Bay Alloy Hangar. (Mick West)

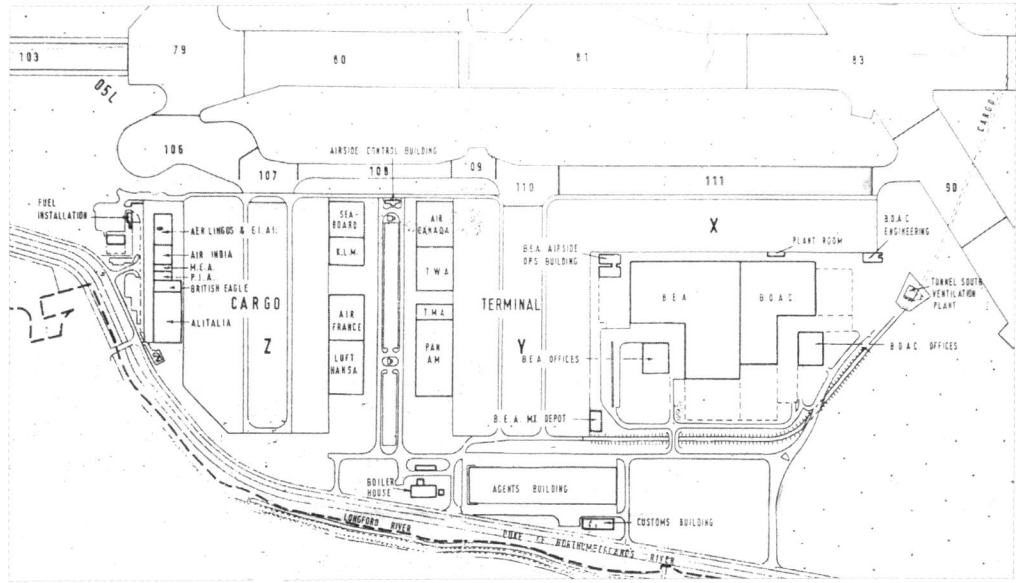

Heathrow, Cargo Area plan, 1967, showing the various airline allocations, plus BEA/BOAC cargo shed, since replaced by the British Airways World Cargo Centre in 1999. (via Author)

6.12. RUNWAY EXTENSIONS

With the advent of the incoming intercontinental jets from 1958 on, it was necessary to increase runway lengths. Boeing 707s needed 10,000 feet, while the Comet 4 was OK with 7,000 feet. Runway 5 (10R/28L) was originally 9,581 feet, and had been extended westwards initially to 11,000 feet from mid-1960 to spring 1961, including the culverting of the Duke of Northumberland's and the Longford Rivers close to the west end. 10R/28L was further extended to 12,000 feet from early 1965 to the year's end. In October 1968 BAA announced that Costain had a £2.1-million contract to extend Runway 1 (10L/28R) westwards, from the original 9,312 feet to 12,800 feet, work having already begun in October, opening for use on 29 April 1970.

6.13. NEW BOAC TERMINAL PROPOSED

Early in 1967 BOAC drew up plans for its own terminal north of the BEA Maintenance Base, fed by tunnels to Central Area, BOAC's reasoning based on the logic of not having to tow aircraft very far from their Maintenance Base, compared to the Central Area. The scheme was turned down by BAA as it involved closing Runway 2 (05L/23R).

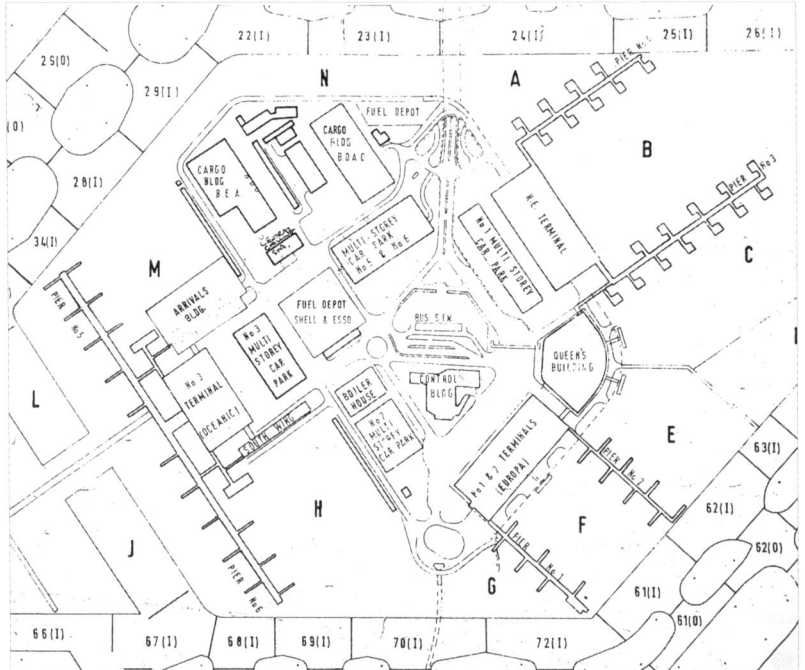

Heathrow plan of Central Area buildings, 1967, inc. Nos 1 and 2 plus No. 3 and NE Terminals with Piers, Queens Building, Control Tower, Cargo buildings, Fuel Depot, Boiler House, Bus Station and Multi-storey Car Parks. (via Author)

6.14. TERMINAL 1

6.14.1. The north-east terminal, otherwise known as Terminal 1, was built to handle British short-haul and domestic operators. Planning began in 1964. Construction, on what was claimed as the largest terminal of its kind in the world at 610 feet by 275 feet plan by 45 feet high, began in 1966, and the terminal was operational by late 1968. It was intended exclusively for domestic and short-haul passengers flying with the British airlines BEA, BKS, Cambrian and Autair plus Aer Lingus, taking over from the existing Europa and Britannic Terminals. It was on two levels, accommodating arrivals on the ground floor and departures on the upper floor, the building having a height limitation so as not to restrict the control tower view over the aprons. The first terminal using this arrangement had been at Prestwick in 1964, and the new Terminal 1 was the largest of any existing or proposed at that time in Europe. One-way roads served each level, the upper road being an elevated steel-concrete composite structure, both roads also giving access to an 800-capacity multi-storey car park in front on the west face, to be known as Multi Storey Car-park No. 1. Airline coaches had a separate road running through the building at ground floor. Airside, there were two piers with a total of twenty aircraft stands, plus twelve stands served by coach. Pier 3, approximately 1000 feet long on the south-east corner, for international passengers had twelve stands, and Pier 4, approximately 700 feet long on the north-east corner, for domestic traffic had eight. Internally the terminal was one large space with

Heathrow Cargo
Area, 20 March
2010, West shed.
(Richard E Flagg)

Heathrow Cargo
Area, 20 March
2010, middle and
East shed, with
BA World Cargo
just visible far left.
(Richard E. Flagg)

Heathrow, Terminal
1 landside.
(Richard E Flagg)

four service cores with lifts and services, plus a central core with toilets and kitchens surrounded by bars, a restaurant and a nursery. The main departures lounge for all flights overlooked the aprons, giving direct access to the piers. Airline offices were at third-floor level on a continuous balcony running around the inside of the building.

6.14.2. The building was steel-framed, with deep trusses forming service space carrying precast concrete floor units. Columns were at 50-foot centres over most of the building and 25 feet on the heavily loaded central service core. 5,600 tons of steel were used in the main passenger building and 1,300 tons on the coach station and the two new piers. The terminal would allow passenger throughput to rise from 12 million per annum in 1966 to 20 million by the early 1970s. The Architects were Frederick Gibberd & Ptnrs and the Structural Consultants Sir William Halcrow & Ptnrs, both having worked on the original Central Area buildings. Main Contractors were George Wimpey & Sons Ltd (substructure) and Tersons Ltd (superstructure). Structural steelwork was by Redpath Dorman Long (terminal) and Dawnays Ltd (piers). Precast concrete floors were by Concrete (Southern) Ltd. Terminal 1 was initially opened for domestic traffic on 6 November 1968, before being formally opened by Her Majesty Queen Elizabeth on 17 April 1969, and was finally open to international traffic on 7 May 1969.

6.14.3. When Terminal 1 opened, the Europa and Britannic Terminals were renamed Terminal 2 and underwent upgrading to be used for foreign airlines' short haul; the Oceanic Building became Terminal 3. Costing £11 million, Terminal 1 was part of a £36-million works programme put in hand by BAA, including a £13-million extension to Terminal 3, and the £8-million cargo area.

6.15. NEW PIERS FOR EUROPA/TERMINAL 2 AND OCEANIC/TERMINAL 3

6.15.1. Between 1967 and 1968, two piers each were added to Europa Terminal 2 and Oceanic Terminal 3 in a £2-million project. Each pier had up to eight stands, with a passenger walkway at first-floor level and ground staff below, controlling the aircraft access systems. All the piers were steel framed for speed, a total of 1,400 tons being used. Pier 1 on the south side of Terminal 2 was approximately 620 feet long, with Pier 2 at the north end 650 feet approximately. Pier 5 extended north-west from Terminal 3 and Pier 6 to the south-east.

6.15.2. An article in *Flight* in August 1967 argued that long fingers where passengers could walk to aircraft, even if 1,000 feet or more, were preferable to the coaches then prevalent at Heathrow to reach distant aircraft stands. The article went on to complain that by 1969, after all the improvements had been made, coaches would still be used for forty-five of the ninety-three stands. Another complaint related to the inadequate waiting lounges that were not large enough for the incoming wide-bodied aircraft, as the fingers were too narrow. This was obviously addressed, as the now standard fingers are generally wider.

6.16. BOAC BOEING 747 HANGAR

6.16.1. When BOAC ordered the new Boeing 747 Jumbo Jet, they were the first in the world to construct a new hangar for 747 maintenance. With a wingspan of 196 feet, length 231 feet and tail height of 64 feet, the specification was going to be large to fit two 747s under one roof. The roof required a clear span of 453 feet, with a clear door opening and area around the tail of 75 feet, clear height around the fuselage of 50 feet, maximum height of construction 110 feet and overall depth into the hangar of 275 feet. The roof was required to carry heavy services and live loads with small deflections, plus front roof higher than rear to give minimum volume to reduce heating costs. Moveable stagings around all aircraft elements were to be incorporated, the tail stagings to be suspended from the roof. The hangar was to be capable of being extended in length and height at a later date. Ancillary blocks were to be provided with workshops, stores, power and heating supply, and control rooms, canteens etc. on the three sides away from the doors. Clear height under the first floor of rear blocks was 14 feet. The chosen design at 560 feet x 275 feet footprint and 109 feet overall height was the world's largest two-layer diagonal grid folded plate structure including the two largest all-tubular welded girders, all site-built. Total accommodation provided was 229,000 sq. ft, equivalent to 6 acres, including the hangar floor at 123,000 sq. ft (9.2 million cu. ft volume gross), and ancillary accommodation on four floors on three sides of 106,000 sq. ft (2.5 million cu. ft gross volume).

6.16.2. The whole roof structure was built at ground level, fitted with some services and partly clad; it weighed 2,100 tons and was lifted into position by twelve jacks. Ten alternative designs were investigated in more detail, all with high entrances for the tail and lower rear, after discounting portal frames, arches, single and double main girders with part cantilevers as well as alternative materials, including rolled steel, hollow sections, concrete and combinations of these. The main roof structure consists of a low-level roof 450 feet wide by 182 feet front to rear, of which the rear 45 feet 6 inches cantilevers from the back girder over the top of four-storey blocks beneath. Gaps between these blocks allow the two aircraft noses between. Four columns support the back girder and were some of the jacking columns. At the front the low-level roof grid joins the lower part of the spine girder, which supports the high-level grid at the top, the fascia girder picking up the other side, in turn spanning 68 feet clear between girders. Both the spine and fascia girders extend beyond the rear roof to accommodate extra working space and as door recesses to give a clear width equal to the maximum span. There are also edge girders picking up the sides of the grids. The whole roof is supported by eight main stanchions, inc. double 8-inch x 8-inch x 40-lb UC at the rear and concrete-encased double 12-inch x 12-inch x 65-lb UC under the spine girder. The footing under the spine girder column, which takes 790-tons maximum, is the largest at 33 feet x 25 feet x 5 feet deep. The plan was to construct as much as possible at 8 feet above ground level and lift up to give 53 feet 4 inches clear below the rear low-level roof. Erection sequence was first the spine girder, second the low-level roof, third the fascia girder, and last the high-level roof.

6.16.3. The spine girder was 558 feet long x 49 feet 6 inches deep x 12 feet 6 inches wide, weighing 360 tons. Top and bottom chords comprise twin 18-inch tubes 19–28 mm thick in Grade 55C steel, latticed together with 6.625-inch-diameter tube. The bottom flange was prefabricated in 64-foot-long sections, and site welded on trestles to a predetermined camber. The vertical cruciform diagonals are twin 14-inch diameter also in Grade 55C, with 5.5-inch diameter cross-bracing, prefabricated in one 59-foot and two 28-foot-6-inch lengths.

6.16.4. The low-level roof is 455 feet long x 182 feet front to rear including the 45 foot cantilever. The depth was 12 feet on module 45 feet x 32 feet 6 inches across the diagonals. The top and bottom chords are 6.625-inch diameter with 4.125-inch-diameter vertical web and 5.5-inch-diameter diagonal web members, all in Grade 50C steel. The back girder comprises two 12-foo-high trusses of rolled sections, including 8-inch x 8-inch UC section flanges, spaced 3 feet apart of maximum span 130 feet between jacking columns. The fascia girder was 617 feet long by 27 feet deep x 6 feet 9 inches wide, built as a Warren truss with vertical infill and with main chords 18-inch diameter; it weighed 305 tons. It had to be lifted 29 feet 6 inches to be connected to the spine girder. Extensive site weld testing was conducted followed by load testing of the high-level roof including the fascia and spine girders. This was carried out using 8.5-ton sand-filled skips to give a total added load of 595 tons on the spine girder and 423 tons on the fascia girder, equivalent to 100 per cent of total dead load + 150 per cent snow + 125 per cent crane + staging loads.

6.16.5. The side blocks were erected first and were used to stabilise the roof during lifting. Hoisting was carried out by Power Rise Ltd using twelve hydraulic jacks, each of 600-ton capacity, with two jacks on each end of the fascia and spine girders, and four along the rear girder, all synchronised from a single control point. The jacking was done in 10-foot lifts every eight hours. At the end of each lift, the roof load was transferred to trestles beneath the jacks, and the jacks moved to a new point at the top of the tower over the next twenty-four hours. Horizontal control during lifting was effected by guide billets at the sides and rear, transferring any horizontal effects to annex bracing. Installation of services and roof cladding continued during the lifting operation. The roof was raised in twenty-one days.

6.16.6. The roof structure was designed to support four 10-ton cranes, four six-level retractable tail staging units at 60 tons each (with platforms at 7-foot intervals from the underside of the tail plane) and various services. The total load of supported equipment is 700 tons, of which 300 tons are moveable. Two of the cranes run on four runway beams from front to back in the low-level roof plus two similar cranes in the high-level roof. Other parts of the aircraft are serviced from a wrap-round steel mezzanine floor 16 feet above floor level, plus two three-level stagings propped off the mezzanine floor at nose end and hung off the roof at tail end to allow access over the wings and along the fuselage.

6.16.7. Six sliding doors are provided, probably the largest in the UK at that time, at 80 feet high x 77 feet wide, weighing 490 tons each, 16 tons of which is the double glazing covering 80 per cent of the faces. The doors run on two running wheels 3-foot diameter spaced 60 feet apart, and are supported at the top by the fascia beam. The consulting engineers for the doors were Bernard Clark & Partners, who were the consultants for the doors on the original Owen Williams' BOAC Wing Hangar and for the extension doors.

6.16.8. The hangar floor is 14-inch-thick concrete comprising 6 inches slab with 18 miles of underfloor heating coils, plus 8 inches concrete, all on 8 inches dry lean sub-base. The 6 acres of apron outside is 12 inches concrete, again on 8 inches dry lean concrete, on cement-stabilised soil. The hangar floor contained 9000 cu. yd and the aprons 36,000 cu. yd of concrete. Normally an aircraft is lifted off the ground with jacks before the undercarriage can be moved, but in this case, to maintain the undercarriage, the aircraft was designed to be supported at ground level and the floor able to be lowered in two pits 60 feet long x 32 feet wide x 17 feet 6 inches deep for the main undercarriage units, and into two 23-foot x 19-foot-6-inch x 17-foot-6-inch pits for the nose wheels. The pits have 3-foot-6-inch-thick walls and 4-foot-6-inch base slabs, all formed using high-yield steel sheet piles. Several heavy steel platforms on jacks within each pit allow undercarriage maintenance and testing of individual units.

6.16.9. The external finishes were mainly metal cladding and glazing. Apart from the glazing on the doors, natural light is provided by sixty-seven pyramid-shaped roof lights each 40 feet x 27 feet. The rest of the roof is metal decking with roofing felt. The heating was provided by a combination of heated coils within the floor and heated air curtain at the door head, capable of restoring the internal temperature fifteen minutes after the doors were closed. An automatic deluge system with 14,000 sprinklers is in the roof for fire protection.

6.16.10. The final design was commissioned in August 1967, and frozen in mid-December. The steel order was placed in February 1968, the main contract being appointed mid-March 1968, beginning on 15 May 1968. The £4-million contract lasted seventy-eight weeks, being handed over to the steelwork subcontractor after 1½ months, and fifty-two weeks for the remainder, topping out occurring on 17 March 1969. Completion was achieved in February 1970, with handover on 12 March 1970.

6.16.11. The overall design and construction was under the control of BOAC Properties Branch, headed by Kenneth J. Joyner. Consulting structural engineer was Prof. Z. S. Makowski (Head of the Civil Engineering Dept at the University of Surrey) and Associates. The computer analysis of the roof was carried out at the University of Surrey. Consulting architects were Norman Royce, Topping, Hurley and Stewart, also the architects for Speedbird House, the BOAC HQ at Heathrow. Main contractor for the £4-million hangar project was Holland & Hannen and Cubitts Ltd, with fifty-three subcontractors. The steelwork subcontractor was Dawnays Ltd with Stewarts & Lloyds for the tubes. The many fabricators were A. E. Watson (Exeter), Sortrac, Unit Superheater, DEC Ltd, London Welding, Hugh Stevenson (Engineering) Ltd, Tubeworkers Ltd, SHS (Structural) Ltd, Blight & White and Graham Wood Ltd. The erectors were McWeeney, Smallman & Co. A total of 2,700 tons of structural steel was used on the project, 1,200 tons of which was tubular sections in the roof. Civil engineering consultants were Edwards & Blackie. Consulting systems engineers were Bernard Clark & Partners, responsible for the six sliding doors, the four 10-ton cranes, the mobile tail staging and the shaped mezzanine floor 16 feet off the ground.

6.16.12. The whole project was for the hangar plus a building containing workshops, car park and offices behind. This building is 506 feet x 207 feet x 138 feet high (the max. allowable height being 150 feet) with workshops on the first two floors rising to 24 feet, a multi-storey car park (to replace a previous one on the site of the new hangar) on six floors with 2,070 spaces (claimed to be Europe's largest at the time), and two storeys of offices at the top, projecting 10 feet out from the floors below. This building was designed by Multidek with consultant structural engineers Rom River Ltd. Now known as Technical Block C it was built by W. & C. French at a cost of £5 million.

6.16.13. A second identical hangar was completed alongside the first in early 1973. There were minor differences to improve the 'buildability'. The spine girder was reduced in width by 455 mm to allow the four-storey ancillary blocks at sides to be built first, including the cladding. The fascia girder was reduced in depth from 8 m to 7.6 m to allow more space over the door head and the width increased from 1.6 m to 2.3 m to give increased lateral stability during lifting. The roof lights were redesigned with more economical framing. The faster British Lift Slab system was used to raise the roof, using redesigned main columns with the jacks placed on top, the roof being supported on screwed tension rods fastened to the roof underside. Connections were simplified by using bolted connections to top flanges of spine, and fascia girders as well as all secondary vertical bracings. This reduced the site welding teams from twenty-four on the first hangar to four on the second, and the site assembly time reduced. The joint between the two hangars was made with expansion joints between the fascia and spine girders and between the new link bridge and the west ancillary block on the original hangar. Load testing using 119- x 8-ton skips plus 594 tons temporary staging/scaffolding was again applied to the fascia and spine girders, the equivalent of 150 per cent imposed and 125 per cent services plus dead load, a total of 1,200 tons, resulting in deflections within 5 per cent of predicted.

6.16.14. The two hangars originally known as Hangars 01 and 02 are now known as Technical Blocks J and K, and, along with Technical Block C, are still in regular use.

6.17. DAILY MAIL TRANSATLANTIC RACE

To celebrate the fiftieth anniversary of Alcock and Brown's first transatlantic crossing, the *Daily Mail* sponsored the Transatlantic Race, which ran between 4 and 11 May 1969. The race was between the top of the Post Office Tower in London to the top of the Empire State Building in New York. Heathrow was the start for some. The headline grabbing contestants, however, were the Harrier taking off from near St Pancras station and the record run by the

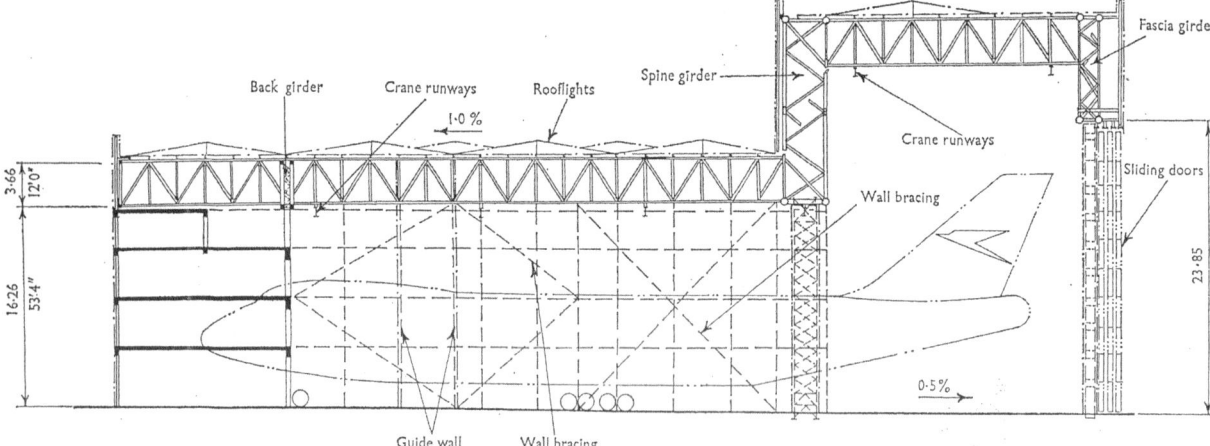

Heathrow, BOAC 747 Hangar roof structural detail cross-section. (Institution of Civil Engineers)

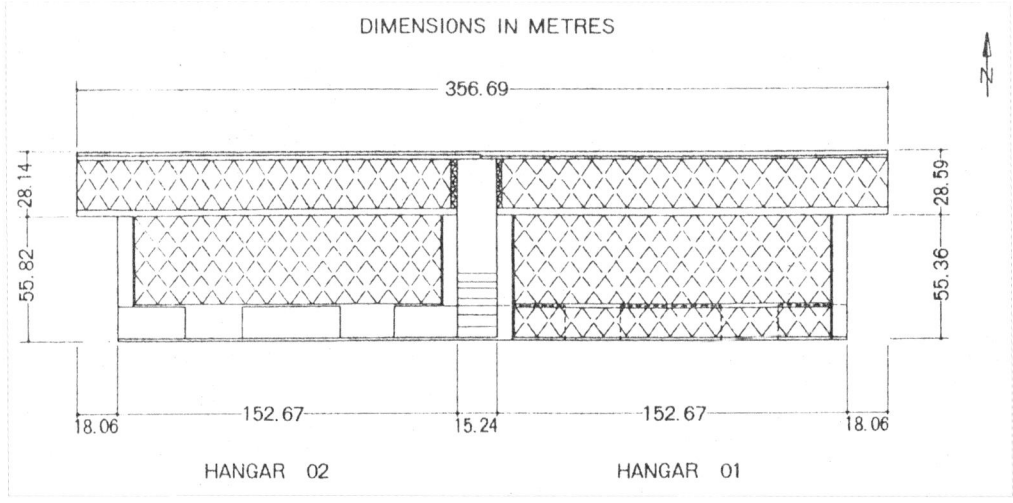

Heathrow, BOAC 747 Hangar structural detail roof plan of Hangars 01 and 02, now TBK on left and TBJ on right. (via Author)

Royal Navy Phantom, neither of which used Heathrow. The Harriers XV741 and XV744 were entered as a ruse to demonstrate the aircraft to the US Marines in the USA, XV741 winning the London–New York sector in a time of 6 hours 11 minutes 57 seconds, taking off near St Pancras station and landing near New York's East River. Pad to pad was 5 hours 57 minutes. XV744 did the return trip New York–London with a pad to pad time of 5 hours 31 minutes, but was beaten by the Royal Navy Phantom. The last run for the 892 Sqn Phantom not only won the prize with the fastest overall New York–London time of 5 hours 11 minutes 22 seconds, but set a new New York–London world air speed record of 4 hours 46 minutes 57 seconds. Both the Harriers and the Phantom were refuelled by RAF Marham Victors, the Harriers needing four A-A refuellings, the Phantom three. Sheila Scott used an Aston Martin to Battersea heliport, where a Bell Jet Ranger took her to Heathrow, setting off in her Comanche G-ATOY *Myth Too* on 4 May, winning the light aircraft prize in 26 hours 54 minutes 20 seconds, just one of her many records. Other successful competitors included Sir Billy Butlin, winning the chartered business jet prize in a HS125.

6.18. TERMINAL 3 UPGRADE

Plans were announced by BAA in February 1968 for the arrival of the Boeing 747, due in 1969. Runway 6 (15R/33L) was to be closed for a £13-million project to build a pier system from the Oceanic Building, as well as a new arrivals building adjacent to the existing Oceanic Building, which would become exclusively for departures. Runway 6 (15R/33L) was closed on 1 July 1968, to allow construction of the new Pier 7, south-west of Terminal 3. The new pier had the UK's first moving walkways, and forward lounges to accommodate 500 passengers. Each of the ten lounges had three telescopic gangways to suit Boeing 747 or Concorde. The new Pier 7 was T-shaped with ten stands on a 1,000-foot-long crosspiece oriented NW–SE attached to a 915-foot moving corridor with four moving walkways to/from the departures building, the first at any British airport. The new arrivals building was, like the original, two storeys, incorporating the ground floor and part of the first floor of the north office block. In addition, Pier 5 was increased to 1,400-feet-long and doubled in width to accommodate moving walkways to serve seven new stands. The inauguration of the 747 facilities at Terminal 3 took place on 1 June 1970. Pier 6, south-east of Terminal 3 also later received similar improvements.

6.19. A NEW RAIL LINK

British Rail had plans for a Heathrow Rail Link from Victoria in 1969. Running non-stop trains on the existing tracks, there was to be a spur west of Feltham direct to Heathrow. There would be six trains per hour, and a journey time of twenty-three minutes was envisaged. There was to be a new flyover near Clapham Junction, and additional lines near Barnes for overtaking. Nothing came of it, and the Heathrow Express became the first overground rail connection, see later. However ,there are plans for rail links from the south side again, see later.

6.20. AIRLINER DEVELOPMENTS IN THE 1960S

6.20.1. During the 1960s, jets began replacing piston engine and turboprop airliners, although numerous older Douglas DC6 and DC7 series and Lockheed piston types were still around. The British were selling the Comet, BAC111, Trident and VC10, the French the Caravelle, and the Russians the Il-18 and Tu-104 for the Eastern Bloc and sympathetic countries. The first Il-62 CCCP-86666, leased from Aeroflot by CSA, was the first of the type to visit Heathrow on 11 May 1968. However, the Americans were – with the Boeing 707, 727 and later the 737, plus the Douglas DC8 and DC9 – making big inroads into the world fleets. The Convair 240/340/440 series would vanish from the scene by the mid-1960s, and the hoped-for successor, the Convair 880/990, tried to compete but had also disappeared by the end of the 1970s. An American Airlines Convair 990 was a particularly unusual sight in 1967, operating the Paris service for Air France. There were still unusual aircraft to be seen, like the TWA Fairchild C82 jet-pack transporting engines within Europe, the Curtiss C46 Commando freighters of Seaboard and Western and Lufthansa (lease from Capitol) plus Air France Breguet Deux Ponts. Two British aircraft types to be seen were BEA Vanguards (the intended Viscount successor) and Argosies on freight duties.

6.20.2. Comets seen at Heathrow were owned by BOAC (until replaced on transatlantic services by the Boeing 707 in 1960, and the VC10 from 1964), BEA, and six other airlines, including Sudan Airways, who operated the last Comet from Heathrow in 1972. Caravelles were competing more successfully for the short-haul market, replacing propeller types, and were operated by eighteen airlines. In turn, Caravelles were to be replaced by Boeing 727s, DC9s and Boeing 737s. BEA originally ordered twenty-four Trident 1s with seventy-nine-seat capacity in 1959, entering service in March 1964, the longer-range Trident 2 following in 1968. Tridents seen at Heathrow were predominantly BEA, but were operated by three other airlines. BAC 111 operators included BEA (replaced by 737s), TAROM and British Eagle. Boeing 727s were operated by seven airlines. On the long-haul side, Boeing 707s dominated, operated by twenty-two airlines. See Appendix D for airline types operated in the 1960s.

Heathrow, originally BOAC 747 hangar TBJ, showing special 747 tail staging. (Tony Szulc)

Heathrow, SABENA Caravelle OO-SRC, July 1961, from Queens Building Roof Gardens, with Fairey hangar, BEA Comet 4B, Viscounts and Vanguard. (Neil Aird)

1970s Developments

7.1. RUNWAY EXTENSIONS

By April 1970, both main runways had been extended, 10L/28R to 12,801 feet and 10R/28L to 12,000 feet, their current length, to accommodate larger jets like the Boeing 747. The other runways were closed to allow terminal expansion, apart from Runway 23L, preserved for crosswind landings until decommissioned on 27 October 2002; it now forms part of a taxiway.

7.2. BEA TRISTAR HANGAR

7.2.1. When BEA were considering purchase of the De Havilland/Hawker Siddeley Trident 3B, it was realised that it was too large for the existing West Base, and the East Base was already committed to the rest of the fleet. The first Trident 3B was due in early 1971, plus BEA had a requirement for an Airbus (A300)-type aircraft by 1975, which eventually settled on the Lockheed Tristar. Thus a new hangar was required to take two Tridents plus two Airbuses. Consultants Scott Wilson Kirkpatrick had previously produced the two-bay hangar at the newly civilianised Glasgow Abbotsinch airport in 1965. The hangar was needed, as Renfrew airport closed in spring 1967, its runway to become part of Glasgow ring road. In use by spring 1967 after a twelve-month contract, the BEA Abbotsinch hangar comprised two 150-foot-square space-frame roofs built at ground level with services and cladding incorporated, and each was raised by jacks on the four corner columns.

7.2.2. By 1967 the need was identified for a new hangar at Heathrow with double the spans of Abbotsinch and 70 feet clear height. The 300-square-foot x 108-foot total height hangar was designed by Consultants Scott Wilson Kirkpatrick, to be constructed on the ground and raised on jacks to rest on four hollow steel columns to give the required 70 feet clear height to the underside of the crane hook. Known as Phase 3 of the BEA Engineering Base Development, approval was given at the end of 1967. The Consultant Team comprising architects, structural engineers, services engineer and quantity surveyor had their first meeting in July 1968 to discuss various options. The Consultant Architect was Murray Ward & Ptnrs. As the required position of the new hangar was to be as close to the Central Area as possible, this meant sacrificing some 3 acres of the West Apron against the north end of the BEA Phase 1 Base, the aircraft parking space being recovered elsewhere. The chosen site meant major services having to be diverted beforehand. The roof design had to take account of the 80–90-foot-high contour lines associated with the side slope clearance on No. 2 runway at the north-west corner. Therefore the corner was restricted to 85 feet in height, resulting in the shallow truncated pyramid roof shape.

7.2.3. The hangar is 340 feet square, 108 feet overall height, with clear height 70 feet. Full-height doors are on the north and south faces, although the roof was designed to allow doors on all four sides in future if necessary. The primary steel frame in the roof comprises two large box lattice trusses spanning diagonally between the corner columns. Secondary trusses carrying purlins span perpendicular to the edge girder on to the main diagonal girders. The top chords of the main diagonal trusses and the secondary trusses follow the roof slope. The main roof trusses are approximately 6 feet square at the eaves to 26 feet deep x 6 feet wide at the apex. These main trusses comprise 14 inch x 16 inch Universal Column chords braced together with battened 7 inch x 3 inch channel and 8 inch x 8 inch Universal Column sections internally. The secondary trusses comprise 8 inch x 3 inch battened channel sections. At the perimeter eaves, box lattice girders form a parapet rising from the corner columns to the middle of each side. These eaves girders, approximately 22 feet deep max. x 8 feet wide, are formed generally from 8 inch x 8 inch column sections. The roof purlins are mainly 10 inch x 4 inch Universal Beams. The door-head track is in a canopy cantilevered from the roof edge girder. Wind bracing is in the top and bottom planes of the secondary trusses around the perimeter. Total weight of the roof is 3,170 tons. The ends of the primary trusses are bolted with V-grade High Strength Friction Grip bolts to cruciform end bearings at the column tops, to allow the roof to deflect freely under vertical loads. Horizontal wind and thermal forces are transmitted through the bearings to the column tops which cantilever off the foundations.

7.2.4. The columns are octagonal, fabricated from welded 36 inch x 1.125 inch plate with internal vertical stiffeners and horizontal diaphragms. They are designed as pure cantilevers above ground-floor level. Foundations for each of the four columns comprised 70-foot-deep steel-lined precast reinforced concrete cylinder caissons 18 feet 9 inches in diameter for the first 22 feet, then 15 feet outside diameter below that. Soils comprise 16 feet of water-bearing gravels beginning 4 feet below floor level, the main bearing stratum being London clay. The caissons were sunk with bentonite lubrication and cast-iron kentledge weights. The tops of the four caissons are joined by peripheral ring beams integral with the floor construction and the door track foundations, all sufficient to transmit horizontal force at the column feet by friction to the subgrade. Roof and side covering is corrugated insulated PVC-coated metal sheeting, with wired PVC translucent sheeting over the central half span of roof. Side cladding is supported by 5-inch x 2.5-inch channel sheeting rails connected to 8-inch x 3-inch channel and 2.5-inch x 2.5-inch angle lattice cladding posts. All the steelwork was bolted using 1-inch diameter V-grade High Strength Friction Grip bolts in the main truss connections, 7/8 inch and ¾ inch diameter General Grade High Strength Friction Grip bolts in the rest, except the cladding steelwork where Black bolts were used, with castle nuts and split pins, the latter to protect from airborne vibration from aircraft.

7.2.5. The hangar was intended to operate twenty-four hours per day on a three shift system, throughout the year. Therefore the doors, on the north and south faces, were required to enable aircraft to pass through and to accommodate forty-eight door movements per day, as twelve aircraft were planned to be serviced daily. Esavian folding leaf doors had been used on earlier hangars, so they were appointed to design the 292-foot clear x 70-foot doors, compacted each side in 32 feet. Because of their height, mild steel tubular door frames were utilised instead of aluminium. The west and east walls above the level of the existing west hangar block were sheeted and glazed. A low-level roof spans between the new hangar and the existing block. Minimal docking facilities within the hangar were fitted. Two double-girder suspension cranes of 11-ton capacity were provided, each serving half the hangar, the long travel being between the doors. In order to maintain a hook height of 70 feet and the total height restriction, only 7-foot depth was allowed for the crane system, which is by Demag Cranes Ltd. An air-conditioned soundproof office for the accommodation of servicing staff is provided inside. The roof space contains a sprinkler system, heating pipes and lighting with a walkway system. The heating comes from an underfloor and high-level system supplied by a hot air booster system plus a foam water deluge system.

7.2.6. The £2.6-million contract was awarded to the Industrial Engineering Branch of John Laing Construction Ltd. Before construction commenced, many major services had to be diverted. Foundations were nearly complete by March 1970. The hangar was near completion in May 1971. Two lifting systems were considered by Braithwaite & Co., the steel fabricators, one by British Lift Slab using hydraulic jacks and tension rods, as had been used at Abbotsinch, and one by Power Rise Constructors Ltd, which pushes up on jacks on temporary trestles around the columns (as was used on the Heathrow BOAC 747 hangar). The British Lift Slab method was adopted as a result of a successful tender by Braithwaite who had the advantage of the technique at the Abbotsinch BEA hangar. The British Lift Slab system limited the load per column to 840 tons due to space restrictions at the top of the columns, so the erection weight had to be carefully calculated so as not to exceed this. In the event, the lift was 3,170 tons. The roof was lifted using sixteen hydraulic jacks on each column with twin 1.75-inch-diameter continuous threaded lifting rods from each jack, running down the side of the columns for fixing to the corner of the roof structure. As the maximum length of lifting rods was 28 feet, and 67 feet was required, the lift was carried out in three 22-foot lifts. The rods were coupled together and as they would not pass through the jack, the jacks were unloaded and the rods lowered to give further increments of lift. To enable the jacks to be unloaded, additional jacks were provided so that they could be released in pairs to allow rod lowering. The rods were connected to the roof by two channels per jack under the main roof trusses. The roof lift was carried out in the autumn of 1970, and took one week.

7.2.7. Consultant Structural Engineers and Project Coordinators were Scott Wilson, Kirkpatrick & Ptnrs, of 5 Winsley St, London W1.
Consultant Architect was Murray Ward & Ptnrs.
Consulting Engineers for services were Donald Smith Seymour & Rooley, London W1.
Main Contractor was Industrial Engineering Branch of John Laing Construction Ltd.
Groundwork Contractor was C. V. Buchan & Co. Ltd.
Steel fabricators were Braithwaite & Co. Structural Ltd, of Great Bookham (Leatherhead), West Bromwich and Newport.
Roof Lifting Contractors were British Lift Slab.

7.3. BOEING 747 AND WIDE BODIES AND CONCORDE APPEAR

The first Boeing 747, Pan American N735PA, arrived at Heathrow on 12 January 1970 on a proving flight, the first of the many wide-bodies to take over long-haul destinations. Concorde G-BSST first landed at Heathrow on 13 September 1970, heralding a new era of supersonic passenger travel, although the first official visit was not until July 1972. As well as the 747, other wide-bodies were entering service, including the Lockheed Tristar and the McDonnell-Douglas DC10, both having three engines and a passenger capacity half that of the 747, but still useful. The first Tristar to visit Heathrow was N305EA in a basic Eastern Airlines colour scheme in 1972, later to be seen at Manchester with Court Lines on the nose, then by September

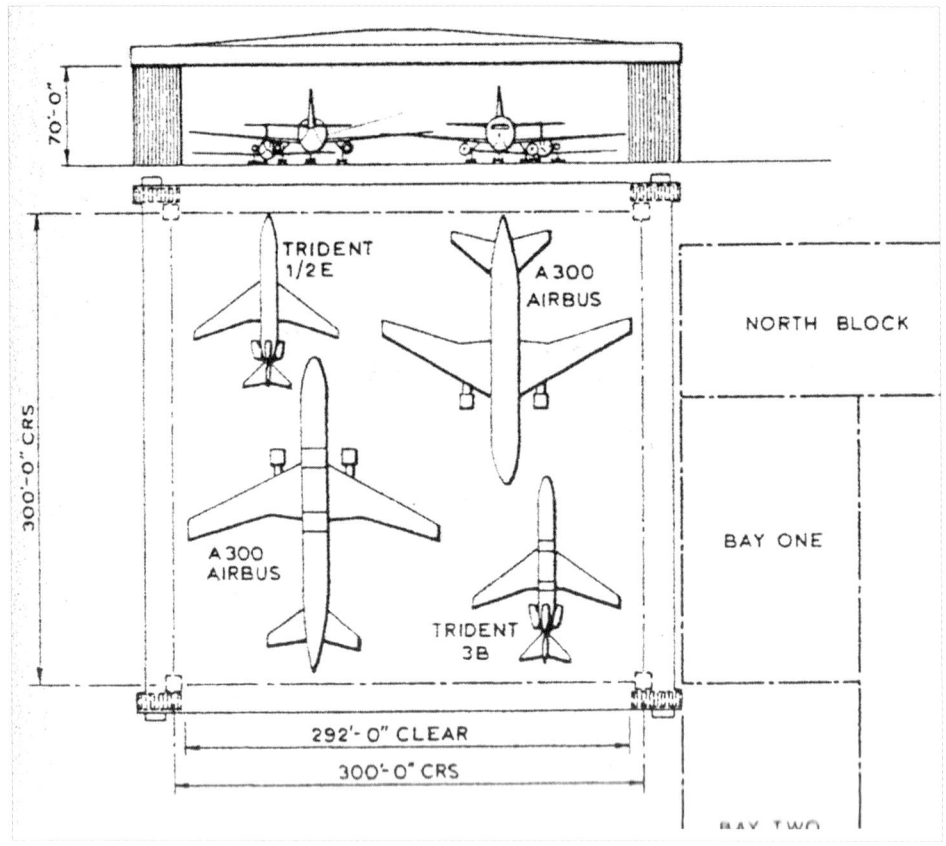

Heathrow, BEA Tristar Hangar plan, with two A300s and two Tridents to show how the hangar works, with doors open both ends. (via Author)

Heathrow, BEA Tristar Hangar with structural steel roof ready to be jacked up the four columns, with Libyan Arab Air Force Hercules 114 landing on Runway 28L. (Mick West)

Heathrow, BEA Tristar Hangar with structural steel roof jacked up into position, showing jacks and cables at tops of columns. (via Author)

Heathrow, BEA Tristar Hangar frame being clad, with Aztec G-AXOW landing on Runway 28L, 1970-1. This hangar is popularly known as the Cathedral hangar. (Mick West)

Heathrow, Pan American Boeing 747-121 N735PA, 18 November 1973, which was the first 747 to visit Heathrow on 12 January 1970. (Barry Collman)

at Farnborough with a BEA coloured tail. The first Airbus to be seen at Heathrow appeared on 20 May 1974 in the shape of Air France A300 FBVGA, three days before introduction on the Paris route. In 1971/2 wide-body movements totalled 13,000, doubling by 1974, and trebling again by 1984. Their holds had plenty of spare capacity after passengers' baggage, and this was filled with freight. The wide-bodies had an unforeseen effect on the Cargo Terminal, as that had been built on the theory that freight would grow with exclusively cargo aircraft. Passenger aircraft carry far more than the freighters, to the extent that the original twenty-nine stands are little used. The freight sheds continue in use, but deal in goods to and from the Central Area via the Cargo tunnel as well as from the other terminals.

Heathrow, first official visit of a Concorde to Heathrow, 1 July 1972, being G-BSST, the British prototype, with the BEA Cathedral Hangar behind, plus PanAm Boeing 707 and Brantly B2 helicopter. (Mick West)

Heathrow, first visit of a Lockheed Tristar to Heathrow, 1972, being N305EA in an Eastern Airlines scheme, to be seen at Farnborough later that year. (Mick West)

7.4. EDINBURGH COMES UNDER BAA UMBRELLA

Edinburgh joined the other airports managed under the BAA flag in 1970. In a sorry state, the airport was eventually to be equipped with a completely new runway away to the west and a new terminal.

7.5. PETER MASEFIELD LEAVES BAA, REPLACED BY NIGEL FOULKES

At the end of 1971, Peter Masefield resigned from BAA after nearly six years guiding the organisation through its formative years, bringing it to profitability. He would be replaced by Nigel Foulkes, Managing Director of Rank Xerox.

7.6. PIERS TOTALS

By 1972, piers gave a total of seventy-two stands, twenty on Terminal 1, the rest on Terminals 2 and 3. Terminal 1 now had 1,260 spaces in its car parks.

7.7. RUNWAY IMPROVEMENTS 1973–4

For many years rapid-hardening cements and resin mortars provided repairs for BAA concrete pavements during night-time or full closures at Heathrow. By the early 1970s BAA had begun major maintenance strengthening of the original concrete runways/taxiways with asphalt overlays at Prestwick, Gatwick and Heathrow, using night-time lulls in traffic. As Heathrow has more than one runway, the south runway 10R/28L was closed each night 21.00–07.30 between May and October 1973, followed by the north runway 10L/28R over the same period in 1974. Temporary centre-line lights and threshold markings were provided, but runway designation and touchdown marks were omitted. Temporary ramps were provided between one layer and the next. On the south runway, slopes of 1 in 60 led to complaints, and they were eased to 1 in 100. The height of the ramp was limited to 80 mm and the ramps were no closer than 110-m intervals. The full width of 91.4 m was surfaced each night, although later resurfacings were only the central 45.7 m. The north runway used similar restrictions. To reduce the effect of the ramps, resurfacing proceeded against the prevailing wind direction such that aircraft ran down the slope. Two mixing plants were provided, both being used for normal production, but allowing for one breakdown in the night, leaving sufficient capacity to leave the running safe. The use of the subsidiary runway was protected as long as possible, and access to the Cargo Area was protected during the south runway work. Intermittent possession of the work area affected the raising of the aviation ground lights and drainage to the new asphalt. On the south Runway 5 (10R/28L), 2,800 lights and pits had to be installed and raised. The lights were bedded with high alumina cement on precast makeup rings 550 mm in diameter. The runways slopes and cross-falls were complicated by the large number of runway and taxiway intersections. Generally the overlay comprised 125-mm base course, 40-mm wearing course and 20-mm porous friction course, which with 1 per cent cross-fall from the centreline led to a maximum thickness of 350 mm. The friction course was open-graded to eliminate aquaplaning. The usual length of asphalt laid each night was 120–150 m with the friction course about twice this.

7.8. MAPLIN, THIRD LONDON AIRPORT

7.7.1. The subject of another London airport was raised in a White Paper – 'London's Airports' – in July 1953, after which all was quiet, until a House of Commons all-Party Estimates Committee of 1960/61 recommended a detailed study of Stansted. An inter-departmental committee was set up in November 1961, the report being published in 1964, again recommending Stansted, which was accepted by Sir Alec Douglas-Home's Government. A decade earlier, in October 1954, John Boyd-Carpenter, Minister of Transport and Civil Aviation had presented a White Paper to parliament recommending go-ahead on Gatwick, with Stage 2 including a second runway. This was endorsed by Roy Jenkins, the Labour Minister of Aviation in June 1965, but set aside while the Stansted debate carried on. Had this been pursued, perhaps Roskill etc. might not have happened, or at least the need would have been delayed.

7.8.2. On 22 February 1968, Anthony Crosland, the new President of the Board of Trade announced his decision to set up the Roskill Commission 'to enquire into the timing of the need for a four-runway airport to cater for the growth of traffic at existing airports serving the London area, to consider the various sites and to recommend which site should be selected'. Aspects to be considered included general planning issues, including population and employment, growth, noise, amenity and effects on agriculture and existing property, aviation issues, including air traffic control and safety, surface access, and cost, including the need for cost/benefit analyses. This last was to upset a lot of people. Roskill began work in June 1968, looking at seventy-eight possible sites, ranking them in a site selection league, then announced a shortlist of four possible sites nine months later. The four chosen sites were Cublington (Wing) in Buckinghamshire and Nuthampstead in Hertfordshire (both disused Second World War airfields), Foulness on the Thames estuary in Essex, and Thurleigh (RAE Bedford) in Bedfordshire, and did not include Stansted, which caused some surprise at the time. After 2½ years, the commission published its report on 21 January 1971, recommending Cublington by a majority of six to one. Sir Colin Buchanan preferred Foulness as the only coastal site, the rest rejecting it on grounds of passenger and cargo inaccessibility, reclamation costs, and its general unpopularity within aviation circles.

7.8.3. Soon afterwards, on 26 April 1971, Peter Walker, the Minister for the Environment, and John Davies, the Minister for Trade and Industry, announced the government's rejection of the Commission's recommendation and chose Foulness, soon to be renamed Maplin Sands to sound more acceptable. Planned for 125 million passengers per year, it was to open in 1980 with four runways all aligned north-east–south-west on reclaimed land. Sited well away from populated areas, it would be served by a new motorway and rail service. Although the environmental lobby campaigned against the development, it was the 1973 oil crisis that finished the project. After some years of speculation and public enquiries, Maplin, as the third London airport, was officially abandoned in an announcement by Peter Shore, Secretary of State for Trade, on 18 July 1974, on the basis that forecasts of passengers' demand were lower than previously thought. Furthermore, capacity until 1990 did not need Maplin, no further runways were required at the four London area airports of Heathrow, Gatwick, Stansted and Luton; passenger capacity could be increased at Heathrow from 20 to 38 million and Gatwick from 6 to 16 million per year.

7.8.4. Stansted as the third London airport would eventually reach fruition. Maplin has reappeared as a suggested site for a new airport, being promoted by the Mayor of London, Boris Johnson, although the likelihood of development is unlikely, at least in the short term.

7.9. NEW ANIMAL QUARANTINE CENTRE

A new animal quarantine centre was announced in February 1975, to comply with the new rabies regulations in force that month, which extended precautions to all mammals. This was sited about 2 km west of Hatton Cross.

7.10. GLASGOW AND ABERDEEN COME UNDER BAA UMBRELLA

In 1975, Glasgow and Aberdeen joined the BAA, bringing the number of airports governed to seven, the three London airports at Heathrow Gatwick and Stansted, plus the four Scottish ones at Prestwick, Edinburgh, Glasgow and Aberdeen. Aberdeen was notable for the large number of North Sea gas- and oil-related flights, particularly helicopters, and was the busiest heliport in the world at the time.

7.11. TERMINAL 2 ENLARGEMENT

On 1 June 1975, work began on a £20-million project at Terminal 2 on enlargement, modernising facilities to cater for wide-bodies, with a new ground-floor check-in concourse, new escalators, lifts and ramps, plus a new shopping complex. Architects were Pascall & Watson with Murdoch Design Associates.

7.12. CONCORDE SERVICES BEGIN

The first visit to Heathrow by Concorde was by the British prototype G-BSST on 13 September 1970 after deliberately diverting from the Farnborough Airshow. It was to be some years before the UK and France were able to convince the USA that Concorde was not too noisy. Because of the consequent delays in permission, prospective sales to the world's airlines evaporated, apart from British Airways and Air France orders; they had seven each.

At 11.40 on 21 January 1976, British Airways Concorde G-BOAA and Air France Concorde F-BVFA took off from Heathrow and Paris Charles de Gaulle simultaneously to become the world's first supersonic airline services, the British one heading for Bahrain, the French for Dakar and Rio de Janeiro. A prestigious check-in area for Concorde passengers was provided at Terminal 3, as well as a special lounge and a stand right next to the main building. Later that year, the US authorities relented, giving permission to open Concorde services to Washington-Dulles airport; services began on 24 May when a British Airways Concorde began the service from Heathrow on the same day that Air France began one from Paris. The second Concorde landed at Washington soon after the first, and both were then photographed nose to nose. However, for New York it was not to be until the US authorities relented in early 1977, both British Airways from Heathrow and Air France from Paris eventually beginning services on 22 November 1977. In January 1979 the British Airways Bahrain service was extended to Singapore in a joint operation with Singapore Airlines, but it finished in November 1980.

7.13. EURO-TERMINAL BETWEEN TERMINALS 1 AND 2

To increase capacity, a new £6.6-million Euro Terminal was announced in January 1977 with work beginning at the end of 1977, to be open in 1979. Occupying 2,400 m^2, and positioned in front of the Queens Building between Terminals 1 and 2, it had moving walkways to link both terminals, and included baggage check-in, shops and bar, and waiting space for 700 passengers to go with the five extra stands.

7.14. NIGEL FOULKES LEAVES BAA, REPLACED BY NORMAN PAYNE

Nigel Foulkes left BAA on 1 March 1977 after five years, to become the Chairman of the Civil Aviation Authority. His successor at BAA was Norman Payne, who had been Director of Engineering in BAA from 1965, then Director of Planning from 1969, before becoming a member of the board in 1971.

7.15. AIRPORT STATISTICS

By 1977 the airport occupied 2,819 acres, and a total of seventy-five airlines were using the airport, five from Terminal 1, twenty-eight from Terminal 2 and thirty-nine from Terminal 3, plus three cargo airlines. By the end of the 1970s, 27 million passengers per annum were passing through.

7.16. PRECISION APPROACH PATH INDICATORS

The Precision Approach Path Indicator system, intended to replace VASI as described earlier, was first installed at Heathrow on the right side of runways 10L and 28L for operational evaluation, beginning 16 February 1979. VASIs continued on the left-hand side with equivalent brilliance settings. The Precision Approach Path Indicators comprise a set of four lights in a single unit perpendicular to the runway, next to the touchdown aiming point, usually on the left-hand side. Each unit of the PAPI has a slightly different angle setting, with the innermost being half a degree higher than required glide path, with progressive reductions of 1/3 of a degree on each until the outermost, which is set half a degree lower than the correct glide path. The correct angle is shown by two whites and two reds. Three/four reds indicates that the aircraft is too low, and three/four whites that it is too high. Runway 28L had an additional wing bar positioned 120 m upwind for long-bodied aircraft, which would otherwise use the three bar VASI system, but this was removed later. Following successful trials, the VASIs were replaced by PAPIs on all runways in early 1984. Early problems with condensation forming on the lenses after switch-on were solved by installing heaters in June 1984.

7.17. AIRLINE DEVELOPMENTS IN THE 1970S

By the early 1970s the increase in air transport passenger numbers caused the rapid replacement of short-haul piston engines and the early jet transports by Boeing 727s, DC9s, and Boeing 737s for Western European countries and Tu-134s and Tu-154s for the Eastern Bloc countries. Boeing 737s would gradually supersede other short-haul airliners in numbers, but only a few operators to Heathrow had them in the 1970s: Aer Lingus, Air Algerie, Lufthansa and Sabena. The required increase in long-haul capacity was being addressed by the introduction of wide-body aircraft, first the Boeing 747, then the Airbus A300, Lockheed Tristar and DC10, which by the end of the 1970s were established in many airline fleets, replacing many of the earlier jets. Concorde entered service on 21 January 1976 with a service to Bahrain, but it would not be until 22 November 1977 when New York services would begin, after objections had been satisfied. Boeing 747s were operated by nine European plus twenty-four other operators. Early DC8s were being replaced with the lengthened DC8-60 and 70 series. The Caravelle would soldier on with Air France until 1980, its other users having moved on to more modern types. The VC10 had all but vanished by 1980 apart from British Airways. Il-18s could still be seen with Soviet-bloc countries, even continuing into the 1980s with Balkan, LOT and Interflug. See Appendix D for airline types operated in the 1970s.

8

Extension of the Piccadilly Underground to Heathrow

8.1. A rail link to Heathrow was first considered in October 1946, then by subsequent working parties and committees in 1954, 1957, 1962, 1966 and 1967, finally being recommended by the Heathrow Link Steering Group under the Ministry of Transport Chairman. The Greater London Council approved the Piccadilly Line extension to Heathrow in December 1970 and agreed to a 25 per cent grant of capital cost. The first contract was let in April 1971. Subsequently the Ministry of Transport made an infrastructure grant of a further 25 per cent of capital cost. The project was to extend the line from Hounslow west to a new station in the Central Area, plus an intermediate station at Hatton Cross on the south side. There would be a total length of 5.5 km, of which 4 km would be cut and cover tunnel, except 0.6 km where it crossed the River Crane, and the remaining length was in twin bored tunnels from Hatton Cross to the centre. The route followed Bath Road from Hounslow West, turning along the A30 Great South West Road and under the airport including Runway No. 2 (05/23), entering the Central Area at the south end of the Queens Building with an overrun length to the north-west, allowing for future extension if necessary.

8.2. The project was let in three contracts. The first one was from Hounslow West to Hatton Cross, about 3.5 km, of which 2.59 km were in covered way, the roof generally being 1 m below ground, except under a sewer where it dips to 5 m. The first 1.83 km and the length adjacent to the British Airways Maintenance Area, plus each side of Hatton Cross station, was constructed with interlocking secant pile walls 890-mm diameter at 0.8-m centres each side with prestressed concrete inverted T-beams for the roof. The deeper portion was a reinforced concrete box between steel sheet pile walls. The resultant tunnel had two tracks within the 7.3-m width and 3.2-m min. height, mounted on precast concrete anti-vibration deck units on rubber bearings where passing through residential areas. The first sod was cut on 28 April 1971. The first year was spent on service diversions involving ten statutory authorities, including 1 mile of sewer tunnel diversion at depths up to 12 m. Designed by London Transport, the Main Contractor was W. & C. French (Construction) Ltd, with piling by A. Waddington.

8.3. The second contract was from Hatton Cross to Heathrow Central. This length involved a reinforced concrete double box cut and cover running tunnel, shield-driven 3.81-m internal diameter twin tunnels, ventilation enlargements 5-m internal diameter, scissor crossovers 9.5-m internal diameter and station tunnel extensions 7.5-m internal diameter. With 300 mm of made ground and 5.5 m of water, bearing sand and gravel, overlying the blue London clay, the twin bored tunnel through the clay offered the ideal solution. The tunnel linings were of two types, the Mott Hay and Anderson 0.6-m-wide rings of twelve segments left over from the Brixton extension of the Victoria Line; and the Halcrow rings, again 0.6-m-wide but in twenty-two segments, similar to those used on the Fleet Line. Consultant was Sir William Halcrow & Ptnrs, the Contractor being John Mowlem & Co. Ltd.

8.4. The final contract was for the Heathrow Central station. The station comprises a 122-m-long by 24-m-wide reinforced concrete box constructed within a concrete diaphragm wall excavated internally from the top, within which are three levels, the ticket hall 6 m below ground, staff accommodation 3.4 m lower and platforms at 14-m depth. The roof is 2 m thick, capable of taking a six-storey building on top. The other floors are concrete flat slabs, propping the walls apart. The Central station is oriented NW–SE between the Tower building and Car Park 1 in front of Terminal 1, with subways to all three terminals. Each subway has two 1.4-m-wide travelators and a central walkway, with a total width of 8.5 m, built using secant pile walls. The Terminals 2 and 3 subways meet in a separate 75-m by 18-m foyer on the south side. Consultant was again Sir William Halcrow & Ptnrs, with Contractor Taylor Woodrow Construction Ltd. The Alcock and Brown statue was moved to a new site close to the west end of the Tower on 25 April 1974, to allow the subways between the terminals and the new underground Central station to begin construction on 10 May 1974. Hatton Cross station opened on 19 July 1975, Heathrow Central following in 1977. The new Piccadilly tube line link was opened by Her Majesty the Queen on 16 December 1977, becoming the first major world airport connected to an urban underground railway system. Heathrow Central was renamed Heathrow Central Terminals 1, 2 and 3 on 12 April 1986.

8.5. It had been hoped that the new underground link would relieve the numbers of passengers arriving by road, but the road tunnel was soon back to its normal peak time congestion. A fifth of passengers still used taxis to get to and from Heathrow. To appease those airlines banished to Gatwick to relieve Heathrow, it was hoped that the opening of the Heathrow–Gatwick Airlink helicopter service in 1978 would help with inter-airline connections. The service proved popular with businessmen, with the ten flights per day each way carrying 60,000 passengers in its first year. However, noise objections from the residents under the British Caledonian helicopter flight path proved sufficient for the government to withdraw the service in February 1986, especially after the M25 had opened, allowing motorway coaches to do the job.

9

Terminal 4 and the Extension of the Piccadilly Line to Terminal 4

9.1. Rejection of the third London airport at Foulness/Maplin led BAA to decide that a large increase in passenger-handling capacity was required by the mid-1980s. The Perry Oaks sewage disposal works on the west side was considered too large an obstacle for an early terminal, so the Terminal 4 site selected was south of the Central Area, near the South Perimeter Road about 2 km west of Hatton Cross. Planning conditions included an extension of the Piccadilly Underground to the new terminal. Alternatives considered included a separate bus/light rail link from Hatton Cross, single or twin tunnel 4-km extensions of the Piccadilly Line from Heathrow Central and a single tunnel 6-km loop with trains running clockwise from Hatton Cross to Heathrow Central via Terminal 4. The bus/light rail link was cheapest but was inadequate for the eventual 8 million passengers at Terminal 4 (about a quarter of Heathrow's total) not using the Underground. The twin tunnel was the most expensive and the single tunnel not considered fail-safe. The 6-km loop line was chosen as the best option, as the existing westbound tunnel from Hatton Cross to Heathrow Central would be available in emergency to ensure continuity to Heathrow Central if a train failed on the loop.

9.2. Powers to construct the line were sought in the London Transport Bill in 1979, in which the Terminal 4 station was below the multi-storey car park adjacent to the terminal. Also the main tunnel works would be from a site and access shaft at Bedfont Road on the west side, adjacent to the animal quarantine centre, about 1 km west of Terminal 4. A further 1980 Bill included provision of permanent ventilation shaft and fan-house at the north end of the Cargo Terminal approximately halfway between the two stations. BAA began construction of Terminal 4 in mid-1981, and, as finance had not been agreed, the station had to be moved. An amending Bill in November 1981 allowed realignment of the railway to the new station site south of the multi-storey car park. After further negotiations on financing the extension, BAA were to construct the station and lease it to London Transport, passenger numbers reducing the fees payable. Due to Terminal 4 construction having already begun, the sole access shaft would have given insufficient time to construct the line, so the main site was moved to Wessex Road on the west perimeter, close to Perry Oaks, with a smaller site on the apron west of the Central Area. Completion of the tunnel and trackbed would take fifteen to eighteen months plus twelve months of track laying and equipment.

9.3. The design was based on a junction with the existing shallow westbound tunnel, west of Hatton Cross station, formed with diaphragm walls and prestressed concrete roof beams. The junction would be linked to a new cut and cover tunnel of similar construction on a descending gradient, to where sufficient cover of London clay would allow shield assembly for the tunnel drive to Terminal 4. This tunnel section, about 1 km in length, connects to the east end of the Terminal 4 station box. The bore continued west of the station on a continuous clockwise curve for approximately 4 km, linking ventilation shafts at Bedfont and Wessex Roads, terminating west of Central station. The Bedfont Road shaft avoided the need to use the cargo area at all. Approximately 5 km of tunnel were in 3.81-m-diameter precast concrete lining, while the ventilation tunnels were lined with 3.85-m-diameter cast-iron bolted linings. Basic details were issued in September 1982 and tenders issued in November 1982. The winning tenderer was a £10.6 million joint venture, Thyssen-Taywood, comprising Thyssen (GB) and Taylor Woodrow. Engineering works began on 31 January 1983. Construction of the bored tunnels used three shields, one each way from the Wessex Road site and one from Hatton Cross. Access to the tunnel at the Wessex Road main site was from a 7.7-m-diameter cast-iron temporary shaft 20 m deep. Tunnel linings used were 0.75-m wedge block sixteen-ring segments 152 mm thick by Halcrow, similar to those used in the original Hatton Cross extension but wider. The 130,000

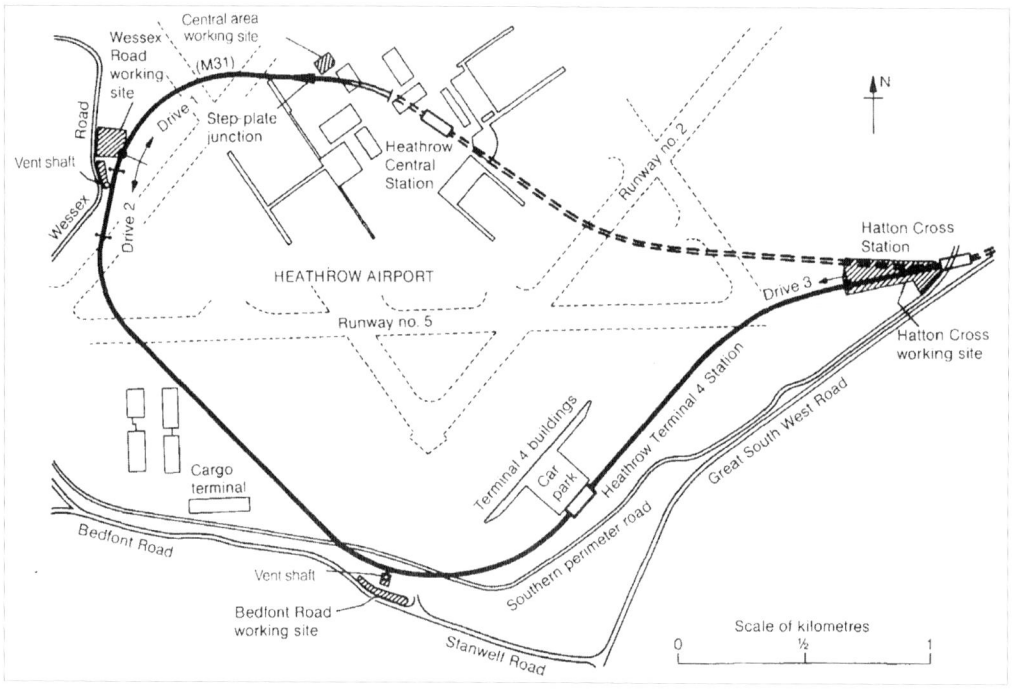

Heathrow, Piccadilly tube line extension, initially Hounslow West to Heathrow Central by 1977, then to Terminal 4 and the loop formed by 1986. (Institution of Civil Engineers)

segments were made at Taywood's precast works set up especially near their Southall HQ. Completion of the Phase 1 basic scheme to track-bed was required by 30 June 1984. The cut and cover tunnel extension at Hatton Cross was altered to use the 3.85-m diameter cast-iron linings left over from the Fleet Line construction, but (unusually) built in cut and cover fashion. Tunnel lengths achieved a maximum of 90 m per week. The whole operation was complete by spring 1986, the Terminal 4 station box construction being within the main Terminal 4 construction. The route from Heathrow Terminals 1, 2 and 3 to Terminal 4 was opened to the public on 12 April 1986 after the main terminal and station were officially opened by the Prince and Princess of Wales on 1 April 1986.

Alitalia DC8 I-DIWR with original B1 hangar group behind with an Eagle Britannia, plus two Esso tankers fuelling a BEA Vanguard foreground. (John Hamlin)

North side, main tunnel entrance to Central Area plus Emirates A380 model, with new Control Tower behind. (Philip Sherwood)

Heathrow Central Area control tower 10 August 1980, showing the Alcock and Brown statue moved from the north side. (Author)

Heathrow Central Area control tower 10 August 1980, taken from Queens Building side, with bus station to the right and Boiler House chimney plus Terminal 3 car park behind. (Author)

Heathrow, original Terminal 2 with newer façade, 8 October 2007, now demolished. (Thomas Nugent via geograph website)

Heathrow, Three-bay Alloy Hangar, the first aluminium hangar in the world, later in its time, when owned by Fields, c. 1991. (Paul Francis)

Heathrow, Three-bay Alloy Hangar, end bay, *c.* 1991. (Paul Francis)

Heathrow, original BOAC Owen Williams' designed hangar, now TBA, South Pen, unmodified due to the Wing Hangar being too close for manoeuvring, 27 September 2009. (Tony Szulc)

Heathrow, TBA from south side 27L approach, 28 July 2001, showing unmodified South Pen, used for Concordes, and modified East Pen. (Juan Rodriguez via airliners.net)

Heathrow, Southern Air Traffic Control Centre, North side, 1965, before the move to London Air Traffic Control Centre (LATCC) at nearby West Drayton. (CAA Archives via Pete Bish)

Heathrow Central Area Boiler House, Building 448, 3 March 2010, soon to be superseded by the new Combined Heat & Power Plant on South side near Cargo Area. (Author)

Heathrow, BOAC Owen Williams' designed Wing Hangar, an early cable-stayed roof hangar, later TBD, demolished 1990. (Geoffrey Negus)

Heathrow, Terminal 2, Pier 2, 1 June 1967, Four Trident 1s including G-ARPW & E, typical of the fleet that utilised the automatic landing technology in fog, taken for granted now, with Hunting hangar behind. (Author)

Heathrow, St George's Chapel, underground by the Central Area tower, 27 February 2008. (John Salmon via geograph)

Above: Heathrow, Central Area Cargo Tunnel entrance, 1991, plus Aeroflot Il-86 and SAS DC9 take-off, with Terminal 4 behind. (Mike Hudson)

Left: Heathrow, Terminal 1 and Pier 3 airside, post 1970 as Terminal 3 Boeing 747 Pier 7 is in use. (via Author)

Heathrow, Terminal 2, Pier 2 and Queens Building foreground, with Terminal 1, Pier4A and Runway 09L/28R behind, 23 April 2005. (Graeme Bolton via airliners.net)

Heathrow, Terminal 2, Piers 1 and 2 foreground, plus Queens Building middle and Terminal 1 Europier plus Piers 3 and 4 behind. (Mike Moores via airliners.net)

Heathrow, TBJ plus TBK hangars, 27 September 2009, built for Boeing 747s. (Tony Szulc)

Heathrow, TBK hangar internal (1) plus British Airways Boeing 747, 17 December 2009, showing the space frame roof. (Tony Szulc)

Heathrow, TBC multi-storey car park plus high level offices, 5 January 2014, behind TBJ and beside TBA, built with TBJ. (Tony Szulc)

Heathrow Terminal 3, 4 November 2006, showing Pier 5 and Pier 7 with the new Control Tower at the far end. (Mike Moores via airliners.net)

Heathrow, Originally BEA hangar for Tristars, 10 August 1980, now part of TBE, known as the Cathedral Hangar, with sloping roof to protect views to Runway 28R approach. Boeing 737 inside with Trident next door in Phase 1 hangar. (Author)

Heathrow, Cathedral Hangar, 20 March 2010, in current British Airways colours. (Richard E. Flagg)

Above: Heathrow, Cathedral Hangar internal, March 1988, with GB Airways Boeing 737 G-DDDV and one of the four columns behind. (Kevin Colbran)

Right: Heathrow Central, Radar Tower by Car Park 1A, 8 October 2007. (Thomas Nugent via geograph)

Heathrow, ex-BMI hangar, now TBD, 5 January 2014, plus Boeing 747 G-CIVE. (Tony Szulc)

Heathrow, ex-BMI hangar internal showing main roof truss, 5 January 2014, recently re-christened TBD. (Tony Szulc)

Heathrow Express construction collapse, October 1994, with terminal damage to Cambourne House on the left. (Institution of Civil Engineers)

Heathrow Express remedial cofferdam 60m/200ft diameter by 30m/100ft deep, 4 November 1996. (Institution of Civil Engineers)

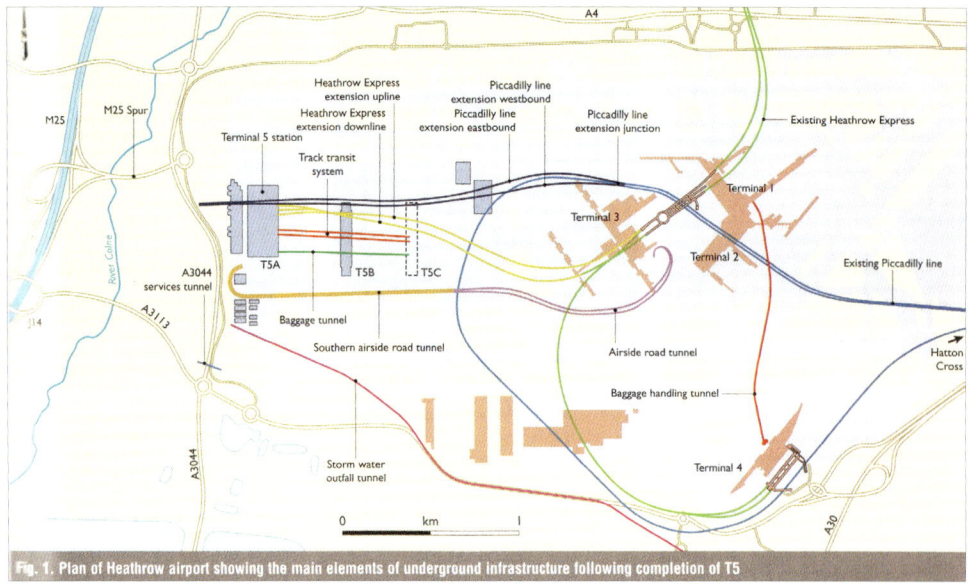

Fig. 1. Plan of Heathrow airport showing the main elements of underground infrastructure following completion of T5

Heathrow, tunnels plan 2005, showing Piccadilly tube line (blue), plus its extension (dark blue), Heathrow Express inc to T4 (green), plus its extension (yellow), airside road tunnels (yellow and purple), stormwater outfall (maroon), and baggage tunnels (red). (Institution of Civil Engineers)

Heathrow, aerial photo, 24 May 2010, with old Central tower plus Queens Building gone and Terminal 2 to follow. Cargo Area lower left and Terminal 4 bottom, with hangar area on lower right. The toast-rack appearance is already apparent with north-south T5A, T5B and T5C on the far left. (Brian G. Nichols-Plane-Images)

Heathrow, New Control Tower, 28 April 2006. (Paul Langfermannd via airliners.net)

Heathrow, TBA West Pen 5 Jan 2014, showing A380 tail modifications, with British Airways' first A380 G-XLEA inside. (Tony Szulc)

Heathrow, A380 F-WWWD special visit to trial modifications to TBA for tail, 11 February 2012. (British Airways via Severfield-Watson Structures)

Heathrow new Terminal 2A under construction, plus adjacent multistorey car park, September 2013. (Allan Huse)

Heathrow, Piccadilly tube line extension to Terminal 4 and back to Hatton Cross, December 1983. (Institution of Civil Engineers)

10

Terminal 4

10.1. Increasing congestion in the Central Area led to the building of Terminal 4 on the south side, connected by road to Terminals 1, 2 and 3 by the existing Cargo Tunnel. The BAA objective was that Heathrow capacity would be 38 million passengers per annum, of which Terminal Domestic had 5 million, Terminal 1 International had 8 million, Terminal 2 had 9 million and Terminal 3 10 million, making 32 million, but, as not all would reach capacity, 30 million realistically. This left 8 million to be catered for in Terminal 4. The site occupied 70 hectares on the south-east side, south of Runway 5 (10R/28L), and east of Runway 7 (05L/23R). It included Air India and Field Aviation Services facilities, restricting development in that area until they were relocated. The planning application was submitted in September 1977, but was called in for public inquiry, which occurred between 31 May and 15 December 1978, resulting in acceptance in principle in the May 1979 report. Detailed planning was submitted in November 1980, preliminary approval being achieved in May 1981, which enabled preliminary works, including earthworks, to begin. Final planning approval came in September 1981. From a BAA concept, the Architects Scott, Brownrigg & Turner created the terminal building, occupying 90,000 m², with a single long airside concourse with direct access to the aircraft rather than departure lounges, piers and gates. The area was split: landside public areas 15,000 m², landside non-public areas 7,800 m², airside public areas 30,000 m², airside non-public areas 23,000 m² and plant and lifts/stairs 14,200 m². To achieve smooth passenger flow, departures are set down on the upper level and move through the airside concourse, 650 m long by 25 m wide, to the aircraft bridges on the same level, with sixty-four check-in desks along a wide frontage. Sixteen aircraft stands are accessible from the concourse, nine airside and seven behind, with four more remote stands to the south-east. Eight of the nine airside stands were designed for stretched Boeing 747s. Arrivals leave the aircraft by bridge to the lower level, where moving walkways transport them to passport control, then down one level to baggage reclaim. From there, passengers can travel under cover to the vehicle pick-up area on the forecourt or the Underground station. The objectives were to keep walking distances between check-in and gates to 120–200 m, car park to check-in average 100–200 m, not less than 60 per cent aircraft stands connected directly to the terminal, avoidance of conflict between arrivals and departures (which occurred at Terminal 1 despite the intended separation), baggage routes to be as short as possible, plus other passenger help standards. Baggage for both arrivals and departures are sorted in one area 180 m by 50 m with baggage vehicles driving into the building.

10.2. In May 1978, Scott Wilson Kirkpatrick & Ptnrs were appointed as civil and structural engineering consultants for the project, except for the aprons, which were to be designed by BAA's Engineering Dept. Geology of the site comprised 0.4 m topsoil, 3-to-7-m-thick Taplow gravel deposits, overlying 65 m of London clay. The sands and gravels had been quarried in places and replaced with fill, and in some areas were overlain by brick earth up to 1.3 m thick. The old backfilled course of the Duke of Northumberland's River ran through the middle of the site north-west to south-east, diverted earlier in Heathrow history. Groundwater level was generally 2–3 m below ground level, so to exclude groundwater during construction and in its permanent condition a continuous cut-off wall encloses the main building, service yards, forecourts, short-term car park and the Underground station. Generally this cut-off wall is a 500-mm-thick reinforced concrete diaphragm wall where required to act as retaining or load-bearing wall; otherwise it is a lighter version of the same, or bentonite-cement-gravel cut-off.

10.3. The original concept for the terminal structure was precast concrete, but steel frame proved cheaper based on quicker build time. The planning module has steel column grids of 10.8 m NE–SW, and alternating grids of 7.2 m and 18 m NW–SE. The main terminal building (184 m by 108 m by 21 m high), except the plant room with metal deck roof, has a concrete slab roof on steel beams supported by tubular triangular lattice steel trusses at 10.8-m centres of spans up to 32.4 m. The airside concourse roofs are similar, spanning the full 25.2 m. The departures forecourt is an elevated deck 184 m long by 51 m wide, 11 m above ground level, providing vehicular access to the terminal building and short-term car park, and is the roof over the arrivals concourse. It carries eight traffic lanes, and comprises a 250-mm-thick reinforced concrete slab spanning 3.6 m on to longitudinal secondary steel beams, in turn supported on steel plate girders with box columns, forming three-bay portal frames of 18-m, 7.2-m and 20-m spans. The departures ramps carry the two-lane gyratory road system from ground level up to the forecourt, and comprise reinforced concrete voided slab deck spanning 19–23 m on to 1-m-diameter columns. The bottoms of the ramps cross the Underground, so the columns are on piled foundations, whereas generally the terminal columns are on pad bases into either the gravels or the London clay.

10.4. The Underground station is south of the short-term car park, with the ticket hall beneath the car park. A 6.65-m-wide subway links ticket hall and terminal via lifts and escalators with a smaller 3-m-wide emergency subway on the south. The station box is surrounded by a 1-m-thick reinforced concrete diaphragm wall, propped by the floor and roof slabs. The box is 135.8 m long, 8.6 m wide and 7 m high internally, planned to allow approach tunnels with reasonable clay cover, to simplify tunnelling. The roof, of precast prestressed inverted T-beams, was designed to support emergency vehicles. Immediately north of the station box is the ticket hall 48 m x 28 m x 7 m high, with internal columns on a 16-m by 7.2-m grid supporting 1.5-m by 1-m roof beams and a 300-mm-thick slab, in turn forming part of the car park floor. Built by cut and cover, the ticket hall has concrete walls 750 mm thick on three sides, the station box forming the fourth.

10.5. The four-level 1,150-space short-term car park in front of the main building, 165.6 m x 64 m on plan, is of reinforced concrete with column centres 16 m x 7.2 m, served by spiral ramps each end. Access from the A30 road from the east is via a three-span dual carriageway concrete bridge over the A30 to an elevated roundabout over the southern perimeter road, from which the ramps to the forecourt lead.

10.6. Associated with Terminal 4 are approximately 150,000 m² of taxiways and 170,000 m² of aprons. The aprons, providing twenty-two stands, were built of 350-mm plain pavement quality concrete on 150-mm lean concrete base course.

10.7. Earthworks were split into two phases owing to the presence of Air India and Fields'

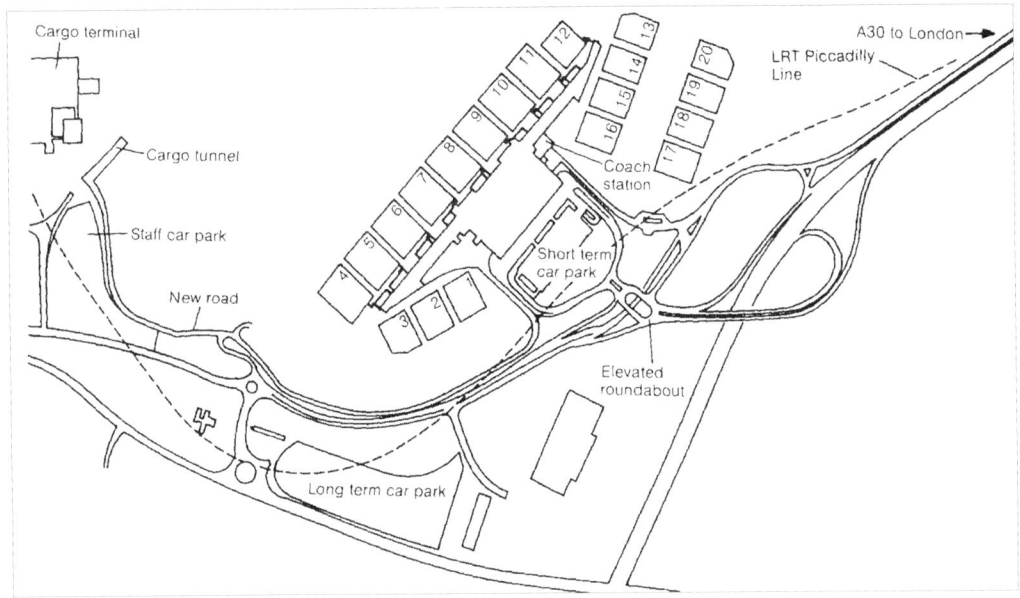

Heathrow, Terminal 4 plan, showing relationship to local features. (Institution of Civil Engineers)

Heathrow, Terminal 4 steel frame under construction, 2 September 1982, with the soon-to-be-demolished Air India freight facility top left and Three-bay Alloy Hangar, Fields and PanAm hangars behind. (Institution of Civil Engineers)

Heathrow, Terminal 4 building frame envelope nearly complete, 3 April 1984, with elevated road entry/exit in place, and Air India facility gone. (Institution of Civil Engineers)

hangars. These were in the north-east of the site and were in use until October 1982 and February 1983 respectively. Phase 1 earthworks extended to the Air India boundary, and lasted from June 1981 to November 1982; they included the terminal and aprons to near formation level. Phase 2 earthworks followed on in February 1983, after demolition of the Air India building in January, and lasted until September 1983.

10.8. The completion of earthworks allowed access for construction of the foundations and substructure of the terminal. This was split into the main centre 200 m x 150 m, split into three areas by expansion joints, the elevated departure forecourt bridge 200 m x 50 m separated from the main building by an expansion joint, and the SW and NE pier extensions also with expansion joints. Terminal steel erection began March 1982, the building structure being complete by mid-1985.

10.9. Costing £210 million including access roads, Terminal 4 was opened by HRH Prince Charles and HRH Princess Diana on 1 April 1986. After an overnight move from Terminal 3 to Terminal 4 by British Airways aircraft, equipment, cars, buses, vans and lorries plus staff, the first use by passengers was on 12 April. 70 per cent of Terminal 4 capacity was used for British Airways, the rest was for KLM, NLM and Air Malta. Terminal 4 Main Contractor was Taylor Woodrow, supervising 320 work packages. There were new problems for controllers, with aircraft needing to cross Runway 5 (10R/28L) to get to Runway 1 (10L/28R), but they manage. The same problem had been present when the Cargo Area opened, but the freight traffic was never large. Earlier in Heathrow's history there had been the same problem for London Airport North traffic crossing Runway 1 to get to Runway 5, but again the number of movements was small compared to today.

10.10. Terminal 4 now accommodates the Sky Team Alliance, having undergone a recent £200-million upgrade to accommodate forty-five airlines, with an extended check-in area, renovated piers and departure lounges, as well as two new stands capable of taking the Airbus A380. Terminal 4 has a total area of 105,481 m².

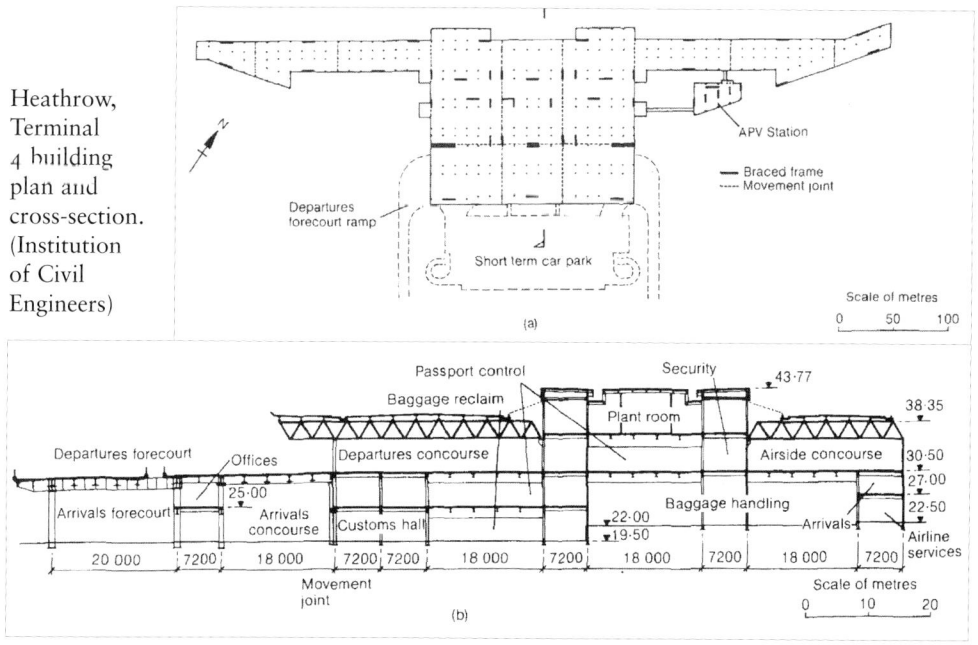

Heathrow, Terminal 4 building plan and cross-section. (Institution of Civil Engineers)

1980s/1990s Developments

11.1. NEW AIRPORT SPUR FROM M4, PLUS M25 LINKED

The M25 Yeoveney to Airport Spur (Junctions 13–14) was opened in August 1982, providing a direct link from the south-west to the airport. The M25 between Junction 14 Airport Spur and the M4 interchange (Junction 15) opened in December 1985, providing direct links to the West Country and Wales. When the M25 was completed in 1986, direct motorway access to the rest of the country was achieved.

11.2. NEW RADAR TOWER IN CENTRAL AREA

The secondary surveillance radar dish mounted on the tall concrete tower on the north side of Car Park 1a near the main tunnel was in use in around 1983. Similar radars were installed by the CAA on towers at Debden for Stansted and Pease Pottage for Gatwick, as well as at Claxby (Lincolnshire), Great Dun Fell and Tiree around the same time. The original lower radar scanners, mounted on frames, were sited on the north-west corner, south of Runway 10L/28R, now 09L/27R, and north of Perry Oaks fuel storage depot.

11.3. FIELDS AIRCRAFT SERVICES LEAVES HEATHROW

When Terminal 4 became operational, Field Aircraft Services desk moved from Terminal 1 to a new general aviation terminal between Terminal 4 and their Executive Jet Centre. However, it had become evident that BAA wanted private executive jets out of Heathrow, and Fields set up a new operation at Biggin Hill in 1988, having set up one at Stansted the previous year. General aviation movements had stayed static at 27,000 over the previous twenty years, whereas scheduled airline movements had increased from 267,000 in 1973 to 310,000 per annum by 1988.

11.4. TRIAL MICROWAVE LANDING SYSTEM INSTALLED

11.4.1. August 1986 saw the fitting of a Microwave Landing System (MLS) on Runway 28R. Selected by ICAO to replace ILS, the choice had initially been between the British Doppler system or the Australian 'Interscan' system, which the USA termed 'Time Referenced Scanning Beam' (TSRB). The Americans favoured this latter system and persuaded other

ICAO countries to vote for its adoption in the early 1980s. MLS had advantages over ILS, including extra channels making siting less critical; no beam bending due to terrain, buildings etc, enabling curved approaches; and being less subject to interference. The TSRB system at Heathrow was an engineering model produced by Plessey, intended for trials and modifications rather than operational use. Originally intended to remain for just over a year, it was finally removed in 1993–4 to be replaced with the production version, the P-Scan 2000 to Cat 3 standards. British Airways were involved at an early stage of evaluation by installing manufacturer's equipment in Boeing 757 G-BIKK and carrying out MLS approaches on 27R. Boeing 767 G-BNWB joined the trials in 1994 to evaluate DGPS navigational data against the MLS signals.

Heathrow aerial from the south-east, 25 February 1982, showing Three-bay Alloy Hangar, Fields apron and PanAm hangar bottom left, and Central Area Terminals 3, 2 and 1, top left to right, with Eurolounge built out from the Queens Building just visible top right with Piers 3 and 4 behind that. (Institution of Civil Engineers)

11.4.2. The Americans veered towards GPS systems rather than MLS at the end of the nineties, which resulted in a loss of interest in MLS in Europe. However, the higher incidence of Cat 3 conditions in Europe, together with concerns about disruption if satellites were switched off for military reasons, revived interest in MLS, and four Thales systems were installed at Heathrow from 2002. As a constituent part of the British Airways

Heathrow vertical aerial circa 1990, showing Cargo Area bottom left, Terminal 4 boittom, Hangars right and Central Area Terminal 1,2 and 3 plus tower centre, and Perry Oaks Sewage farm on west side (*left*) to be replaced with Terminal 5. (via Philip Sherwood)

order for A318, A319 and A321 in the mid-2000s, Thales multimode receivers were fitted, with GPS, ILS and MLS sensors. The presentation of guidance information for pilots on approach using MLS is identical to ILS.

11.5. BAA PRIVATISED

The Conservative government under Margaret Thatcher was in the process of privatising the nationalised industries, and BAA was not to be left out. It was realised that airports could not compete against one another in the normal sense, and since BAA was making profit, it would be a mistake to split it up and make each airport completely independent. The government instead saw a way of allowing more financial transparency and inhibiting cross-subsidy, by making each airport a separate company under the overall umbrella of BAA as a holding company. So in August 1986 each of BAA's seven airports became separate under BAA, owned by the Secretary of State for Transport until 1987, when the British Airports Authority was privatised and renamed BAA plc, controlling Heathrow and the six other UK airports: Gatwick, Stansted, Edinburgh, Glasgow, Prestwick and Aberdeen.

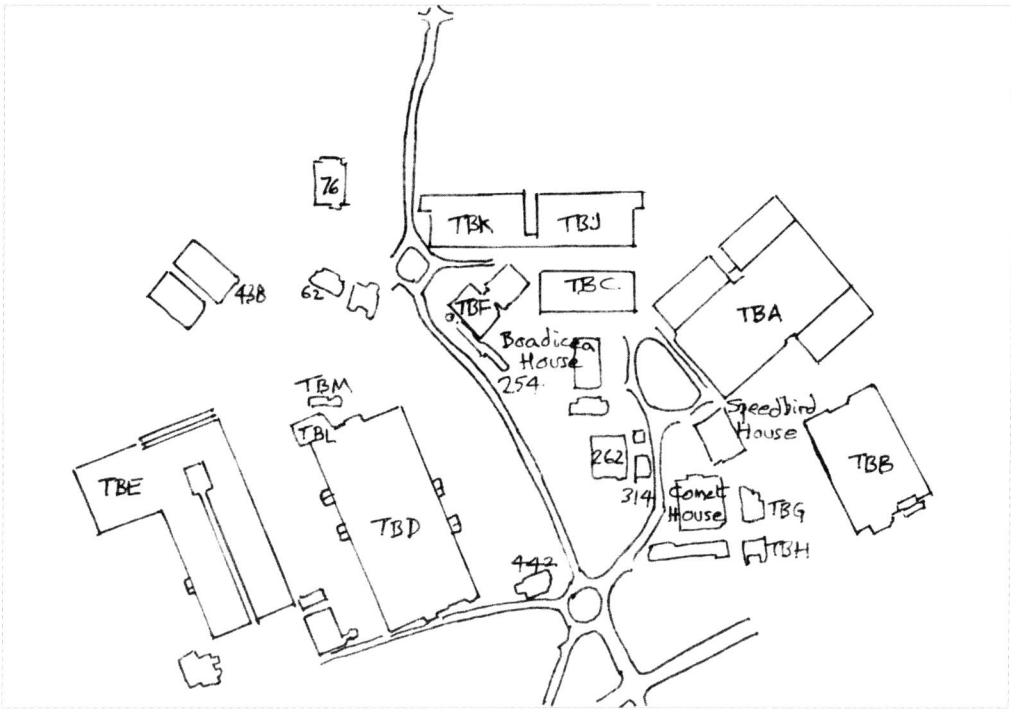

Heathrow, No. 1 Maintenance Area, now sole hangar location, *c.* 1989, showing labelling of Technical Blocks and offices (latter soon to be demolished). (via Author)

11.6 STANSTED BECOMES THIRD LONDON AIRPORT

BAA having acquired Stansted in 1966, a terminal was developed on the south side in 1969, and extended in 1972. There had been a public inquiry into a three runway plan for Stansted in 1965–6, but the case was not proven then. The Roskill Commission did not include Stansted in its final four for detailed consideration in 1969. The second public inquiry resulted from a BAA planning application to expand Stansted. Conducted by Graham Eyre QC between 1981 and 1983, the public inquiry accepted the need to expand Stansted, but using the existing single runway. In June 1985 Nicholas Ridley, the Transport Minister, announced approval for Stansted to expand from 2-million to 8-million capacity, with acceptance that 15-million capacity would follow when the 8-million figure had been reached. The final report of the inquiry had recommended that eventually a fifth terminal would be required at Heathrow to increase its capacity, and Nicholas Ridley recommended that BAA and Thames Water study the removal of Perry Oaks sludge works to make room for T5. Nicholas Ridley also confirmed that neither Gatwick nor Stansted would get a second runway. There were objections to the London airport developments as agreed from provincial airports, particularly northern ones including Manchester, who believed that limiting development in the south would drive airlines north, but Ridley believed that airports should be supported everywhere to ensure that traffic did not go abroad. With the M11 already in place from 1977, the new Richard Rogers terminal on the north side of Stansted began construction from April 1986 and opened in March 1991, with a new direct rail service to London, the Stansted Express, terminating underground at the terminal.

11.7. RUNWAY COMPASS BEARING CHANGES PLUS RESURFACING

On 2 July 1987, the main runways changed from 10/28 to 09/27. Runway and major taxiway resurfacing by asphalt overlay was undertaken at Heathrow in 1981, 1985, 1986, 1989 and 1990 plus later contracts. These later overlays stripped away only what was necessary, worn/damaged courses, to be replaced with thin carpets, plus dealing more effectively with cracking of the asphalt reflecting cracked concrete underneath. Due to the failure of the earlier thicker mortar beddings under the raised ground lighting rings, thin rapid-hardening mortars between precast or metal ring extensions was used instead.

11.8. TERMINAL 3 UPGRADE

Once British Airways long-haul services had been transferred from Terminal 3 to the new Terminal 4 in 1986, redevelopment of Terminal 3 in a four-year £73-million refit could begin. Phase 1 began in April 1986. Improvements to the departures building included demolition of the north end, the south end was rebuilt with a 40 per cent increase in check-in area, more lifts, better escalators, better shops, and a 30 per cent increase in the departures lounge, overall a 67 per cent increase in floor area. January 1988 saw the opening of new check-in desks in the rebuilt departures concourse. The arrivals building had new catering, open in July 1987, and new baggage reclaim would increase by 70 per cent, open in November 1987. Phase 2 included a new computer-controlled baggage-handling system incorporating lasers, and the second part of the arrivals hall extension, complete in October 1988. Phase 3 was the final extension of the arrivals building, complete in October 1989, increasing floor area by 65 per cent from 7,500 to 12,300 m². The last of the new check-in desks were complete in April 1990. Architects were D. Y. Davies Associates of Richmond, Consulting Engineers for departures were British Airports Services and for arrivals were A. Hunt Associates.

11.9. NEW BMI HANGAR

Of approximate plan dimensions 81 m frontage x 86 m depth, the bmi hangar was constructed by Costain Construction in an £8.5-million contract in mid-1991. The hangar comprises a main 78-m-span truss, weighing 90 tonnes, spanning the width. The truss was approximately 11 m deep with 7-m bays and approximately 20-m height clearance. Positioned one fifth of the way in from the doors, it carries five secondary trusses at 14-m centres spanning front–back. Small trussed purlins span between the secondary trusses parallel to the main truss. An additional shallower truss over the doors picks up smaller trussed purlins spanning between it and the main truss. Steelwork subcontractor was Robert Watson in a £1.2-million contract. Dutch firm Airfacts designed the structure with radar-absorbing panels to eliminate interference with the air traffic control system.

11.10. TERMINAL 1: PIER 4A

In 1993 a Pier 4A was completed extending westwards approximately 350 m from the existing Pier 4 on the north side of Terminal 1. It provided an extra nine stands, serving Great Britain, Ireland and the Channel Islands. The pier was built over an existing airside road, so was suspended 6 m up on steel portal frames spanning the road with concrete floors spanning between portals and a hoop-shaped external envelope clad in aluminium sheet. Designed by Nicholas Grimshaw & Partners, the cost was £25 million, and with the adjacent Pier 4 could now handle 10 million passengers a year.

11.11. TERMINAL 2 REDEVELOPMENT

In mid-1996 Terminal 2 was redeveloped in the £30-million Airside scheme, including an extension to the departures lounge on two levels, the existing floor being extended out and the upper level being roofed over on the original open-roof terrace, all for catering and seating with shops. The development also included a new immigration hall, which opened in November 1995. Soon afterwards, Terminal 2 check-in area was redeveloped in another £30-million project.

11.12. EUROPIER

11.12.1. By January 1992 Runway 2 (05R/23L) was close to the end of its life before major work was needed, but it severely limited expansion of the eastern apron. Stand demand in Terminals 1 and 2 exceeded supply, and daily overspill of approximately six aircraft to the western apron was necessary, which in turn caused problems there. By April 1992 options were proposed for the development of the eastern apron, including provision of four extra stands at Terminal 4, which was also suffering from stand shortage. It was proposed to downgrade Runway 2 (23L) from instrument to visual status, displacing the centre line 15 m eastwards, curtailing its length to 2,000 m landing distance, and discontinuing Runway 05R . By restricting the runway to visual landings only, this allowed expansion of the eastern apron eastwards and for five Boeing 747 stands at Terminal 4 to be constructed.

11.12.2. Prior to Europier, the existing Eurolounge had been built out from the Queens Building in the 1970s with four jetties serving stands plus five nearby stands. In November 1993 BAAS approved expenditure for construction of Europier to achieve 90–95 per cent jetty service at Terminals 1 and 2, compared to 80 per cent and 90 per cent existing for Terminals 1 and 2 respectively. Extending eastwards in line with the Queens Building but coming from the south-eastern corner of Terminal 1, it provided an extra ten stands with seating for 1,130 passengers and 600 m² of retail space. The existing link between Terminal 1 and Eurolounge had to have an extra-high-level floor added by extending the existing steel frame to provide an arrivals route. The Eurolounge itself was spanned by a 50-m bridge. The west link was an entirely new steel frame with main columns at 9-m centres. The Europier itself was 284 m long by 16.2 m wide by 13 m approximate height, providing jetty service to ten stands plus four remote stands. The three-storey structure has arrivals on the top floor, departures on the middle and maintenance accommodation on the ground floor. Two jetty stands were retained at Eurolounge. The departures level in Europier seats 1,140. The Europier construction comprises a high curved roof on pairs of steel tree columns at 7.2-m centres. Walking distances were reduced by linking Europier at mid-length and having moving walkways in all links for departures and arrivals levels. The new pier was based on a 1.8-m module, on overall grid dimensions 10.8 m x 7.2 m, all steel framed. Construction began July 1994 and became operational 4 December 1995. The building, costing £30 million, and designed by the Richard Rogers Partnership, with structural engineers Waterman Partnership, incorporated 1,600 tonnes of steel, and 4,000 m² of glass. Europier was the last phase of a £150-million upgrade of Terminal 1. The other Terminal 1 improvements included a refurbished International Departures Lounge, opened in September 1995. and a new Flight Connections Centre on the south end of Terminal 1 for passengers in transit, opened in December 1994, both also designed by the Richard Rogers Partnership. After this work Terminal 1 was able to handle 22 million passengers a year

11.13. HEATHROW EXPRESS

11.13.1. In 1988 Paul Channon, the Minister of Transport approved a new scheme to link Heathrow with the Paddington Line, 2 miles north of the airport. After amendments, principally on environmental grounds, royal assent to the joint British Rail-/BAA-promoted parliamentary Bill was received in May 1991, but was shelved because of other priorities. Funding was eventually agreed in March 1993. The new track was to dive under the M4 into a tunnel to a new Underground station serving Terminals 1, 2 and 3 at the Central Area, with a single track onwards to Terminal 4. Intended to run every fifteen minutes, the electric trains would cover the 27 km from Central Area to Paddington in seventeen minutes non-stop. BAA was to put up 80 per cent of the £190-million construction, the other 20 per cent from British Rail, although by 1996 BAA had bought out British Rail's share due to the latter's preoccupation with privatisation. The total cost of the Heathrow Express was originally put at £260 million, with British Rail putting up £53 million for electrification and the airport junction, and BAA £208 million for the stations, tunnelling and trains. By 1993 the estimates had risen to £300 million in 1993, and the eventual cost was £450 million.

11.13.2. The original fuel depots at Central Area were relocated to west of Terminal 3 in advance of the Heathrow Express project.

11.13.3. Balfour Beattie won the £60-million contract in January 1994 for the Heathrow Express airport tunnels and stations. The contract comprised a new viaduct at the junction with the main line, twin 5.5-m-diameter shield-bored tunnels from the M4 to Central Area and from there to Terminal 4 in a single tunnel, with the Central Area and Terminal 4 station tunnels and concourses built using a modified version of the New Austrian Tunnelling method (NATM), which utilised sprayed concrete linings. Tunnelling work near the M4 began in December 1993, with 600 m of cut and cover tunnel between the main line and the M4, followed by the main bored tunnel from August 1994, which would cover the 3 km of twin running tunnels to the Central Area, a series of 9-m-diameter station caverns under the Central Area, continuing to Terminal 4 with a smaller station area. The original target date for opening was 1 December 1997. Works in the Central Area began on 9 May 1994. By June the concourse tunnel had passed under Cambourne House, a small two-storey office building, close to the Tower. By July settlement was being recorded in Cambourne House. By early August the Up line tunnel had begun, and by September tunnels were being constructed on five faces. Settlement was continuing as well as movement of tunnels, which culminated in a collapse of the workings on 20 October 1994, taking Cambourne House with it, fortunately with no fatalities.

11.13.4. The potential delay to the project as a result of the collapse was estimated at eighteen months. A Solutions Team was swiftly formed, drawn from the main players,

BAA, main contractor Balfour Beattie, lead design engineers Mott MacDonald and the loss adjusters Brocklehurst with their consultant Ove Arup & Ptnrs. Their task was to find a recovery solution that included all the tunnels including the sprayed concrete tunnels and the Central Terminal Area collapse zone. The resulting solution had to encompass the disturbed ground, the mass concrete fill placed to limit further damage, collapsed tunnels, and large buried construction plant. By December 1994 it was agreed that the preferred method was a 60-m-diameter cofferdam 30 m deep surrounding the collapsed zone. It had to encompass the concrete piled surface slabs and escalator box, the original 20-m-diameter 30-m-deep fuel depot shaft, and the three partially completed large-diameter sprayed-concrete-lined platform and concourse tunnels. The shaft and tunnels had been filled with 13,000 cu. m of concrete as a short-term stabilising measure. The large size of cofferdam was chosen to enable safe access and removal of major obstructions. The circular shape was chosen as it eliminated any cross-strutting that a rectangular cofferdam would have needed, and offered 20,000 cu. m less bulk excavation. The original ground conditions were 6 m of Terrace gravels over 60 m of London clay on the Woolwich and Reading beds in turn on the chalk at 90 m below ground level. A series of boreholes was initiated soon after the collapse to reveal the extent of where the disturbed ground was, which were two areas of the Up line tunnel and one area of the Down line tunnel, all contained within the cofferdam perimeter, plus one in the station concourse just outside the perimeter. After careful investigation and stabilisation, 182 secant piles were installed to form the outer ring of the cofferdam. These were 1,200-mm diameter for the top 20 m, stepping down to 900-mm contiguous piles for the next 20 m, the pile centres being set at 1,060 mm. Permanent lateral support was provided by reinforced concrete rings cast against the piles as excavation progressed in 1-m lifts, increased to 1.2-m lifts after 7-m depth, the maximum achievable on a five-day lift cycle. The 20-m depth was the original tunnel crown depth and the majority of excavation was thus protected from groundwater. The area of disturbed ground under Cambourne House over the concourse tunnel was outside the cofferdam and was further protected by an elliptical ring of secant cement/bentonite piles 30 m deep adjacent to the concourse tunnel. Further piles were installed inside this ring to further guarantee soil stability over the concourse tunnel. The piling was carried out late 1995/early 1996 allowing excavation within the cofferdam to begin in March 1996. Once the cofferdam excavation had reached tunnel level, pilot tunnel breakthroughs were gradually enlarged and temporarily plugged with concrete to preserve the cofferdam integrity. In total, 255 bored piles 900-mm diameter x 15 m long for the base slab were placed in July 1996. They limit long-term heave and control hydrostatic uplift. The base slab was completed by September 1996. Piling contractor was Stent.

11.13.5. Stent Foundations completed piled foundations at Terminal 4 for the new station, 30 m below ground level, in mid-1994. The platform tunnels, crossover and turnout tunnel were all built using the sprayed concrete lining method, after careful review after the Central Area collapse. The new flyover at the Airport Junction with the Paddington–Reading main line, just west of Hayes and Harlington station, was completed in September 1996. It was needed so as to avoid conflict with the main-line high-speed services.

11.13.6. In the summer of 1996, as civil works on the Heathrow Express were nearing completion, an opportunity was taken to extend the scheme by the inclusion of an underground train siding, called a headshunt, between the two stations to store a four-carriage train. This increased the capacity of Heathrow Express trains from eight to fourteen per hour for an additional 1.4 per cent of project cost. The 5.675-m-internal-diameter headshunt tunnel was 135 m long from the crossover cavern in Central Area to its end, and was positioned so as to allow possible extension of HEX to Terminal 5. The go-ahead for main design was given in November 1996, to start construction in January 1997. Sprayed concrete was again used for the lining. Breakthrough into the crossover cavern was made on 26 April 1997, three months ahead of programme, at a final cost of £6 million.

11.13.7. The Heathrow Express was able to run an interim service from 19 January 1998 by investing £1.9 million in an interim service from a temporary station located on the new airport line a short distance south of the junction with the Paddington–Reading main line, called Heathrow Airport Junction. It was ten minutes from the Central Area via a special dedicated coach link. The Central Area cofferdam remedial operation allowed the Heathrow Express to be completed only six months late, also saving an estimated £100 million in extra costs, opening throughout on 25 May 1998 to stations at Heathrow Terminals 1, 2 and 3 and onwards to the terminus at Terminal 4. The temporary Heathrow Airport Junction station closed at the same time and was subsequently removed. Heathrow Express was officially opened by Prime Minister Tony Blair on Tuesday 23 June 1998. Heathrow Express trains run both ways every fifteen minutes with journey times of fifteen minutes from Central Area, with additional slower Paddington trains between.

11.14. 50TH ANNIVERSARY FLY-PAST

The 50th anniversary of Heathrow was celebrated on 2 June 1996 by a fly-past of aircraft visible at the airport over the years; it was organised by the International Air Tattoo. The first aircraft was the Battle of Britain Flight's Lancaster PA474, representing the original first commercial aircraft to take off from Heathrow, Lancastrian G-AGWG of British South American Airways. In order of appearance were DH Rapides G-AGSH and G-AIDL, Bristol Freighter C-FDFC, DH Dove G-OLPC, DC3 G-AMPZ, C47A G-DAKK, DC4 ZS-BMH, DC6 G-SIXC, Viscount G-BFZL, Herald G-CEAS, HS748 G-AVXJ, DH Comet 4C XS235, DC8-71 N805DH, BAC-111 G-AVMT, Boeing 727 EC-GCK, Boeing 737-500 G-OBMY, Boeing 747-400 9V-SMS, Boeing 767 C-FMWP, MD-11 N1768D, Airbus A340 G-VBUS, Concorde G-BOAA with nine Red Arrows Hawks, Boeing 777 G-ZZZD.

11.15 BRITISH AIRWAYS NEW HQ WATERSIDE OPENS

Construction of a new headquarters building for British Airways at Harmondsworth Moor, north-west of Heathrow between the M25 and the M4 began in September 1995, and began transferring staff between December 1997 and May 1998, the building officially opening in June. Costing £200 million, the building is arranged in six sections around a central 175m/574ft long atrium/street, each section representing a continent. It has been likened to aircraft grouped around a terminal. The Architects were Niels Torp, Consulting Engineers Buro Happold, Building Services Cundall and Main Contractor Mace. Following transfer of staff, the old Comet House and Speedbird House near to TBA Hangars were demolished.

11.16. BRITISH AIRWAYS WORLD CARGO CENTRE

The new British Airways World Cargo Centre opened in January 1999. Designed by W. S. Atkins, on a budget of £250 million, it consists of a bull-nose-profile metal-clad building, dictated by the need for a low-radar signature, occupying 87,000 m² of floor space, including 5,000 m² of offices, with £80 million worth of mechanical handling equipment. It increased Heathrow's cargo capacity by two-thirds, boosting BA's share from 600,000 to 1 million tonnes per year, almost all in passenger aircraft's baggage holds. The building has a 300-m x 100-m footprint x 35-m height, one-third of its volume (360,000m³) comprising mechanically accessed racking holding 2,000 Unit Load Devices, which fit into aircraft holds. Next to this space is the 150,000 m³ ventilation and structure slot running the full length of the building. Beyond this is the largest element, a 9,600-space consignment store occupying 540,000 m³ on four floors.

11.17 ALCOCK AND BROWN STATUE MOVED AGAIN

In 1999 the Alcock and Brown statue at the west end of the Central Area Control Tower was moved to outside the Visitor Centre on the North side, close to the Renaissance Hotel. The statue remains there although the building is now the Heathrow Academy. The statue is on a smaller plinth than its previous site by the tower.

11.18. AIRLINE DEVELOPMENTS IN THE 1980S AND 1990S

11.18.1 The 1980s: On 27 September 1981 Karair DC6 OH-KDA performed the last scheduled piston-engined transport movement from Heathrow to Manchester and Helsinki. Earlier jets like the Caravelle and Boeing 707 were being sold on to smaller airlines and upgraded by Boeing 737s and DC9s. Smaller types seen in small numbers at Heathrow were ATR42s, DHC6 Twin Otters, DHC7s, DHC8s, HS/BAe 748s, BAe ATPs, BAe 146s and Saab 340s. By the mid-1980s the earlier marks of DC9 were being upgraded by the MD80 series, in use by five European airlines. By the end of the 1980s, sixteen airlines were using the 737, which by now were being upgraded to the 300 series and greater. Other older types being disposed of included Viscounts, Il-18s, Tu-104s and VC10s. Boeing 727s were still being widely used, but would vanish by the 2000s except on a few Middle Eastern airlines and JAT. The sole Heathrow operator of the Trident by now was British Airways, with the last flight from Manchester to Heathrow on 31 December 1985. Boeing 747s (fifty-three Heathrow operators), DC10s and Tristars were being widely used and newer types were coming on-stream like A310, Boeing 757 and 767. On 14 December 1988, Antonov An124 CCCP-82008, then the largest aircraft in the world, was the first of the type to visit Heathrow, to be followed by several more later that month collecting relief supplies for the Armenian earthquake. On 16 December 1988 there was the first and only visit of an even rarer beast, the Antonov An22 CCCP09319, the largest ever propeller aircraft, also collecting relief supplies for the Armenian earthquake. On 16 August 1989 Qantas Boeing 747-438 VH-OJA departed on a proving flight to Sydney non-stop, a distance of 9,638 nautical miles, taking 20 hours 9 minutes. See Appendix D for airline types operated in the 1980s.

11.18.2 The 1990s: The Boeing 737 was being operated by thirty-six airlines into Heathrow by 1999. The 1990s saw an influx of new ex-Soviet state's airlines with their Tu154s and Il62s, as well as western products from the Airbus and Boeing stables. The Il-86 and Il-96 would appear in Aeroflot colours. The McDonnell-Douglas MD11 was being introduced as an upgraded DC10. By the end of the 1990s, Airbus A330s, A340s and Boeing 777s began being seen by a few airlines. The short-haul A320 was introduced, and later the A319 and A321, although it would not be until the 2000s that the last two would arrive in quantity. Fokker 70 and 100 derivatives of the F28 Fellowship appeared in the early 1990s. The Saab 2000 would only appear in Crossair colours. See Appendix D for airline types operated in the 1990s.

11.18.3. The demise of Pan Am in December 1991 saw its Heathrow slots given to United Airlines. Similarly the financial difficulties with TWA saw its slots handed to American Airlines in 1991, TWA finally being taken over by American in 2001. By 1998 the transatlantic Open Skies agreement allowed US Airways to operate services to Heathrow from March 2008, to be followed in April by Continental Airlines.

12

Terminal 5

12.1. The main Terminal 5A building was the largest single-span structure in the UK. It provides forty-seven aircraft stands, ten capable of taking the A380, with thirteen more stands completed by 2011, making sixty in all. Terminal 5 has a total area of 353,020 m². The complex included the building of a 3,800-capacity multi-storey car park, a new 600-bed hotel, the diversion of the Longford and the Duke of Northumberland's rivers along the western side (costing £45 million), a link road to the M25 and the extension of the Heathrow Express rail and Piccadilly Tube lines. Architect was the Richard Rogers Partnership, with architectural services and design management at scheme stage by HOK. Architectural services at T5B were by Pascall and Watson. Structural engineer for the above-ground structure was Arup, and for the substructure was Mott MacDonald. Main Contractor was Laing O'Rourke. Roof and façade steelwork was by Watson Steel, and for the superstructure was Severfield Rowen plc. Pavements were by Amec Group (Civils), fit-out by Mace, tunnelling by Morgan Vinci JV. There was a total of eighty main suppliers.

12.2. When Terminal 5 opened on 27 March 2008, it was almost twenty-five years since the White Paper – Airports Policy, 1985 – that encouraged its development. The site for T5 was on the old Perry Oaks sludge works, for which a joint study was conducted by BAA/Thames Water between July 1985 and April 1986. In August 1985 a Heathrow Surface Access Working Group was set up and reported in June 1987, which resulted in the Heathrow Express direct rail service from Paddington to Heathrow Central, and improvements to the A4, M4 and M25. In spring 1988 BAA commissioned engineers W. S. Atkins to begin airport access feasibility studies, initial planning for extra airport facilities began and legal counsel was appointed. The concept/design competition for Terminal 5 was won by Richard Rogers Partnership in 1988. When planning for T5 began in February 1988, the initial concern was the boundaries. The north, east and south sides were constrained by taxiways, while the west was more variable, with roads and rivers plus the perimeter road. Also, to cater for future large aircraft, an 85-m taxiway box around the site was defined, which allows for a wingspan of 80 m for the A380-800. By 1988 the idealised form for T5 was identified as a core terminal building with aircraft stands on three sides plus two or three satellites with Underground links for passengers, luggage and vehicles.

12.3. The Perry Oaks sludge dewatering plant was being cleared from February 1989, with centrifuges eventually being installed at Iver South to accelerate the rate of disposal. The Perry Oaks site was replaced by pipes linking Iver South sewage treatment works to Mogden sewage treatment plant in Twickenham, and the Perry Oaks site was cleared by 1998. In a £106-million contract, Costain not only carried out the pipe diversion, but both Mogden and the Iver South facility were upgraded, with new bridges over the A4 for Iver South site entrance. Contracts were split as follows: pipeline from Perry Oaks to Iver South – £8 million; new junction on A4 to Iver South – £2.5 million; upgrade of existing A4 junction to Iver South – £3.5 million; pipeline upgrade Mogden to Iver South – £14 million; Mogden modifications – £34 million; design and management – £6 million; dewatering plant at Iver South – £38 million; total £106 million.

12.4. Orders for the extension of the Heathrow Express were published in September 1994 and for the Piccadilly Line extension in November 1994. Roads orders for the T5/M25 spur road were published in May 1996, and proposed M4 improvements published in March 1997.

12.5. In March 1992 BAA approved in principle the scheme that formed the basis of the planning application, to cater for an additional 30 million passenger a year. BAA publicised its intentions between May 1992 and January 1993, before the T5 application was submitted in February 1993, and was called in a month after by the Secretary of State for Transport. By this stage the concept had been arrived at of long north–south runs of aircraft parking aprons, plus a multilevel main terminal with aircraft stands on three sides, departing passengers being above those arriving. The terminal access had a direct M25 spur plus Heathrow Express and Piccadilly Line extensions from Central to T5.

12.6. The resulting public planning inquiry for Terminal 5 on the west side was the longest in UK history, lasting 525 days from 16 May 1995 to 17 March 1999 and costing £80 million, £64 million being BAA's costs. The inspector delivered his report on 21 November 2000, the Government giving its approval on 20 November 2001. Work on Terminal 5 began in September 2002 on a 260-hectare site, topping out occurring in 2005. The £4.3-billion terminal, capable of handling 30 million passengers a year, was officially opened by Her Majesty the Queen on 14 March 2008 to a juddery start, but is now fully operational. Being British Airways' main hub, it comprises a four-storey main terminal (T5A), 396 m long by 158 m wide by 39 m high with curved roof on the western perimeter and two separate satellite buildings (T5B and T5C) between it and Terminal 3, with space for a third satellite, T5D.

12.7. Key to the development were 14 km of mainly bored tunnels with precast concrete rings to provide road, rail and drainage. The twin 8.1-m-internal-diameter Airside Road Tunnels (ART) were 1.27 km long from near T3 to the south-west corner of T5, with cut and cover portals each end. Driven just 8 m beneath a live taxiway, the tunnels had to pass over the Heathrow Express tunnel. A 6-m-wide road width is provided in each tunnel with one-way travel. Rings in the Airside tunnels comprised eight bolted segments 350 mm thick by 1.7 m wide. In June 2002 the first of 1,500 concrete rings were placed in one of the two bores. The two parallel bores were connected by 3-m-diameter cross passages every 130 m. The tunnels were £59 million of the total £140 million contract, the balance being civil engineering work on the portals and approaches. They were completed in June 2003 and opened in 2005.

12.8. The existing Heathrow Express linked Central Area to T4, with stub tunnels being left 200 m west of the Central station. The £44-million, 1.7-km Heathrow Express twin tunnel extensions were 5.675-m internal diameter, driven from a cut and cover launch

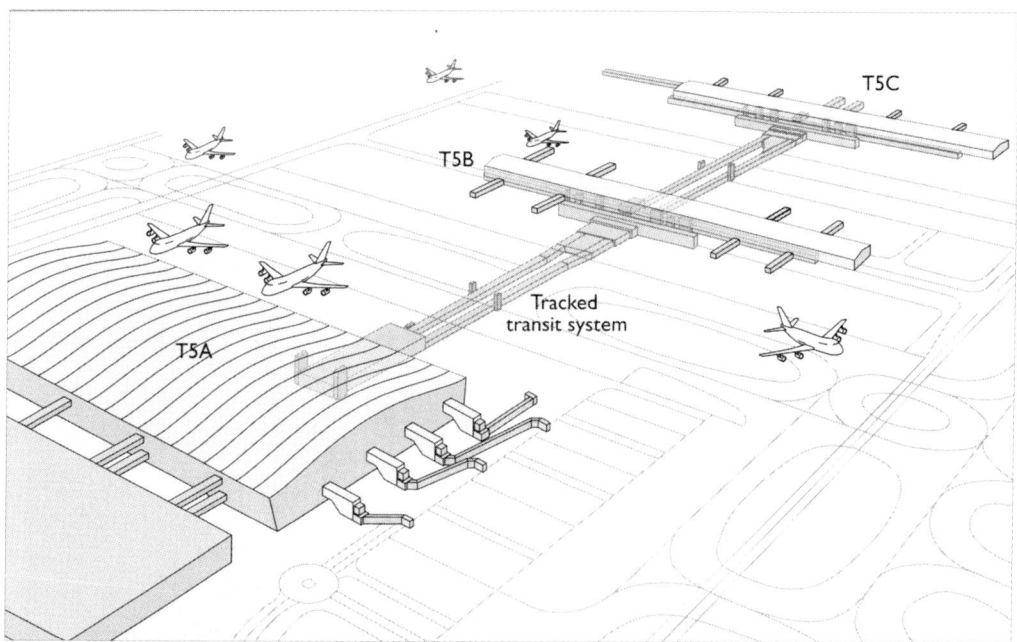

Above: Heathrow, Terminals T5A, T5B and T5C, isometric drawing showing tracked transit system for passengers and freight using driverless trains. (Institution of Civil Engineers)

Right: Heathrow, Terminal 5 aerial from North, 24 November 2011, with Staines Reservoirs behind and Queen Mary Reservoir beyond. (Thomas Nugent)

Heathrow, Terminal 5A and Satellite T5B on left, aerial from the north, 27 July 2010. (Andres Ramirez)

Heathrow, Terminal 5A internal, 7 July 2010. (Andres Ramirez)

chamber adjacent to the Piccadilly tunnel extensions. Rings for the Heathrow Express tunnels comprise ten segments 220 mm by 1 m wide. The Heathrow Express link from Central Area to Terminal 5 opened 27 March 2008. The £30-million, 1.6-km Piccadilly Line twin tunnels were 4.5-m internal diameter, driven from a chamber 300 m west of T5B satellite, one passing under the existing T4 loop. The connection with the existing Piccadilly T4 loop comprised a 40 m by 23 m by 17 m deep diaphragm-walled box. Rings for the Piccadilly tunnels comprised eight segments 150 mm thick by 1 m wide. The Heathrow Express and Piccadilly Line extensions lie adjacent to each other in the Terminal 5 station, the Heathrow Express occupying Platforms 3 and 4, the Piccadilly Line Platforms 5 and 6. Platforms 1 and 2 remain unused, reserved for future rail extensions westwards. The 2.91-m-internal-diameter storm water outfall covers 4.1 km along the south-western perimeter between T5 and the Clockhouse Lane Pit 2 km south of T5, with seven segment rings 220 mm thick by 1 m wide, and was handed over in January 2004. The contractors for the tunnels at T5, including the ART, Piccadilly Line and Heathrow Express extensions, the storm water outfall and the A3044 services tunnels, were an alliance of Morgan Vinci JV (tunnels), Laing Civil Engineering (portals), Amec (production design and mechanical and electrical work) and Mott MacDonald (consultant).

12.9. The Terminal 5 project involved extensive foundations and paving works. The basement structures for the three terminals, core terminal T5A, and satellites T5B and T5C, are up to 20 m deep, and are supported on large diameter piles. Single piles are at each column position. The associated earthworks comprises the excavation and reuse of 6.5 million m³ of material, and the compaction of 7.2 million m³ within a contaminated, waterlogged site of 1 km² on the old Thames Water Perry Oaks sludge disposal works, bisected by the two man-made rivers previously mentioned. With ground water 3 m below ground level, dewatering of the gravels had to be undertaken before excavations could begin. Open steep-sided excavation, sheet pile walls and temporary reinforced soil walls were used to reach depth. The terminal buildings are on piles up to 2.1-m diameter, some under-reamed to 6.2-m diameter, reaching to 35 m below basement level. Main piles are laid out in a 9-m by 18-m grid with more lightly loaded piles located midway between the long side piles. The basements and Underground stations extend beneath T5A, T5B and T5C to 20 m below apron level. The largest beneath T5A is 400 m by 168 m running north–south, and incorporates the rail station box. This box is 280 m by 90 m running east–west beneath the public transport interchange and the main multi-storey car park. All three terminals are also connected by an underground tracked transit system, including stations, running tunnels, pedestrian tunnels and a maintenance base. The basements generally have three floor levels. T5A generally has composite steel-concrete floors incorporating 1,200-mm-deep welded steel plate girders except over the station box, which is roofed over with precast concrete inverted T-beams with *in situ* concrete deck. The T5A grid was 18 m by 9 m to accommodate the rail station track and platforms as well as baggage-handling systems, but for T5B and T5C a 9-m by 9-m grid was adopted. Floors in the satellites are of flat slab construction, except for the roof over the tracked transit system in T5C where precast concrete double T-beams are used.

12.10. Aircraft pavements had to take account of A380 wheel loads of 28 tonnes, compared to 23 tonnes for the Boeing 747-400. Compared with other parts of Heathrow, where 450-mm-thick concrete on 150-mm lean concrete on 300-mm sub-base had been adequate, the underlying soil had a much lower bearing capacity. Initial designs led to a required depth of 800 mm of concrete, which was beyond the slip-forming capability available, so stronger concrete was proposed, enabling the depth to be reduced to below 600 mm.

12.11. The two terminals T5A and T5B made up Phase 1 of the £4.3-billion development. Designed by consulting engineer Arup, the main building was the largest single-span structure in the UK, using 40,000 tons of steel to create 280,000 m² of space with a clear span roof 156 m by 396 m, with views out to the airport. In T5A departing passengers arrive on bridges from the rail interchange, forecourt and car park, check in and clear security on the upper level. From there they go to the middle level of T5A or go to T5B by tracked transit system for gate seats and retail. Arriving passengers use the lower level of T5A to clear immigration, collect baggage and out to onward journey transport. T5A is surrounded by a 3,800-space car park on the west side beyond the transport interchange, and apron on the other three sides. The terminal comprises a three-storey steel frame supporting 280,000 m² of composite floor slabs above the basement up to five levels deep. The roof, 156 m span by 396 m long by 40 m high, is the most spectacular part visually, comprising twenty-two pairs of 914-mm-diameter steel legs reaching down to apron level with arched steel box girders rafters at 18-m centres with a central span of 107 m, the latter being 800 mm wide with depth varying from 1.8m to 3.8m, together forming tied portal frames. Total weight of steelwork in the roof rafter/column portals is 1,500 tons per bay x eleven bays, so 16,500 tonnes. The rafters are tied at high level by pairs of 115-mm-diameter pre-stressed strand cables to control spread of the arches. The rafters were assembled near ground level, partially clad, and lifted 30 m to height using strand jacks on temporary towers with two pairs of girders being lifted each time. The secondary beams acting as purlins span 18 m and comprise 610-mm-deep steel box sections at 5.4-m centres approximately. The infill cladding was completed using mobile cranes. The column legs comprise pairs of tube at 18-m centres at apron level meeting higher up at the main node, then splitting into a four member tree, two canted in to pick up the main rafters, the other two canted out to the rafter ends. The outer sections of rafters, named tusk rafters, are of I-section tapering to 900-mm depth at their ends, and are secured to the main feet nodes by tie-down straps. The main upper node has a 400-mm-diameter steel pin through all the members meeting there. Façade steel was then erected and the superstructure frame erected under the completed roof. Work on the basements began at the end of 2002, concluding at the end of 2004. The roof structure began in October 2003 up to early 2005 in six phases from the south end, five of 54-m length and one of 18 m. Roof cladding was completed between the end of 2003 and the end of 2006. The façade was begun at the end of 2004 through to summer 2005, with the internal structure between summer 2004 and autumn 2005. In order to confirm erection methods, a complete section of roof was assembled at Dalton in North Yorkshire, trialling the erection method, roof cladding, façade and glazing installation, and lighting, which produced over 100 improvements to shorten the programme. The façade on the east and west elevations is supported by 400-mm by 200-mm elliptical hollow sections spanning 18 m horizontally between the roof tie-down straps. The glass and steel weight is carried to apron level by 139-mm diameter steel props. The west face steelwork was designed to resist the pressure from a car bomb in the car park. The north and south gable ends are conventional steel-framed cladding carried down to apron level, transferring wind forces vertically to ground and roof. Internal steelwork has a grid 18 m by 18 m with a drop to 18 m by 9 m in less critical areas.

12.12. The first satellite T5B, 442 m long by 51 m wide by 19.5 m high, comprises a clear span steel roof on two floors, using 600,000 m² of post-tensioned flat slab floors, to minimise formwork and labour. Compared to T5A it is smaller, but still larger than T4. The steel roof has a similar curved profile to T5A, the steel plate girders being supported on four-member tubular column trees each end.

12.13. The second satellite T5C, costing £300 million, is similar to and between Terminal 5B satellite and the new tower. Occupying a total of 51,000 m² on three levels above ground and three below, the basement structure was built as part of Terminal 5 works, incorporating the passenger transit system. T5C already had six remote stands in use before opening. While the design is similar to T5B, the construction and stages are different. T5B was built from one end and worked on one front, whereas T5C will start at the central services core and work outwards both ways. T5C has a steel frame and composite slab, compared to concrete frame and post-tensioned concrete slab on T5B, to speed up construction by 15–20 per cent. T5C has twelve aircraft stands, eight of which are A380 capable. T5C opened officially on 1 June 2011, in conjunction with a relaunch of a San Diego service by British Airways.

13

2000s Developments, Terminals 1 and 3 Upgraded

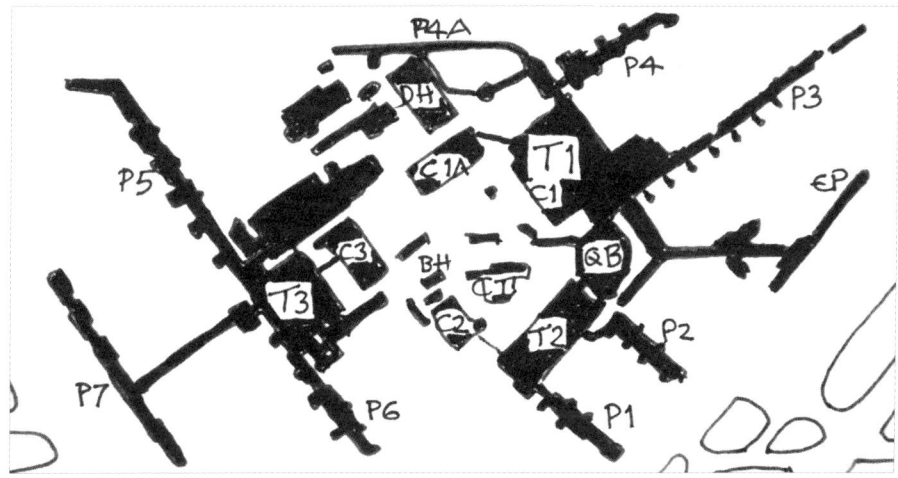

Heathrow Central Area sketch as at 2003, showing Terminals T1, T2 and T3, Piers P1 to P6, EP-Europier, CT-Control Tower, QB-Queens Building, Multi-storey Car Parks C1, C1A, C2, C3, BH-Boiler House Bldg 448, and DH-D'Albiac House. (Author)

Heathrow Central Area Bus Station and Terminal 1 behind from Car Park 3 by Terminal 3. (Author)

Heathrow, Singapore Airlines A380 9V-SKD by Terminal 3, 20 March 2010. (Richard E. Flagg)

Heathrow, Virgin Hangar under construction, 2001, showing steel frame. (Watson Steel)

Heathrow East Fire Station, 5 January 2014, at the east end of Runway 28R.

13.1. RUNWAYS RESURFACED

The main runways were resurfaced again between 2001 and 2002 in a £40-million contract. The BAA/Amec Pavement Team resurfaced the north runway first in 2001, overnight, by planing off the top 65 mm and replacing it with 65 mm of base course of Marshall asphalt. Later a 50-mm Marshall asphalt wearing course was added. Eight or nine shifts were used to lay an area 70 m long by 50 m wide of base course, then five shifts of wearing course at 110 mm per shift. After seventy-two hours, the wearing course was grooved to create friction for landing aircraft, with a maximum of between 300 and 700 m of ungrooved surface being left. The new wearing course was blended with the old at a gradient of 1:100. Work proceeded from east to west, the predominant aircraft landing direction. Timing was critical with all equipment ready and lined up near the runway for handover at 22.30, planing from 22.45, and asphalt at 1.30. By 2.30 they were halfway across the runway, with completion by 4.30. The handover began at 4.00, so that by 5.00 an airport checker team could carry out an hour-long safety inspection, the handover being complete by 6.00. The south runway followed in 2002, by planing off the top 40 mm, laying 60 mm of base plus 40 mm top course to ready the runways for the A380. After trials on the north runway, all planings were recycled for reuse in the base course. In addition, 2,000 lights and 1,000 pits had to be raised.

13.2. PIER 5 FOR A380

By May 2002 work was underway on the £34-million 450-m-long new Pier 5, with 5.5-m-high windows, and the first two gates for the A380. Architects were Pascall & Watson, with structural engineers Buro Happold.

13.3. NEW VIRGIN HANGAR

The Virgin hangar, of approximate plan dimensions 83 m frontage x 72 m depth, was built by Tilbury Douglas in a £20-million contract from June 2001 to December 2002. Large enough to accommodate an A380, the hangar comprised an 11,500-m² hangar with workshops, crew rooms and a three-storey office block.

13.4. TERMINAL 3 UPGRADED

In November 2003 work was underway on £300-million refurbishment of Terminal 3 on a four-year programme to extend the arrivals area, to segregate the arrivals and departures within the piers, to be complete by April 2005. Principal Contractor was Mace. Terminal 3 was further upgraded in 2006 by the addition of the new £105-million Pier 6, replacing the original Pier 6 on an east–west orientation to accommodate the Airbus A380, with four new stands comprising 450-mm-thick pavement concrete on 150-mm cement bound material base. Terminal 3 forecourt was upgraded in 2007 with a new £90-million 40-m-deep pedestrianised plaza, new drop-off area and a new canopy, see below. Terminal 3 has a total area of 98,962 m².

13.5. NEW MULTI-STOREY CAR PARK OVER HEATHROW CENTRAL STATION

In late 2004, work began on installing piled foundations on a £50.6-million seven-storey 1,560-capacity Short Stay car park building above the Central Area Heathrow Express station, ten years after the tunnel collapse. Bounded by Chester Road on the north-east, Camborne Road to the south-east, Cromer Road on the north-west and the drop-off area to Terminal 3 to the south-west, this was a new car park to replace the original multi-storey Terminal 3 car park, which had been replaced by the new Terminal 3 drop-off area. After fourteen months of geological investigation and modelling by Buro Happold to study the ground conditions after the tunnel collapse, piling began. Principal contractor Laing O'Rourke, engineering consultant Buro Happold and piling contractor Expanded Piling devised a solution using 1.8-m-diameter piles driven precisely between the Heathrow Express tunnels, passenger walkway and passenger terminal to keep the Heathrow Express running. The piles also had to avoid ground alongside reserved for Crossrail tunnels proposed. The piling operation comprised more than 360 piles of 60 mm diameter capped in groups of six to eight, plus nine 1.8-m-diameter piles, the latter up to 60 m deep, driven in casings for the first 40 m to reduce friction passing the tunnels, ending up 6 m below the tunnels so as to not affect pressure on the tunnel linings. The new car park comprising steel and concrete sits on a rectangular transfer deck of steel girders that sit on the original circular footprint of the site, originally planned for a hotel. This transfer deck is above the Heathrow Express control room and plant room that break the surface.

13.6. OTHER HEATHROW CAR PARKS

With approximately 35 per cent of passengers arriving at Heathrow by private car, there is still a need for car parks. The other Central Area multi-storey car parks, both Short Stay, are the 1,693-space Terminal 1a car park, and the 564-space Terminal 1 car park. Car parks on the south side near Terminal 4 are the 892-space Terminal 4 Short Stay car park and the 1,873-space Long Stay/Business car park. Terminal 5 has the 3,800-space Short Stay multi-storey immediately to the west, with the 1,200-space T5 Business car park north of T5 along the Western Perimeter Road, and the 2,755-space T5 Long Stay car park, 1,499-space Business T1 and T3 car park and the 740-space Business Parking Plus car park along the Western Perimeter Road on the north side near the Central Area tunnel. Finally the 4,386-space Long Stay T1 and T3 car park is on the Eastern Perimeter Road, east of Central Area.

13.7. FUEL SUPPLY

After the first fitment of two hydrants per aircraft stand at the Cargo Area in 1968, followed by pipes serving the Boeing 747 stands on the Central Area south-west apron, a programme of fitting hydrants to as many stands as possible was implemented. By 1983 the older tankers were being replaced by the Volvo F7 with 4,000-gallon plus 6,000-gallon trailer capacity, which was designed to suit the tight turns of ramps and roads at Heathrow. While tankers could cope with the smaller aircraft like the A320 at 5,250 gallons, aircraft like the Boeing 747 at 50,000 gallons or the A380 at 68,000 gallons could only be refuelled from hydrants at pier stands. Fuel is delivered to Heathrow mainly by pipeline. In total, 25 per cent comes from the West London Terminal at Stanwell, just south of the Cargo Area, which is fed by pipe from Fawley Refinery, Hampshire. Another 35 per cent comes by pipe from Buncefield (Herts Oil Storage Terminal, HOSL), fed from Lindsey Refinery, Lincolnshire and Coryton Refinery, Essex. A further 25 per cent comes from Walton-on-Thames and 15 per cent by rail. After the Buncefield fire in December 2005, the one-third reduction in availability led to reduced aircraft fuel loads, necessitating additional stops for fuel elsewhere, e.g. at Manchester, until the Buncefield pipeline was diverted around the affected area. The main Heathrow suppliers are BP, Esso, Texaco, Q8 and Total.

13.8. TERMINAL 1 UPGRADED

In 2005 Terminal 1 underwent redesign and redevelopment, including a new eastern extension doubling the departure lounge in size and increasing seating and retail space, the terminal now occupying an area of 74,601 m², and being home to bmi and Star Alliance airlines. Terminal 1 is due to close in 2013/14 to allow construction of Phase 2 of the new Heathrow East Terminal, to be complete by 2019.

13.9. A NEW FIRE STATION

There are technically three fire stations at Heathrow: Fire Station HQ between T5 and T3, Fire Station East at the east end of 27R, and the original HQ site (Bldg 450) on Northern Perimeter Road/Newport Road, although the latter is an ambulance station partly leased to London Fire Brigade. By 1967 the main fire station was on the Northern Perimeter Road, west of the tunnel, with a Central Area satellite fire station on the end of T2/Pier 1. The northern fire station, Building 450 off Newport Road, latterly became the ambulance station, but has been partly leased back to London Fire Brigade since 1997. The eight-bay Fire HQ is between T5 and Central Area, and was opened in around 1998. The new (five-bay) Fire Station East, south-east of and close to the east end of runway 27R, was opened early in August 2008, to replace the thirty-year-old (believed to have been three-bay) fire station, due to be demolished, to make way for the new Terminal East/T2.

13.10. A NEW TOWER

13.10.1. It was realised that by the time Terminal 5 became operational the original 122-feet-6-inch-high 1955 tower would not have adequate viewing over the western aprons. A new, enlarged tower was needed at a different location at the centre. The new tower controls over 1,000 aircraft approaching and departing daily as well as all taxiing. A team of thirteen air traffic controllers operate visual control from the cab on top. The new tower was moved atop the geographic centre 500 m west of the old tower, and raised to 87 m, on the end of Pier 7, west of Terminal 3. The location needed 360° views from the cab, and taxiways and stands at the base demanded a very low viewing angle. The result, with a 10-m-high glass façade affords the largest cone of vision of any tower in the world.

13.10.2. The traditional form for the cantilever mast would have been slip-formed concrete requiring an uninterrupted supply of concrete on a twenty-four-hour basis, plus a crane to fit out stairs, lifts plus the top cab, which did not suit BAA's restriction to night working or height considerations. Alternatives considered included a much smaller-diameter steel mast, cable-stayed for lateral strength and stiffness, allowing a diameter half that of the equivalent cantilever mast. In steel it could be fabricated in 12-m lengths with pre-fitted stairs, lift cores and service risers. The smaller-diameter mast allowed construction of the cab at ground level, which could then be jacked up the mast. With three temporary towers supporting a yoke with strand jacks, each new mast section could be inserted under the previous section, the whole then being lowered to the ground to reposition the yoke and repeat the process.

13.10.3. Extensive wind tunnel testing was undertaken to confirm acceptability under dynamic conditions for the controllers on top, the three 150-mm-diameter cables and two 5-ton mass dampers under the cab controlling the axial stiffness.

13.10.4. The tower site was a Boeing 747 stand for Terminal 3, which was closed, allowing foundation construction with 1.05-m- and 0.75-m-diameter piles and a pile cap up to 4.1 m deep, supporting the tower, a three-storey base building and the permanent cable anchorages, installed in 2004 by Laing O'Rourke. No other concrete was used until the base building was erected, BAA being unwilling to sacrifice aircraft stands during constructing, and effectively moving construction off-site until necessary. By adopting all-steel construction, Arup and Mace, the main contractor, could limit movements across airside space to no-fly hours at night.

13.10.5. The cab of the tower was prefabricated and assembled in late 2003 just inside the airport southern perimeter near Terminal 4, away from taxiways to allow cranes. At 32 m in height by 17-m diameter the cab was formed from twenty-four radial roof trusses spanning on to twenty-four steel façade mullions, acting as portal frames to support the roof and façade glass. The mullions also support the three levels of floor slabs and transfer load to the cab lower skin, thence to the three main support points, where the top cable anchorages are. The cab weight of 862 tonnes, being more than twice the 400 tonnes of a 747, for which the pavement had been designed, necessitated special arrangements. The 32-m-high cab section was lifted on to six multi-wheeled trailers arranged in pairs under each corner of a temporary cable-stayed heavy steel girder tripod base by a 500-tonne-capacity crane. All the 144 wheels were raised to allow transport, and moved 1.5 km into position in two hours in November 2004. The Italian lift specialist Faggioli PSC handled the transportation using the trailers, all three being computer controlled to synchronise steering. Once in position, during spring 2005 it was then jacked up progressively using three 16-m-high towers on which 600-tonne hydraulic strand jacks were mounted, again by Faggioli PSC, allowing the insertion beneath the cab of the seven triangular steel sections, with a maximum horizontal dimension of 4.8 m/16 feet. The triangular mast sections, fabricated in Bolton and Sheffield, comprised 30 mm steel skin with internal vertical stiffener plates spanning vertically 3 m between horizontal stiffener hoops with flanges top and bottom to allow bolting of sections internally on site. The mast sections comprised one 80-tonne section 14 m long and six 60-tonne 12-m-long sections, each section incorporating numerous service holes. Each individual jacking process allowed the insertion and bolting of one 12/14-m mast section. All of this work, especially the main cab move, took place overnight. After final mast assembly, the internal staircase, landings and lift were fitted out. Once the cab had reached full height, the three-storey steel-framed base building was erected, 250 tonnes of steelwork being used. Finally the temporary guy cables were replaced by three pairs of 150-mm-diameter cable stays attached to the top of the tower's tripod mast and anchored to the ground. Also installed was a 100-m pedestrian bridge from the base building to Pier 7, erected overnight in prefabricated glazed 30-m lengths.

13.10.6. The tower was handed over to NATS in March 2006 for fit-out, going live in February 2007. The original tower closed to operations on 20 April 2007 after fifty-two years' service, to be replaced on 21 April 2007 by the new £50-million cable-stayed control tower, becoming the tallest in the UK. Architects were Richard Rogers Partnership, with Consulting Structural Engineer Arup, Foundations Engineer Mott Macdonald. Main Contractor was Mace, Foundations Contractor Laing O'Rourke, Steelwork Contractor Watson Steel, and temporary works concept and design was by the Rolton Group, with jacking and cab transport by Faggioli. The tower was officially opened on 13 June 2007 by the Secretary of State for Transport Douglas Alexander.

13.11. NORTH SIDE MAJOR GENERAL ROY SURVEY TABLET MOVED

The Ordnance Survey slate plaque marking Major General Roy's original north-west triangulation point on the Nene Road Police Station on the North side had to be relocated in late 2013 due to the relocation of the Police Station and the demolition of the original building. The plaque has been remounted on a masonry plinth 20 metres away from its original position, on the north-western side of the adjacent Nene Road Roundabout. Thus the origins of the Ordnance Survey may still be seen.

13.12. AIRLINE DEVELOPMENTS IN THE 2000s

Following the Air France Concorde F-BTSC crash after take-off from Paris on 25 July 2000, all Concordes were grounded. The crash occurred when debris on the runway burst a tyre, which led to a fuel tank rupture and a fire; the plane crashed with the loss of 100 passengers, nine crew and four on the ground. Following Kevlar lining to the fuel tanks and new strengthened tyres, Concordes came back into service from 7 November 2001, but the economics of the service saw the end of Concorde in the UK on 24 October 2003, when three Concordes landed in quick succession, one in service and two on charters, bringing to an end supersonic passenger services. See Appendix D for airline types operated in the 2000s.

13.13. AIRPORT HOTELS

Things have come a long way from the early hotels built in 1959, when passenger numbers were only 4 million per annum; today there are fifteen times that figure – within a short bus ride on the Hoppa bus, passengers can be taken to the airport from at least twenty-four hotels on the perimeter of Heathrow. Working clockwise around the airport, along the Bath Road from the north-west corner are the Thistle London Heathrow (4*, 264 rooms); Premier Inn Heathrow Airport Terminal 5 (3*, 400 rooms on five floors); Sheraton Heathrow (4*, 426 rooms on three floors); Arora Heathrow (4*, 350 rooms on four floors, built 1999); Holiday Inn London Heathrow, just west of the Central Area tunnel (4*, 230 rooms in two blocks of six and ten floors); further east of the tunnel still on the Bath Road is the Park Inn Hotel (Radisson, 4*, 895 rooms on four floors); Renaissance London Heathrow (Marriott 4*, 649 rooms on four floors). Then comes a group near Harlington Corner/Northern Perimeter Road: Radisson Blue Edwardian (4*, 459 rooms); Sheraton Skyline (4*, 350 rooms), London Heathrow Marriott (4*, 391 rooms on five floors); and the original Holiday Inn Ariel (3*, 184 rooms on four floors). Next are the Bath Road easterly hotels: Premier Inn Heathrow Airport (Bath Road) (3*, 590 rooms on three floors); Ibis (3*, 351 rooms); and lastly Double Tree by Hilton London Heathrow (4*, 200 rooms). Above the Bath Road along the M4 corridor are the Novotel London Heathrow

(4*, 178 rooms on four floors); the Crowne Plaza (4*, 465 rooms on five floors); and the Comfort Hotel Heathrow (184 rooms). On the south side are the Jurys Inn Heathrow on Eastern Perimeter Road at Hatton Cross (3*, 364 rooms on eight floors, built 2003), and two at Terminal 4 – the Hilton London Heathrow (4*, 398 rooms on six floors); and the Yotel Heathrow Airport within Terminal 4 comprising thirty-two Japanese style cabins. Lastly, on the west side close to Terminal 5A is the Sofitel Heathrow (Arora 5*, 605 rooms on three floors, built 2008), and three just west of the M25: the Travelodge Heathrow (3*, six floors); the Hilton London Heathrow Terminal 5 (4*, 350 rooms); and the Arora Park Hotel (3*, 119 rooms on five floors).

13.14 PLANE SPOTTING AT HEATHROW

Several hotels mainly along the Bath Road on the north side, plus near Terminal 5 offer plane spotting packages, including Renaissance London Heathrow Hotel (Marriott) (Bath Road, widely regarded as the best views), Thistle Hotel (northern perimeter west end), Holiday Inn London Heathrow Ariel (east end Bath Rd), Ibis Hotel (Bath Road east of Holiday Inn), Premier Inn Bath Road (Bath Road east of Ibis), Jury's Inn (behind BA Maintenance Area close to 27R approach), Park Inn Heathrow (Bath Road near Ibis), plus Premier Inn T5 (west end Bath Road) and Travelodge Terminal 5. For more details see: http://www.plane-spotting-hotels.com/index.php/plane-spotting-heathrow/

   Also available is a covered viewing stand with car pak next to the Heathrow Academy (ex-Visitor Centre) close to the Bath Road on the north side near the Sheraton Skyline Hotel, charge applies.

Recent Developments

14.1 QUEENS BUILDING, TERMINAL 2 AND OLD TOWER DEMOLISHED

14.1. *Terminal 2 Closed*

14.1.1. In order to facilitate construction of the new Terminal East or Terminal 2A, the Queens Building was demolished in late 2009, with the original Terminal 2 later. Terminal 2 with an area of 49,654m², Heathrow's oldest, closed on 23 November 2009 with the departure of an Air France flight to Paris. It was originally designed to handle 1.2 million passengers annually, but by its' end it was handling up to approx. 8 million. It was demolished by November 2010.

14.1.2. For 2009, before closure, Terminal 2 throughput was 3.9 million passengers; Terminal 1 was 12 million, Terminal 3 was 20.4 million, Terminal 4 was 5.1 million and Terminal 5 was 24.5 million, totalling 65.9 million.

14.1.3. The 1955 Central Area Tower was demolished in January 2013. Although Air Traffic Control staff had moved to the new tower in 2007, the old building offices continued in use to the end. The sole red brick building from the original development that will remain is the Boiler House.

14.2. BAA'S £6.6 BILLION PROGRAMME ON ITS SIX AIRPORTS

In April 2008 BAA embarked on a £6.6-billion five-year programme to modernise its seven airports, with thirteen individual work programmes. Heathrow accounts for two-thirds of this spending at £4 billion, and BAA anticipate 75 per cent of passengers using twenty-first century facilities by 2013/4.

14.3 BAA FORCED TO SELL GATWICK, STANSTED AND EDINBURGH

In March 2009 BAA were forced to sell off Gatwick, Stansted and one of the Scottish airports by the Competition Commission. After much legal positioning, Gatwick, Stansted and Edinburgh were progressively sold off. Gatwick was sold to Global Infrastructure Partners (GIP) in October 2009 for £1.51 billion. Edinburgh was sold in April 2012 for £807 million to GIP. GIP also own London City Airport. Stansted eventually went to

Manchester Airports Group in January 2013 for £1.5 billion. Manchester Airports Group also own Manchester, East Midlands and Bournemouth Airports. BAA still own Heathrow, Aberdeen, Glasgow and Southampton/Eastleigh Airports.

14.4. TERMINAL 1 REFURBISHMENT, AGAIN

Terminal 1 is undergoing another refurbishment, with project manager Mace completing £60-million work on the arrivals and departures areas, Taylor Wimpey on £20-million work on immigration and connections, while Balfour Beatty are on pier refurbishment and £100 million worth of work on construction of the northern section of the new satellite pier for Heathrow East, to be ready in August 2010. Terminal 1 departures' check-in desks have been replaced by e-ticket and self-service facilities, opening up the whole area.

14.5. TERMINAL 3 UPGRADE, AGAIN

Terminal 3 has been refurbished in a £120-million programme with new glass-clad forecourt and piazza, and a new £34-million airside bus terminal, as well as moving baggage sorting to a new airside building, releasing space and allowing an increase in passenger capacity of 17,000 a day. Also Terminal 3 will have new areas to standardise security searches, having commonality with other BAA airports.

14.6. TERMINAL 4 UPGRADE

Terminal 4 is being refurbished for the first time in a £120-million project. To create more space for check-in desks, an extension to the front of the original building has been constructed. The new extension is a steel-framed glass-clad canopy-covered entry piazza 180 m long, 25 m wide and 13 m high. Most importantly the structure had to be bomb-blast resistant in case of terrorist attack. Comprising seventeen bays, 10.8 m wide, each bay is formed by a steel portal frame, with the long column-free interior formed with 2 m deep by 25 m, span braced trusses on columns each end with mezzanine offices over. The steel frames were strengthened in weaker areas after dynamic modelling of the structure for explosives. The trusses span on to 650-mm x 250-mm box columns, which had to be positioned on the original structural grid below, as the area was previously the terminal forecourt, essentially a bridge structure for departures. The existing construction of the forecourt meant that all steelwork erection had to be carried out using one 80-ton-capacity crane, the largest that the deck could support, positioned on 6-m x 4-m mats to spread the loads on the bridge deck. Before work could begin, the original terminal canopy was removed, allowing strengthening of some of the original steelwork. In front of the extension a new 10-m-deep steel canopy cantilevers off the new extension, clad in ETFE, which disintegrates in a bomb blast rather than becoming shrapnel. All this work was necessary, with the terminal needing to accommodate thirty-nine airlines compared to the previous seven. Structural engineering consultant was Buro Happold, and steelwork contractor was Watson Steel Structures.

14.7. HEATHROW EAST TERMINAL, OR TERMINAL 2A

14.7.1. Heathrow East, or Terminal 2A, the new terminal, is being built to replace the original Terminal 2 and the Queen's Building. Its satellites will eventually be capable of handling 30 million passengers a year; this is Heathrow's largest project, with a new terminal aligned perpendicular to the main runways on the north and south sides.

14.7.2. Heathrow East will also have a new slim satellite T2B opposite on the east side, with a further satellite T2C for the future. T2B has a contract value of £580 million and is the largest ever airside project procured by BAA. It will be 522 m long by 35 m wide, with sixteen pier-served stands. Balfour Beattie as construction partner for works worth £750 million is responsible for realignment of taxiways, new aircraft stands east of Terminals 1 and 2, as well as design, management and construction of the £100-million first phase of the Heathrow East satellite, or Terminal T2B. This phase of T2B with six stands was ready in 2009, linked to Terminal 1 by Europier. Balfour Beattie was awarded the £450-million second phase of T2B as a complete design and build contract comprising the remaining ten stands, due for completion in October 2013, with flights operating from early 2014. Parsons Brinckerhoff as part of the team is providing project controls, planning, project management, commercial and design management, systems engineering and design. As part of this process Parsons Brinckerhoff, part of the Balfour Beattie Group, are introducing Building Information Modelling (BIM), providing the project team with visualisation of all planned construction sequences, and the means to understand the overall construction/logistics management requirements at all levels of detail, in order to achieve the daily key performance indicators. The completed T2B will have a passenger tunnel with moving walkways to the main Terminal T2A, and eventually a train system as at T5, but only after T2C is constructed. Ten of the sixteen stands are capable of taking the A380 and the other six Boeing 747s. The 365-m-long by 60-m-wide second phase of T2B will have a 15-m-deep basement varying in width from 65 m at the ends to 99 m in the middle for the train station, a baggage tunnel, space for baggage sorting, space for vertical circulation, tunnel space for T2C connection, as well as plant and service rooms. The basement wall comprises a 1.2-m-thick diaphragm wall of 26.5 m in depth with 232 ground anchors 35–42 m long in the central part, inside of which are 705 bored concrete piles of 1.2–1.8m diameter up to 57 m depth. The largest are necessary for the 167 steel columns allowing top-down construction. As with many other sites the area is criss-crossed with existing services including cable bundles and fibreoptic data links into the control tower, plus other communication lines, fuel pipes, power lines, some unrecorded, but all having to be relocated. After completion of the new tunnels, the old Europier can be demolished.

14.7.3. Demolition of Terminal 2 had to be complete before the new Terminal 2A could start, but before that all the services had to be lifted on to a gantry in front of both buildings being demolished, to allow safe demolition and to keep Terminal 1 going. Like Terminal 5, Terminal 2A has a multi-storey car park and entry point divided from the main building by a covered 'canyon'. It is steel-framed and glass-clad, but instead of one arch across the shorter span, the roof will have a wavy truss with three peaks and two troughs corresponding to distinct points in the terminal. The three waves correspond with the three activities on the top floor: check-in, security and departures. At check-in the roof rises, then dips towards the exit, rises into security, falls on exit to rise into the integrated departure lounge. Secondary trusses span between the wavy trusses, running from the lower boom on one to the upper boom on the adjacent truss, creating a sloping roof between each wavy truss. The north-facing 4-m-high vertical face produced on the saw-tooth profile acts like a north-light roof, allowing light in with no glare. Also the 6-m floor-to-floor height will add to the airiness of the four-storey building. Ground level will contain offices and ramp storage, with arrivals on the first floor, departure gates at second floor, and check-in and security on the top floor. The composite steel and concrete floors span between columns on a 9-m by 9-m grid. The footprint of the new building is 200 m by 300 m, and will be built with twelve zones, each with its own power and lighting service core, which can be opened progressively, before all being joined into one as a single building. Learning from T5, extensive modularisation and repetition will speed construction and commissioning, e.g. 12-m-long pipe trays in the floors, with all pipes fitted, instead of individual pipes; they are manufactured off site, minimising the amount of working at height. A total of 1,483 off-site modules are planned. Every service core is a 9-m by 9-m box, 18 m tall. Each core can be split into modules 2.5 m square by 9 m long, manufactured off site, for road transport. Module installation begins in August 2010. The winning Architect is Foster & Ptnrs, with Arup as concept structural engineer, and Amey and Ferrovial's technical office taking over the design from Arup. Mace are providing consultancy services, and construction is by Hetco, the joint venture team of Ferrovial Agroman and Laing O'Rourke. The £800-million deal with Hetco to build Terminal 2 was signed on 15 March 2010, encompassing site excavation, foundations, main structure, including façade and roof, plus ten aircraft stands.

14.7.4. Phase 2 will involve the demolition of Terminal 1, allowing Terminal 2A to be extended northwards, together with construction of Terminal 2C, and continue with Terminal 3 demolition. Once complete, Terminal 2 will have a similar footprint and capacity to Terminal 5. Together, Heathrow's Terminals 2 and 5 with their parallel north-south orientation, so-called toast rack appearance, will allow much easier access to taxiways and runways. No date has been fixed for Phase 2 as yet, dependent on capacity requirements.

14.8. HEATHROW BAGGAGE SYSTEM UPGRADE

By 2012 Heathrow's baggage system will have been upgraded with Terminal 3's system being replaced, and Terminal 1's and Terminal 4's systems refurbished; new systems will be put in place for the new Terminal 5C and Heathrow East. For the new system to be capable of handling 110 million items a year by then, it will have a new underground tunnel connecting all the terminals. At present there is a baggage tunnel between Terminals 1 and 4 built in 1997, and another shorter tunnel linking Terminal 5A with T5B and T5C, which takes baggage in small rail-mounted carts. BAA bought a 5-m-diameter boring machine to bore a tunnel linking Terminals 5, 3 and 1 round the north side of the Central Area, construction beginning in 2009. The system will use Destination Coded Vehicles, which are trolleys holding one item of baggage running at speeds up to 800 m/min. The new tunnel accounts for 30 per cent of the £1 billion being spent on the baggage-handling upgrade.

14.9. HEATHROW T5 AND EAST APRON ENLARGEMENT

Heathrow's Terminals 5A, 5B, 5C Heathrow East and its satellites are all oriented north–south, in what is likened to a toast-rack alignment, improving connectivity with the runways. An £800-million programme of apron enlargement is underway, including new apron and stands for the new Terminal 5C, the new eastern campus, including the new east satellite. The old diagonal runways have been removed, to be replaced with new north–south taxiways to enable the toast-rack arrangement. Old taxiways are also being upgraded to take Airbus A380s. Lastly, infrastructure improvement will include multi-storey car parking for the new Heathrow East Terminal.

14.10. FINAL TERMINAL AIRLINE ALLOCATIONS

2012 figures for each terminal:
Terminal 1, 13.6 million passengers on 119,183 flights
Terminal 2 closed for construction
Terminal 3, 18.6 million passengers on 96,326 flights
Terminal 4, 9.8 million passengers on 59,955 flights
Terminal 5, 28.1 million on 193,440 flights

The eventual aim is for BA to be at Terminal 5, the Skyteam Alliance at Terminal 4, Oneworld Alliance at Terminal 3, and the Star Alliance at Terminal 1 and eventually Heathrow East. In all, the changes will see fifty-four of the ninety-three airlines at Heathrow relocated.

Heathrow, TBA West and North Pens, 29 September 2009, showing the 1980 modifications for larger aircraft tails, with 747 G-CIVV inside. (Tony Szulc)

Heathrow, TBA West and North Pens, 5 January 2014, showing the 1980 modifications for the A380, with British Airways G-XLEA inside West Pen. (Tony Szulc)

14.11. NEW RAIL LINK PROPOSED

From 2007 figures, of the total of 43.7 million non-transfer passengers travelling to Heathrow, 35 per cent arrive by car, 27 per cent by taxi, 13 per cent by bus/coach, 15 per cent by tube and only 10 per cent by rail. Of the total, 15 per cent originate from the south-eastern counties – Hampshire eastwards – and BAA have firm plans to increase rail connectivity with southern region lines. BAA plan to operate Heathrow Airtrack services from Terminal 5 to Waterloo, Guildford and Reading. In addition there are plans to extend Heathrow Express from Terminal 5 to Staines. The two unused platforms at Terminal 5 would be used for this purpose. Planned to start on site in 2012, and be in use by 2016, frequencies for the services would be two trains each way per hour for Waterloo and Reading, and a minimum of one per hour each way to Guildford.

14.12. MIXED-MODE RUNWAY OPERATION

On 1 November 2011, Heathrow began a four-month trial of mixed-mode operations, allowing both runways to be used for departures or arrivals. The trial was one of the recommendations made by the coalition government's South East Airports Task Force in July 2011, after the previous government's abandonment of the third runway. Usually one runway is used for departures and the other for arrivals, but certain events will allow mixed-mode operation. If a flight is going to be delayed on arrival or departure by ten minutes, or the headwind component on approach is greater than 20 kt at 3,000 feet, then the new procedure can apply. It can also be applied if an arrival or departure schedule is going to be more than thirty minutes late, if 30 per cent of flights are running beyond the fifteen-minute punctuality target, or if time is needed to recover from disruption like snow. Once operations are back to normal, the trial would revert to normal practice. The trial would also include tests on landing an A380 on the runway closest to its stand, reducing the effects of wake vortex on other aircraft, as well as using the southern runway 09L/27R for departures and arrivals to Terminal 4, and testing landing small aircraft on the designated departures runway. There was also a second phase of trials in late summer 2012.

14.13. HANGARS MODIFIED TO TAKE A380S

British Airway's West and North Pen Hangars in TBA were modified from late 2010 to early 2012 by installing steelwork to raise the clear height of the doors locally by 3.5 m from almost 23 m, creating a central slot capable of allowing an A380 tail fin (24.1-m-high) access, giving two bays for the fleet of twelve A380s odn order. The existing hangar pens can accommodate a Boeing 747 plus an A319 side-by-side. The additional openings allow a single A380 to be accommodated. Air France and Lufthansa have built new hangars to accommodate their A380s at Paris Charles de Gaulle and Frankfurt respectively, bdut BA is unable to do the same due to space restrictions at Heathrow. The modifications had to be kept to a minimum, as the hangars are Listed Buildings, and involved 138 tonnes of steelwork. The larges 'eyebrow' section, enclosing the tail fin and weighing 24 tons, had to be lifted into position overnight to avoid interference with Runway 09L/27R operations. Contractors were Mace, steelwork was by Watsons, with analysis by Arup and Watsons.

14.14 NEW BIOMASS ENERGY CENTRE GENERATING PLANT INSTALLED

A new Organic Rankine Cycle biomass power plant was being installed 2012–13, on a site between the British Airways Cargo centre and Terminal 4 on the south side. Using clean woodchip waste, the plant costing £46 million will generate 1.8MW of electricity and 8MW of thermal heat and cooling for Terminals T2A and T2B plus heat to Terminal 5. Eventually when the system is connected to Terminals 1 and 3, the Central Area Boiler House Building 448 will be decommissioned and demolished. There is also a Combined Heat and Power Plant within the Cargo Area, installed c.2006, which will eventually be superseded.

14.15. THIRD RUNWAY

In the future was the planned third runway to the north, which had government approval, but a judicial review said that more consultation was necessary. Both parties on the current coalition government have said that there will be no third runway at Heathrow, and no second runways at Stansted and Gatwick. At the time of writing, the third runway has become a major issue in the discussions about airport capacity in the South East and the UK as a whole, including hub airports and the competition from airports in France, Germany and Holland. On 7 September 2012, the Department for Transport announced that Sir Howard Davies was asked to chair an Aviation Commission, whose task will be to investigate options for maintaining the UK's status as an international hub for aviation. It will look at additional capacity and how it could be met in the short, medium and long term. The interim report considered an extra runway at Gatwick, an extra runway at Heathrow, and a new Thames Estuary airport. Any report recommendations would be taken on board by the future government.

Bibliography

GENERAL

'Airlines and Airliners: No. 1 Trident', in Phil Lo Baod (ed.), *Aviation Data Centre* (1992).
A Surface Access Strategy for Heathrow: Sustaining the Transport Vision 2008–2012 (BAA Heathrow, 2008).
Allward, Maurice, *London's Airports: Gatwick and Heathrow* (Ian Allen, 1964).
'BAA Starts Business', *Flight* (31 March 1966), pp. 502–3.
'BOAC's Plan for Heathrow (BOAC Terminal Proposal)', *Flight* (1 June 1967), p. 885.
'Britain's Biggest Airport', *Concrete Quarterly* (February 1948), pp. 38–41.
'Costain Finds There's Brass among Heathrow's Muck (Perry Oaks and Associated Diversions)', *Construction News* (25 November 2004).
Hayter, George, *Heathrow, The Story of the World's Greatest International Airport* (Pan Books, 1989).
'Heathrow 50' series of articles, *Aircraft Illustrated* (June 1996), pp. 40–59.
Heathrow General Information and Chronology (BAA, January 1977).
'Heathrow Squeezes GA', *Flight International* (25 June 1988), p. 22.
Hurren, B. J., 'The Great West Aerodrome, a London Airport Landmark, Last Link with Fairey's about to Vanish (Hangar used by Fire Service)', *Flight* (15 August 1952), pp. 170–1.
Housego, Maurice, *Gateway to the World, the Illustrated Story of London Airport*, (Thames Valley Art Productions, 1959).
'ICAO Adopts VGPI (VASI)', *Flight* (22 June 1961), p. 878.
'Kindly Light, VASI origins', *Flight* (15 August 1958), p. 245.
Lo Bao, P., 'A History of British Airways Helicopters and Its Predecessors since 1947', *Air Britain*, 1985.
London Airport Central, New Terminal Area (i) Control Tower, (ii) Passenger Building and Southern Air Traffic Control Centre (Ministry of Civil Aviation, March 1955).
London Airport (Central Terminal Area) (Ministry of Civil Aviation, September 1953).
'Maplin Abandoned', *Flight* (25 July 1974), p. 76.
New Complete Guide to London (Heathrow) Airport (Pitkin Pictorials Ltd, 1964).
'Noise: Maplin and the New Technology (Third London Airport)', *Flight* (16 August 1973), pp. 301–9.
Piket, Brian and Bish, Pete, 'Heathrow ATC the First 50 Years' (Zebedee Balloon Service, 2005), inc. Heathrow Accidents.
'Precision Flight, VASI tests', *Flight* (20 February 1959), p. 268.
'Serving the Corporate Customer', *Flight* (9 November 1985), pp. 22–6.

Sherwood, Philip, *Heathrow, 2000 Years of History* (Sutton, 1999).

'Southern Air Traffic Control', *Flight* (1 April 1955), pp. 414–5.

Spencer, Philip, 'NZ Air Race, October 1953', *The British Roundel* (November/December 2003).

The Airport Visitor, Annual Guide, Squadron Leader N. J. Freeman and G. D. H. Linton (eds) (Penman Enterprises, 1953).

'The Great West Aerodrome, Last Link with Fairey's about to Go', *Flight* (15 August 1952), pp. 170–1.

Woodley, Charles, *Heathrow Airport, The First 25 Years* (The History Press, 2010).

'World Air Gateway, Recent Progress at London Airport', *Flight* (10 October 1952), pp. 478–81.

CENTRAL AREA, EARLY BUILDINGS

'Civil Aviation, L.A.P.'s New Tower', *Flight*, p. 464.

'Development of Central Terminal Buildings at London Airport', *The British Constructional Engineer*, (June 1955), pp. 22–3 and 57.

'Development of London Airport', *The British Constructional Engineer* (December 1953), pp. 21–3.

'L. A. P. Advances, New Buildings for Britain's Premier Airport', *Flight* (25 September 1953), pp. 432–3 and 430.

'L.A.P Road Traffic', *Flight* (15 April 1955), p. 474.

'L.A P. Terminal Transfer', *Flight* (25 February 1955), p. 252.

'London Airport', *Flight* (8 April 1955), pp. 446–8.

'London Airport Central, Progress Report on the New Central Area Facilities', *Flight* (21 January 1955), pp. 72 and 91.

'Requirements of Civil Airport as Typified by London Airport', *ICE Proc* (Vol. 4, Pt 3, June 1955) pp. 298–336, and 'Discussion' pp. 336–54.

'The Development of London Airport', *Engineering* (Vol. 176, 25 September 1953), p. 397.

'The Main Access Tunnel at London Airport', *Concrete and Constructional Engineering* (March 1952), pp. 91–6.

'The Queen at London Airport, Inauguration and Naming of the Newest of the Three Main Buildings', *Flight* (23 December 1955), p. 935.

'Tower of London', *Flight* (29 April 1955), pp. 565–6.

TERMINALS 1, 2 AND 3

'A New Front Door for Britain, London Airport's Long Haul Terminal (Terminal 3)', *Flight* (14 December 1961), pp. 911–913.

'Building for the 747 at Heathrow (Terminal 3)', *Flight* (8 February 1968), pp. 177–178.

'Building the Heathrow of the Seventies (Terminal 1)', *Flight* (5 October 1967), pp. 561–562.

'Facelift for Heathrow Terminal 3', *New Civil Engineer Online* (15 February 2007).

'Heathrow "Refurb' is more a Rebuild (Terminal 3)', *Construction News*, 28 January 1988), p. 22.

'Heathrow Terminal 2 Closes for Demolition', *Construction News* (23 November 2009).

'Heathrow's New Terminal (Terminal 1)', *Flight* (5 December 1968), pp. 938–40.

'Heathrow's No. 1 Terminal, Triumph or Tragedy?', *Flight* (7 August 1969), p. 196.

'Heathrow's Short Haul Terminal (Terminal 1)', *Flight* (12 May 1966), p. 782.

'Modern Airport Design – 2: Longer Fingers or Passenger Coaches?', *Flight* (31 August 1967), p. 327.

'Modern Airport Design – 3: Holding Lounges in Fingers or on the Aprilon', *Flight* (7 September 1967), p. 361.

'Queen Opens Heathrow Terminal (Terminal 1)', *Flight* (24 April 1969), p. 650.

'Steelwork Speeds Civil Airport Expansion', *Building With Steel* (1967).

'Terminal 3 Pier 5', *New Civil Engineer Online* (16 May 2002).

'Three of the Very Best (Terminal 3)', *New Civil Engineer Online* (27 November 2003).

CARGO TERMINAL

'A Giant from the Future (BA World Cargocentre)', *Architects Journal* (7 May 1998).

'Air France's Heathrow Cargo Terminal', *Flight* (17 July 1969), p.65.

'Building the Heathrow of the Seventies (Cargo Terminal)', *Flight* (5 October 1967), pp. 562–3 and 566.

'Combi Economics Is on the Rise', *Flight* (21 September 1985).

'Design and Construction of Cargo Tunnel at Heathrow Airport', *ICE Proc* (Vol. 48, Pt 1, January 1971) pp. 11–34, and 'Discussion' (Vol. 48, Pt 2, October 1971), pp. 187–201.

'Exercise in Cooperation (New Cargo Centre)', *Flight* (19 January 1967), p. 83.

'Heathrow's New Cargo Tunnel', *Flight* (9 June 1966), p. 934.

'London Airport Tunnel', *Concrete Quarterly* (No. 77, April–Jun 1968), p. 31.

'New BEA/BOAC Freight Complex at Heathrow', *Flight* (28 May 1970), p. 877.

PICCADILLY TUBE EXTENSION

Jobling, D. G. and Lyons, A. C., 'Extension of the Piccadilly Line from Hounslow West to Heathrow Central', *ICE Proc* (Vol. 60, Pt 2, May 1976) pp. 191–218, and 'Discussion' (Vol. 60, Pt 4, pp. 719–37).

Sabine, G. D. and E. Skelton, 'Extension of Piccadilly Line Tunnel to Terminal 4', *ICE Proc* (Vol. 78, Pt 6, December 1985), pp. 1261–78, and 'Discussion' (Vol. 80, Pt 4, August 1986) pp. 1141–52.

RUNWAYS

'All in a Night's Work', *New Civil Engineer Online* (19 September 2002).

Austin, G. E., 'Runway Resurfacing Experience', *ICE Proc* (Vol. 90, Pt 1, June 1991), pp. 575–86.

Francis, Paul, 'Heathrow Airport 1946–56 Pt 1', *Airfield Review* (August 1992), pp. 17–23.

'Heathrow Begins Mixed-Mode Runway Operation', *Flight* (8–14 November 2011), p. 21.

Newton, K., 'Resurfacing of Airport Runways', *ICE Proc* (Vol. 61, Pt 1, February 1977), pp. 119–32, and 'Discussion' (Vol. 62, Pt 4, November 1977), pp. 671–3.

'Night Shift on the North Runway', *Construction News Online* (7 June 2001).

HANGARS

Early Type B1 Hangars
Flight (10 May 1962), pp. 761–2.
Engineering (20 April 1962), p. 526.

Aluminium Hangars

'Aluminium Alloy Aircraft Hangar', *Engineering* (1 June 1951), pp. 654–55.

'Aluminium Alloy Aircraft Hangar (London Airport)', *Engineering* (Vol. 171, 1 June 1951), pp. 654–5.

'Aluminium Alloy Hangar, London Airport; Architects: A. F. Hare and Partners', *Architect and Building News* (29 June 1951), pp. 763–765.

'Aluminium Alloy Hangars at London Airport', *Airports and Air Transportation* (July–August 1951), pp. 220–222.

'Aluminium as a Structural Material (inc 3-bay Hangar, Heathrow)', *Engineering* (Vol. 175, 19 June 1953), pp. 793–5.

'Aluminium Hangars at London Airport', *The Engineer* (1 June 1951), p. 721.

Flight (various issues).

'The First Aircraft Hangar in Aluminium Alloy', *Architects Journal* (7 June 1951).

'The Hunting History', ed. Penelope Hunting (Hunting plc, 1991).

Ward, L. E., 'The Design and Construction of a Three Bay Aluminium Aircraft Hangar at London Airport', *The Structural Engineer* (April 1953).

BEA Hangars Phase 1

'BEA's New Engineering Base, London Airport', *Airports and Air Transportation* (May–June 1952), pp. 36–37.

'Engineering Base for BEA (London Airport)', *Engineering* (Vol. 174, 24 October 1952), pp. 521–4.

'Engineering Base Building for BEA (London Airport)', *Engineering* (Vol. 174, 31 October 1952), pp. 556–8.

'Engineering Base for BEA, the Prestressed Concrete Hangars, London Airport', *Airports and Air Transportation* (May–June 1953), pp. 33–37 and 43.

'Hangar Doors at BEA Engineering Base, London Airport', *Airports and Air Transportation* (July–August 1953), p. 67.

'Hangar Lighting in BEA Hangar', *Architects Journal* (18 September 1953), p. 359.

Harris, A. J., 'Hangars at London Airport, Design of Large Span Prestressed Concrete Beams', *The Structural Engineer*, October 1952), pp. 226–235, and 'Discussion' (February 1953), pp. 61–67.

Holt New, Dudley, 'Design and Construction of the British European Airways Hangars at London Airport, with particular reference to Prestressed Concrete', *Inst. Civil Engineers, Eng. Div* (Vol. 2, April 1953, and Discussion in same), pp. 15–56, and 'Correspondence' (August 1953), pp. 327–30.

'New Hangars at London Airport (BEA)', *Concrete Quarterly* (No. 15, July–September 1952), pp. 22–29.

Photo of BEA Hangars at London Airport, *Architects Journal* (23 April 1953), p. 525.

Photo of BEA Prestressed Beams, *Architects Journal* (15 January 1953), p. 104. 'Prestressed Concrete Hangar at London Airport', *Architects Journal* (4 December 1952), pp. 686 and 690 (BEA hangars).

'Prestressed Concrete Hangars at London Airport', *Concrete and Constructional Engineering* (Vol. 48, January 1953), pp. 28–32.

'Prestressed Concrete Hangars at London Airport', *The Engineer* (31 October 1952), pp. 579–581.

BEA Hangars Phase 2

Edwards, P. B. and Rigg, R. B., 'The Design and Construction of the BEA Hangars Engineering Base at London Airport', *The Structural Engineer* (January 1961), pp.

17–31, and Discussion (December 1961), pp. 411–13.

'Hangars and Workshop at London Airport', *Concrete and Constructional Engineering* (January 1959), pp. 19–23 (separate extension of BEA five bay hangars).

BOAC Owen Williams Hangars

'Accommodation for a Turbine Fleet (BOAC hangar)', *The Aeroplane* (26 June 1953).

'Airport Hangar Doors in Aluminium Alloy (BOAC at London Airport), Architects: Sir Owen Williams and Partners', *Consulting Engineer* (June 1954), pp. 142–3.

'Aluminium Alloy Doors for BOAC's New Hangar, London Airport', *Airports and Air Transportation* (May–June 1954), pp. 28–29.

Articles on BOAC Hangars ref. Owen Williams, 1950–55 in Cottam, David, *Sir Owen Williams: 1890–1969* (Architectural Association, 1986).

'BA Finds Heathrow Slot for A380', *Flight* (13–19 March 2012), p. 12.

'BA Raises Eyebrows to Grow Heathrow Hangars for A380', *Flight* (29 November–5 December 2011), p. 8.

'BOAC Headquarters at London Airport', *The Builder* (4 November 1955), pp. 768–72.

'Doors for BOAC Hangars', *Architects Journal* (8 July 1954).

'Folding and Sliding Doors for an Aircraft Hangar (BOAC)', *The Engineer* (Vol. 197, 14 May 1954), pp. 718–19.

'Hangar Doors of Aluminium Alloy (BOAC, London Airport)', *Engineering* (Vol. 177, 21 May 1954), pp. 658–9.

'Lift-off for Heathrow Hangar (extensions to British Airways Owen Williams hangar)', *Contract Journal* (20 November 1980), p. 31.

'New BOAC Buildings London Airport', *Concrete and Constructional Engineering* (Vol. 51, 1956), p. 302.

Smallpeice, Sir Basil, 'Of Comets and Queens', *Airlife*, 1980.

'Two hangars. (1), Aluminium hangar for the Comet for De Havillands; Architects: James M. Monro and Son; (2), B.O.A.C. central maintenance building at London Airport; Engineers: Sir Owen Williams and Partners', *Architectural Design* (May 1954), pp. 124–8.

Williams, Owen, BOAC Hangars, *Architects Journal* (26 March 1953).

Williams, Owen, Photos BOAC Hangars, *Architects Journal* (26 February 1953).

BOAC Wing Hangar

'Hangar Doors of Unusual Design at London Airport', *The British Constructional Engineer* (July 1958), p. 49.

Payne, N. J. and K. F. Shadbolt, 'Structural Aspects of the Extension of a Hangar for the BOAC at London Airport', *The Structural Engineer* (November 1965), and Discussion (November 1966).

Two articles on BOAC Hangars ref. Owen Williams, 1950–55, (inc. Wing Hangar) in Cottam, David, *Sir Owen Williams: 1890–1969* (Architectural Association, 1986).

'Unusual Doors for BOAC Maintenance Hangar', *Engineering* (23 May 1958), p. 665, (Wing Hangar).

'Use of Slow–Rusting Cor-Ten Steel (BOAC Wing Hangar Doors, London Airport)', *Engineering* (Vol. 192, 24 November 1961), p. 683.

'Extensions to the Wing hangar at Heathrow Airport', in Sir Frederick Snow and Ptnrs 1943–68 25th Anniversary book, pp. 88–89.

BOAC Boeing 747 Hangar

'BOAC 747 Jetliner Hangar', *Civil Engineering and Public Works Review* (March 1970), pp. 269–90.

Jeffs, Eric, 'Heathrow Home for the 747', *Engineering* (20 March 1970), pp. 284–5.

Crook, G. M. and Hanlon, K. G., 'BOAC 747 Project', *Consulting Engineer* (April 1970), pp. 39–53.

Crook, G. M. and Makowski, Z. S., 'Analysis, Design and Construction of the Space Frame Roofs for the BOAC 747 Hangars at London Airport (Hangars 01 and 02)', Proc 1971 IASS Symposium on Tension Structures and Space Frames (pub. 1972), pp. 905–16.

'Jet Hangar Roof in Position (BOAC 747 London Heathrow)', *Contracts Journal* (228, 27 March 1969), pp. 404–5 and 408.

Joyner, K. J., Taylor, R. G. and Makowski, Z. S., 'The Boeing 747 Hangar 01, Heathrow, London', *Tubular Structures* (15, March 1970).

Joyner, K. J., Makowski, Z. S. and Taylor, R. G., 'Structural Aspects of Boeing 747 Hangar for BOAC London Heathrow', *ICE Proc* (47, December 1970), pp. 483–513.

'Jumbo Jet Hangar-Coordination (BOAC 747)', *Contracts Journal* (234, 19 March 1970), pp. 281–2.

Makowski, Z. S., 'Double layer long span roofs (BOAC 747 hangar Phase 2)', *Consulting Engineer* (July 1973), pp. 23–29.

'Massive Hangar and Car Park Projects (BOAC 747), *Contracts Journal* (224, 1 August 1968), pp. 516–7.

Matthews, D., 'Jumbo Jet Hangar, London Heathrow', *Light and Lighting* (63, August 1970), pp. 224–5.

'Raising a Hangar Roof (BOAC 747)', *Engineering* (Vol. 207, 10 January 1969) pp. 59–60.

Self, J. R., 'The Tail of a Giant (Moveable 747 tail stagings), *Consulting Engineer* (November 1970), pp. 50–53.

'The Construction of the Roof of BOAC Hangar 01 at Heathrow Airport', *Acier Stahl Steel* (No. 2, 1970), pp. 53–64.

Taylor, R. G., 'BOAC Hangar 01 at Heathrow Airport for Boeing 747 Airliners', *The Structural Engineer* (September 1970), pp. 343–52, and (Discussion, 1 September 1971), pp. 425–9.

BEA Tristar Hangar

'BEA Airbus Hangar, Foundations Nearly Complete', *Civil Eng and Public Wks Review* (March 1970), p. 283.

Edwards, P. B., 'BEA Servicing Hangar nears Completion at Heathrow', and Williams, P. L., 'Lifting the Roof Structure', *Construction Steelwork* (May 1971).

Edwards, P. B., 'Construction of the New Service Hangar for BEA', *Civil Eng and Public Wks Review* (65, October 1970), pp. 1149–53.

Wilkinson, K. G. and Mottershead, G. E. , 'BEA Servicing Hangar at Heathrow, Specification for', *Civil Eng and Public Wks Review* (65, October 1970), pp. 1145–7.

EUROPIER

Binney, Marcus, 'London Airport Europier (Terminal 1) (Richard Rogers Partnership)' in *Airport Design* (1999).

Duncombe, L. F., 'Heathrow Airport Europier', *ICE Transport* (Vol. 135, Pt 1, February 1999), pp. 1–8.

TERMINAL 4

Bell, G. D., 'Heathrow Airport Terminal 4: Planning', *ICE Proc* (Vol. 80, Pt 2, April 1986), pp. 343–66.

'Heathrow Airport Terminal 4, Discussion', *ICE Proc* (Vol. 82, Pt 3, June 1987) pp. 683–95.

'Heathrow T4 Gets Makeover', *New Civil Engineer* (12 August 2008).

'New Extension Lands at Heathrow', *New Steel Construction* (May 2010), pp. 12–13.

Williams, G. M. J. and Rutter, P. A., 'Heathrow Airport Terminal 4: Design Civil and Structural', *ICE Proc* (Vol. 80, Pt 2, April 1986), pp. 367–84.

Williams, K., 'Heathrow Airport Terminal 4: Mgt and Construction', *ICE Proc* (Vol. 80, Pt 2, April 1986), pp. 385–411.

TERMINAL 5

'BAA Threads New Tunnel Through Heathrow (Airside Tunnel for T5)', *New Civil Engineer Online* (20 June 2002).

'Heathrow Airport Terminal 5', Engineering Special Issue One, *ICE Proc* (Vol. 161, May 2008), including 'Gaining Permission', R. Pellman, pp. 4–9; Tunnelled Underground Infrastructure, I. Williams), pp. 30–37; Building Substructures and Pavements, T. Dawson, K. Lingham, R. Yenn, J. Beveridge, R. Moore and M. Prentice), pp. 38–44; Terminals 5A and 5B, S. McKechnie, D. Mitchell, W. Frankland and M. Drake), pp. 45–53; and Rail Transportation Systems, .I Fugema), pp. 54–59.

'London Heathrow Airport, Terminal 5 (Richard Rogers Partnership)', in Binney, Marcus, *Airport Design* (1999).

McKechnie, S., P. Hulme, G. Thind and D. Mitchell, 'Design and Construction of Terminal 5 Roof', *The Structural Engineer* (2004, Vol. 82, No. 18), pp. 25–31.

'Subterranean Saga (T5 tunnels)', *New Civil Engineer Online* (1 February 2004).

NEW CONTROL TOWER

Construction News (various, including 27 January 2005, 7 April 2005).

'Heathrow Tower under Control', *New Steel Construction* (March 2006), p6.

New Civil Engineer International (1 January 2005).

New Civil Engineer (various issues, including 24 February 2005, 3 March 2005, 7 April 2005, 18 August 2005).

'New Control Tower Checks In', *New Steel Construction* (April 2006), pp. 20–21.

Matthews, Richard, 'Creating Heathrow's New Eye in the Sky', *ICE Civil Engineering* (Vol. 161/CE2, May 2008), pp. 66–76.

HEATHROW EXPRESS

'Airport Parking Expanded (New Multi-storey Car Park above Heathrow Central Station)', *Construction News* (6 October 2005).

'Arrival Procedures (Heathrow Express Cofferdam)', *Ground Engineering* (September 1996), pp. 18–21.

'Disaster Chronology (Heathrow Central Station collapse)', *New Civil Engineer Online* (1 March 1999).

'Heathrow Express', New Railways for London Special (No. 3, 1999).

Powderham, A. J., *Heathrow Express Rail Link: Design and Construction of Deep Piled Circular Cofferdam* (Private via Institution of Civil Engineers, 1998).

Powderham, Alan. 'Heathrow Express Cofferdam: Innovation and Delivery through Single-Team Approach, Pt 1: Design and Construction', *Civil Engineering Practice* (spring/summer 2003), pp. 25–40.

Rust d'Eye, Chris, 'Heathrow Express Cofferdam: Innovation and Delivery through Single-Team Approach, Pt 2: Management', *Civil Engineering Practice* (spring/summer 2003), pp. 41–50.

Thomas, A. H., *Fast-track: The Heathrow Express Headshunt Tunnel – Design and Construction* (Miller Prize, Institution of Civil Engineers, 1999).

Thomas, Gareth and Bone, Roger, 'Innovation at the Cutting Edge: The Experience of Three Major Infrastructure Projects (Newbury Bypass, the Heathrow Express Cofferdam and London Underground's Earth Structures Project)', *CIRIA* (C548, 2000).

'Thrilled Tony Blair opens HEX', *New Civil Engineer Online* (25 June 1998).

HEATHROW EAST/TERMINAL 2A

'BAA Special Report, Transforming Airports', *New Civil Engineer* (3 July 2008).

'Balfour Beatty picked for £750m Heathrow Work (T2B)', *Construction News* (27 January 2009).

'Foster's Heathrow East Gets off the Ground', *Architects Journal* (1 June 2007).

'Heathrow: Flying High (Heathrow East/T2A)', *New Civil Engineer* (10 August 2009).

'Journey into the Future: Terminal 2', *New Civil Engineer* (6 June 2013).

'Managing Major Programmes', *New Civil Engineer* (12 July 2012).

'Remake, Remodel, Rebuild (Terminal 2B)', *New Civil Engineer* (13 October 2011), pp. 16–18.

Appendix A

RUNWAY DIMENSIONS

Gateway to the World (1959)
No. 1 (10L/28R) 9,316 x 300 feet, No. 2 (05R/23L) 7,735 x 300 feet, No. 4 (15L/33R) 5,823 x 250 feet, No. 5 (10R/28L) 9,581 x 300 feet, No. 6 (15R/33L) 7,570 x 300 feet, No. 7 (05L/23R) 6,260 x 250 feet

Pooleys for Europe (1962)
05/23R: 6,255 feet, 05/23L: 7,734 feet, 10L/28R: 9,312 feet, 10R/28L: 11,000 feet, 15R/33L: 7,560 feet

Aerad Flight Guide (September 1965)
No. 1 10L/28R: 9,312 feet, No. 2 05R/23L: 7,734 feet, No. 5 10R/28L: 11,000 feet
No. 6 15R/33L: 7,560 feet, No. 7 05L/23R: 6,255 feet

Pooleys UK 1967, five concrete runways, 80 feet AMSL
05L/23R: 6,255 x 250 feet, 05R/23L: 7,734 x 300 feet, 10L/28R: 9,312 x 300 feet, 10R/28L: 12,000 x 300 feet, 15R/33L: 7,560 x 300 feet

Esso Map 1968
05L/23R No. 7: 6,254 x 250 feet, 05R/23L No. 2: 7,734 x 300 feet
10L/28R No. 1: 9,312 x 300 feet, 10R/28L No. 5: 12,000 x 300 feet
15R/33L No. 6: 7,559 x 300 feet

Airports (Stroud, 1970)
05R/23L: 7,734 feet, 10L/28R: 12,801 feet, 10R/28L: 12,000 feet

BAA Information, 1977
05/23 No. 2: 2,357 x 7,734 x 150 feet, 10L/28R No. 1: 3,902 x 12,800 x 150 feet
10R/28L No. 5 3,658 x 12,000 x 150 feet
Nos. 1 and 5 have 75-foot shoulders and 25 feet on the extensions

ABC British Airports, Ian Allan (1980)
05/23: 7,733 feet, 10L/28R: 12,802 feet, 10R/28L: 12,000 feet
Airports UK, Peter Crook and John Crooks (Jarrold, 1983)
05/23: 2,357 x 7,734 x 150 feet concrete,

10L/28R: 3,902 x 12,802 x 150 feet, 10R/28L: 3,658 x 12,000 x 150 feet
10L/28R and 10R/28L concrete with friction course, with 75-foot paved shoulders and
  25-foot shoulders on west extensions.

Pooleys UK and Ireland, 1985
05/23: 2,357 x 45m concrete, 10L/28R: 3,902 x 45m concrete/asphalt
10R/28L: 3,658 x 45m asphalt

Main runways changed from 10/28 to 09/27 on 2 July 1987

ABC British Airports, Ian Allan, (1988)
05/23: 7,733 feet asphalt, 09L/27R: 12,802 feet concrete/asphalt
09R/27L: 12,000 feet concrete/asphalt

RAF Flight Information Publication, Supplement, 7 February 1991
05/23: 7,733 feet concrete, 09L/27R: 12,800 feet concrete/asphalt
09R/27L: 12,000 feet concrete/asphalt

Last use of Runway 23 on 27 October 2002.

UK VFR Flight Guide (2000)
05/23: 1,966 x 45m, 09L/27R: 3,902 x 45m, 09R/27L: 3,658 x 45m

Appendix B

PASSENGER/MOVEMENTS/CARGO STATISTICS

Calendar Year	Passenger Flow	Aircraft Movements	Cargo tonnes Except 1946–55	Heathrow Employees
6–12.1946 (1)	63,151	2,046	2,386	
6–12.1946 (2)	57,109	3,783	1,083	
1947	281,638	17,962	2,912	850
1950	523,351	37,746	15,812	
1951	796,092	49,341	14,457	
1952	860,760	50,859	15,330	
1953	1,205,000			
1954		79,649		
1955	2,633,642	119,612	49,085	
1956		122,952		
1957	3,539,855	117,332	61,033	
1958	3,601,191	117,286	70,194	
1959	4,295,870	122,174	86,925	
1960	5,587,236	137,913	107,901	25,000
1961	6,307,272	147,710	121,664	
1962	7,066,854	146,801	141,500	
1963	8,450,118	160,870	167,466	
1964	9,693,509	180,051	202,618	34,000
1965	10,839,962	194,486	245,772	
1966	12,208,259	214,786	287,175	39,872
1967	12,729,993	223,808	289,772	42,016
1968	13,528,943	228,855	342,930	43,469
1969	14,622,555	241,526	367,739	48,123
1970	15,698,419	246,614	366,452	48,576
1971	16,926,379	253,711	382,995	50,404
1972	19,139,693	258,095	463,899	50,608
1973	20,946,141	268,701	510,014	50,669
1974	20,688,664	267,726	505,724	51,609
1975	21,989,825	253,908	440,130	51,899
1976	24,102,777	254,768	472,395	52,918
1977	23,979,712	245,646	496,891	55,464

1978	26,991,549	269,872	534,696	56,614
1979	28,909,657	280,690	550,486	57,207
1980	27,512,945	266,822	524,810	54,002
1981	26,839,911	245,789	501,549	48,080
1982	26,608,429	252,839	505,522	43,675
1983	27,290,005	263,313	552,713	44,312
1984	30,172,447	274,184	615,814	45,880
1985	31,744,531	285,734	602,636	47,106
1986	31,309,785	293,914	537,145	
1987	34,743,1965	308,031	574,128	
1988	37,509,104	330,377	642,127	
1989	39,585,394	347,017	686,150	
1990	42,950,512	368,440	774,093	
1991	40,494,575	362,032	729,805	
1992	45,242,591	388,166	831,731	
1993	47,899,081	396,082	924,247	
1994	51,713,366	411,511	1,043,049	
1995	54,461,597	421,268	1,114,418	
1996	56,044,625	428,275	1,128,718	78,000
1997	58,185,398	430,706	1,156,105	
1998	60,356,414	451,382	1,300,961	
1999	61,975,028	458,300	1,355,071	
2000	64,277,045	466,799	1,401,920	
2001	60,453,330	463,567	1,263,589	
2002	63,035,489	466,545	1,310,579	
2003	63,208,042	463,650	1,300,348	
2004	67,109,174	476,001	1,412,019	
2005	67,683,317	477,887	1,389,298	
2006	67,339,227	477,048	1,342,646	
2007	67,852,387	481,476	1,393,243	
2008	66,906,954	478,693	1,482,662	
2009	66,036,957	460,026	1,348,914	72,000
2010	65,881,660	450,016	1,551,308	
2011	69,433,230	476,295	1,569,304	76,500

NOTES

1. 1946–55 figures from BAA Heathrow publicity brochure, January 1977. Cargo figures in short (American) tons. 6–12.1946 (1) from BAA brochure, 6–12.1946 (2) from *Flight* (10 October 1952), and movements 6–12.1946 (2) and 1947 for scheduled services only

2. BAA employee figures given in annual reports for 1966–85 only.

3. 1957–84 from BAA annual reports. Figures are based on financial years rather than calendar years, but given above in previous year, e.g. 1966 actually 1966/7. Passengers include Scheduled, non-Scheduled and Transit. Aircraft Movements or Air Transport Movements (ATMs) include Scheduled and non-Scheduled. Cargo figures include mail.

4. 1986–2012 from CAA figures based on calendar years. Passengers include Scheduled, Charter and Transit, except 1986–9. Aircraft Movements include Scheduled and Chartered. Cargo, called Freight, includes Chartered, but excludes mail 1986–9.

Appendix C

ACCIDENTS AND INCIDENTS

On 5 June 1947 Halifax C8 G-AIHW made a heavy landing with an apricot cargo from Valencia. The aircraft was written off with wireless operator slightly injured.

On 25 July 1947 Skyways Avro York G-AIUP suffered brake failure after landing on Runway 28 normally, overran on to turf, over a ditch, across a road, ending up across the Duke of Northumberland River. The aircraft was severely damaged, but there was no fire and most of the passengers suffered only cuts and bruises, with four more seriously injured.

On 23 October 1947 BSAA Lancastrian G-AGUL ground-looped after landing, with no injuries.

On 2 March 1948, Sabena Douglas DC3 Dakota OO-AWH made a night-time GCA approach on Runway 10L with visibility 200 yards. Following a routine approach, it was concluded that that the pilot lost visual contact after passing the last sodium approach lights, when the aircraft was 80 feet to the right of the centreline. He then attempted to turn left, and stalled at 50 feet. The aircraft hit the ground nose first, followed by the port wing, wheel and propeller, and caught fire. Three crew and nineteen of the twenty-two passengers died, a further passenger dying later.

On 12 September 1948 Air France Languedoc F-BATX overran the runway after landing with some damage, but no injuries.

On 28 October 1949 Grumman Mallard NC2956 took off, but swerved to port at a height between 30 and 50 feet, lost height and crashed on the airport, bursting into flames, killing two crew and four passengers, and injuring another crew member.

On 31 October 195, BEA Vickers Viking G-AHPN on a flight from Paris to Northolt was diverted because of fog to Heathrow, where the fog was just as bad, and crashed at Heathrow after hitting runway 28R during an attempted go-around in poor visibility of 40–50 yards. Three crew and twenty-five passengers died, with two surviving. The subsequent court investigation recommended a mandatory prohibition of landing in weather conditions below the operators' minima by a certain percentage. The court also recommended greater clarity and simplicity in the operator's manual's minimum height and visibility.

On 3 January 1951 Pan American Stratocruiser N1036V, on landing in slush, inadvertently selected undercarriage retract instead of flap retraction, and right gear retracted.

On 30 May 1952 Pan American Stratocruiser N1029V had electrical failure on approach and the gear retracted on landing.

On 1 August 1952 DH 89 Rapide G-ALBB, on approach behind a Stratocruiser, encountered turbulence at 300 feet and crashed before the runway threshold, throwing the pilot out who was severely injured and causing lesser injuries to five of the eight passengers.

On 29 November 1954 BEA Ambassador G-ALZR lost both nose wheels on take-off, burned off fuel, and landed on 10R with passengers and baggage moved to the rear to move the centre of gravity back. On stopping, additional people entered the aircraft to lift the nose, enabling refitting of the nose wheels.

On 16 June 1955 BEA Viscount G-AMOK taxied out in poor visibility along 28R attempting to get to 15R, but lined up on disused Runway 15 (closed 1949) and attempted to take off, but crashed into a barrier set up for construction work, with considerable damage to the aircraft but no casualties.

On 22 June 1955 DH Dove G-ALTM was filming the approach lighting when the pilot noticed a drop in airspeed and a low oil pressure on his fourth approach to 10R, and shut down the port engine instead of the starboard engine, which lost power soon after. The aircraft crashed short of the runway, with no fire or casualties.

On 18 August 1956 Central African Airways Viscount VP-YNE landed on runway 23L at dusk, with severe vibration on touching down, the starboard undercarriage leg having retracted. No fire resulted and all forty-six on board disembarked safely.

On 1 October 1956, Avro Vulcan XA897, strategic bomber of the Royal Air Force, approached runway 10L in heavy rain and low cloud, struck ground 2,000 feet short of the runway, sustaining damage, then crashed on the runway. The Vulcan was the first to be delivered to the RAF, and was returning from a demonstration flight to Australia and New Zealand. The Captain and Air Marshal Sir Harry Broadhurst were able to eject and survived, but the four other occupants were killed.

On 11 August 1957 BOAC Lockheed L749A Constellation G-ANNT landed on runway 23L after starboard main undercarriage and nose wheel were unlocked manually due to a hydraulic fault, resulting in damage to the port wing.

On 2 May 1958 Iraqi Airways Viscount YI-ACM sustained structural damage due to a heavy landing, with no injuries to the thirty-eight passengers and six crew.

On 7 January 1960, BEA Viscount G-AOHU landed on runway 28L in deteriorating visibility. After a heavy landing the aircraft went into what was described as wall of fog, and full braking was applied, resulting in nose wheel collapse. By the time the fire brigade arrived nine minutes later a severe fire had developed, which burnt out the fuselage. There were no casualties among the fifty-four passengers and five crew on board.

On 2 March 1960 Hunting Clan Viking G-AGRV swung left after a normal touchdown, coming to rest with the fuselage touching ground and the port main undercarriage tyre deflated, the aircraft sustaining substantial damage.

On 8 March 1960 Skyways Hermes G-ALDH carried out a normal landing when the starboard main gear collapsed, with no injuries.

On 24 December 1960 BOAC Boeing 707 G-APFN made a too fast approach to runway 23L and landed halfway down. When the captain realised that braking before the runway end was impossible, he attempted a 100° turn on to runway 33L but the aircraft skidded on to grass where the undercarriage collapsed, with substantial damage but no injuries to the eleven crew or ninety-five passengers.

On 14 August 1962, on the Lufthansa Boeing 720 D-ABOM, on final approach the crew realised the nose landing gear could not be lowered. After a go-round and unsuccessful attempts to lower the gear, a landing was made on runway 10L.

On 11 October 1962 BOAC Comet 4 G-APDA suffered an explosion within No. 3 engine on applying power for take-off. The take-off was abandoned and the engine shut down, but the fire warning persisted. Fire engines appeared on the scene and extinguished the fire, but the engine was extensively damaged along with the engine bay. Investigation established a fatigue failure of a compressor blade.

On 6 November 1963 Trans Canada DC8 CF-TJM taxied out in fog to runway 28L, needing the extra length compared to 28R due to the weight. Take-off was begun but abandoned as insufficient runway lights could be seen. Performance figures were rechecked and showed that 28R with acceptable visibility was acceptable, so the aircraft taxied over for departure from 28R. Take-off was begun but attempts to take off failed, the conclusion being drawn that they had no elevator control. The Captain therefore decided to abort at a speed well above V1. Spoilers were not used and the aircraft overran the runway end by 800 yards into a cabbage field, with extensive damage but only five minor injuries out of the ninety passengers and seven crew. The first emergency vehicles took twenty-three minutes to arrive due to the fog and position. The aircraft was subsequently successfully repaired.

On 27 October 1965, BEA Vickers Vanguard G-APEE, from Edinburgh, attempted an ILS approach to 28R in poor visibility, but went round to attempt a talked down landing on 28L from which another go-round resulted. After holding a while a third approach was requested, on 28R this time. The ILS approach was monitored and the pilot reported 'overshooting'. The aircraft was seen on radar to begin climbing but then dive steeply on to the runway some 2,600 feet from the threshold. All thirty passengers and six crew on board were killed. A number of reasons were felt to have combined to cause the crash, including reduced-visibility light settings inaccurate, tired pilot initiating overshoot with rapid elevator movement, incorrect flap setting, aircraft instrument reading lag, and lack of experience of overshoots in fog.

On 31 December 1965 Beech Travel Air G-ASZC landed on runway 28R and taxied to cross 28L behind a Britannia ready to take off. After receiving confirmation to proceed behind the Britannia, the engines of the latter opened up blowing ZC sideways, resulting in collapse of the port undercarriage leg. No one was injured but the standard phraseology changed from 'behind the departing' to 'after the departing'.

On 31 March 1967 BOAC Boeing 707 G-APFP was returning from crew training at Stansted and selected undercarriage down. Main wheels locked down normally but the nose gear failed to extend. Attempts to extend it failed and the aircraft landed with nose gear up, resulting in a small fire, quickly extinguished by fire vehicles.

On 22 June 1967 Piper PA30 G-ASOO landed without flaps as there was an 18–20 knot headwind. Before landing on Runway 23 he checked undercarriage green light was on, but after flaring out for the landing, the propellers struck the runway and the aircraft came to rest on its belly, with substantial damage.

On 8 April 1968, BOAC Flight 712 Boeing 707 G-ARWE, departing to Australia via Singapore, suffered a No. 2 engine fire just after take-off from runway 28L. Runway 28R was initially offered to return, and then Runway 05R to speed up the return. The fire increased in intensity and unbeknown to the crew the engine and part of its pylon fell from the wing into a nearby gravel pit in Laleham, before the plane managed to perform an emergency landing on 05R with the wing on fire. On stopping, the fire intensity increased and the fuel in the port wing tanks exploded. Emergency evacuation began as soon as it stopped, but four of the 116 passengers and one stewardess of the eleven crew were overcome by smoke and did not survive. The fire was caused by fatigue failure of the fifth stage low pressure compressor wheel and was made worse by failure to shut off fuel during the engine fire drill. Barbara Harrison, a flight attendant on board who helped with the evacuation, was posthumously awarded the George Cross. The Air Traffic Control Officer John Davis received an MBE. The Airport Fire Service efficiency was criticised, resulting in a new Fire Service alert 'Aircraft Accident Imminent', and the development of a new smaller faster vehicle capable of containing a fire before the rest arrived.

On 3 July 1968, a BKS Airspeed Ambassador, carrying eight horses and five grooms, banked steeply to the left over the threshold of Runway 28R, causing the aircraft to contact the grass and swerve towards the terminal building, ending up inverted. It hit two parked British European Airways Hawker Siddeley Tridents, chopping off both their tail sections, burst into flames and came to rest against the ground floor of the terminal building. The three crew and three of the passengers died, as did the eight horses that were on board. The two other passengers and twenty-nine people on the ground were injured, four of them seriously. Trident G-ARPT was written off, and Trident G-ARPI was badly damaged, but subsequently repaired, only to be lost in the Staines crash in 1972. Also, Viscount G-APKF fuselage underside was damaged by a catering vehicle struck by AD. Investigation showed that fatigue failure of a flap operating rod allowed the port flap to retract while the starboard flaps increased extension from 40° to 50°, resulting in an uncontrollable roll to port.

On 22 January 1970, British Midland Viscount G-AWXI had an explosion then fire in No. 4 engine shortly after take-off from Runway 28R. The fire could not be extinguished, but an immediate return was made at Runway 28R and an emergency evacuation carried out. The fire was extinguished on the ground. Five passengers of the thirty-four were injured in the evacuation, one severely.

On 18 June 1972, Trident G-ARPI, operating as BEA548, crashed in a field close to the Crooked Billet Public House, Staines, two minutes after taking off. All 118 passengers and crew on board died. The recommendations from the subsequent public inquiry led to the mandatory requirement for cockpit voice recorders to be installed on British-registered airliners. Two memorials in Staines were dedicated on 18 June 2004 to those who died in the accident.

On 13 November 1973 BOAC Boeing 707 G-APFB starboard main undercarriage bogie fractured forward of the central pivot, while taxiing to take off, with 10 crew and 102 passengers. The front wheels and axle became detached, resulting in substantial damage.

On 25 March 1978 Boeing 707 TF-VLB was operating an Aer Lingus flight. During the landing by the co-pilot, it bounced. The Captain took over, but during the recovery the nose gear struck the runway hard and partially collapsed, the aircraft stopping on the runway.

On 27 December 1979 Pan American Boeing 747 N771PA was on a cargo flight from New York with three crew. After a heavy touchdown, the No. 4 bulkhead, which supports the engine, began to break free of the pylon, causing the engine to tilt down. In turn this caused the engine fuel pipe to rupture plus several other connections including fire monitoring and warning circuits. As the aircraft turned off the runway, a severe fire developed, which was dealt with by the fire service, the fire resulting in substantial damage to the No. 4 engine supports, plus outer starboard wing, engine and pylon fairings.

On 12 February 1980 Cessna 421 HB-LFQ, inbound from Vienna, landed on Runway 23 veering away from the centreline to the right soon after touchdown. The starboard landing gear broke off soon after and the aircraft turned sharply to the right and stopped at the side of the runway. Investigation showed that the torque link coupling bolt had fallen out allowing the wheel to pivot freely. The bolt was found near touchdown.

On 16 September 1980 PanAm Douglas DC10 N83NA was on the take-off run on 28R with 237 on board, when the BAA checker vehicle spotted debris from a tyre burst. He informed the tower on the departure runway frequency, which was overheard by the aircraft commander, who abandoned the take-off. Full reverse thrust and braking were applied, stopping 110 m from the runway end. Two small fires developed, extinguished by the fire service, and a full evacuation was carried out with one passenger suffering a broken leg.

On 12 May 1981, HS-125 G-BHSU diverted to Heathrow after realising that the left main landing gear had failed to come down. The aircraft carried out a two wheel touch and go on Runway 10L to shake the gear down, which failed, so a two wheel landing was made on Runway 05, resulting in substantial damage. Investigation revealed rubber material in the left main gear pressure line.

On 5 May 1982 MEA Boeing 707 OD-AGV made a normal landing on Runway 28L, but as the nose wheel made contact, vibration and bumping was felt. The Captain selected reverse thrust and held the nose off as long as possible. When the nose wheel touched down, a loud bang was heard and the nose dropped 18 inches, the aircraft stopping on the centre line, when the engines were shut down. The fire service arrived but there was no fire and the Captain called for a full evacuation, using steps provided by the fire service, which avoided any injuries. Examination revealed that the nose wheel was down and locked but the oleo outer casing had fractured vertically early on in the landing run.

On 8 December 1996 KLM Cityhopper Fokker 50 PH-KVK showed a left main gear fault when the gear was selected down. The gear was raised and a go-round from Runway 27L was made, then the aircraft was put on hold. Unsuccessful attempts were made to lower and lock the gear, and ATC were advised of the likelihood of a gear failure on landing. Due to a change in wind direction, the crew were advised that Runway 09R would now be the landing runway. A normal touchdown was made but shortly after the left main gear collapsed and the left wing tip, propeller and rear left fuselage contacted the runway, causing the aircraft to veer to the left and come to rest clear of the runway. A full evacuation of the forty-one passengers and four crew was carried out with three minor injuries. Investigation found one of the two bolts needed for the locked position was missing, the other one being loose), preventing correct alignment.

On 5 November 1997, after numerous attempts to shake free the jammed left main landing gear, a Virgin Atlantic Airbus A340-300, G-VSKY, made an emergency landing on runway 27L. Part of the undercarriage collapsed on landing, and both aircraft and runway were damaged. An evacuation of the ninety-eight passengers and sixteen crew was carried out, resulting in minor injuries to five passengers and two crew. Investigation found that a torque rod had come loose and jammed in the keel beam, the torque rod pin subsequently being found off the end of Runway 24L at Los Angeles. Airport Recommendations made as a result of the accident included one that aircraft cabin door simulators should more accurately reproduce operating characteristics in an emergency, and another that cockpit voice recorders should have a two-hour duration in aircraft registered before April 1998.

On 17 January 2008, a British Airways Boeing 777-236ER, G-YMMM, operating as flight number BA038 from Beijing to London, at a height of 600 feet and 2 miles from touchdown, experienced loss of power on the right engine and soon after on the left engine, crashing 1,000 feet short of Runway 27L on grass just inside the airfield boundary, then slid to the edge of the runway and stopped on the threshold, its undercarriage having collapsed. It was the first accident resulting in a Boeing 777 hull loss, and eighteen minor injuries were confirmed, with thirteen people being admitted to hospital. In 2009 a second interim report from the UK's Air Accidents Investigation Branch (AAIB) said that ice may have formed in the fuel lines during the flight, restricting the flow of fuel to the engines. Air accident investigators called for a component on the Rolls-Royce Trent 800 series engine to be redesigned

On 12 July 2013 Ethiopian Airline Boeing 787 ET-AOP landed at 05.37 on a flight from Addis Ababa and parked at Stand 326 on Pier 5 at Terminal 3. After disembarkation of passengers and crew, the aircraft was towed to Stand 592 near the Central fire station to await its next service later that day. At 15.34 an employee in the Control Tower noticed smoke coming from the aircraft and activated the crash alarm, causing a temporary shutdown of the airport. Fire station staff attended at 15.40 and extinguished the fire in the passenger compartment at the rear end at the crown, close to the Emergency Location Transmitter powered by Lithium-Manganese Dioxide batteries.

Appendix D

AIRLINES AND AIRLINERS OPERATED BY DECADE

D1. Airlines to Heathrow 1940s
BEA, Aer Lingus, Alitalia, Hellenic Airlines, Luxembourg Airlines, Scandinavian Airlines System (inc. DDL (Danish), DNL (Norwegian) and ABA (Sweden) were still operating from Northolt. They gradually transferred to Heathrow as facilities improved, BEA continuing to operate services from Northolt as well as Heathrow even before the completion of the Central Area.

British airlines at Heathrow in the 1940s included BOAC (Lancastrian, Liberator, Halton, Dakota, Constellation, DC4M Argonaut), BSAA (Lancastrian, York and Tudor), Lancashire Aircraft Corporation (Halifax), London Aero and Motor Services (Halton), Skyways (Lancastrian, York).

European airlines operating services from Heathrow included Aer Lingus (Constellation), Air France (Dakota, Languedoc), Ceskoslovenske Aerolinie (CSA) (DC3), Iberia (DC4), KLM (DC3, DC4), Sabena (C47/DC3), Swissair (DC3 and DC4), TAP (Transportes Aereos Portugueses) (DC4).

African and Middle Eastern airlines included Iraqi Airways and South African Airways (DC4).

Intercontinental airlines included Air India (Constellation), American Overseas (DC4 and L049 Constellation), FAMA (Argentina) (DC4, York), Iraqi Airways, Pan American (DC3, DC4 and L049 Constellation), Panair do Brasil (L049 Constellation), Qantas (L749 Constellation), and Trans Canada (Lancaster, DC4M North Star).

D2. Airlines to Heathrow 1950s
In the 1950s, British airlines at Heathrow included Airwork (DC4, Viscount), BEA (Ambassador/Elizabethan, Dakota, Viking, Viscount, Vanguard), BKS Air Transport (Ambassador, Viking), BOAC (Britannia, Comet 1, Comet 4, DC4M Argonaut, DC7C, Hermes, L049/749A Constellation, Stratocruiser, York), Cambrian Airways (C47/DC3), Eagle Aviation (DC6, Viking), Hunting Clan Air Transport (DC3, DC6A, Viking, Viscount, York), Skyways (Hermes, York), Transair (Viscount).

European airlines included Aer Lingus (Bristol Freighter, DC3/C47, Viscount), Aeroflot (Il-18, Tu-104A), Air France (Breguet Deux Ponts, DC3, DC4, L749 Constellation, L1049C/G Super Constellation, L1649A Starliner, Viscount), Alitalia (Convair 340, DC4, DC6B, DC7C, SM95, Viscount), Balair (Viking), Finnair (Convair 340/440), Iberia (Convair 440, DC4, L1049C Super Constellation), Icelandair (DC3, DC4, Viscount), JAT (Jugoslovenski Aerotransport) (Convair 340/440), KLM (Convair 240/340, DC3, DC4, DC6A/B, DC7C,

L749A Constellation, L1049E/G Super Constellation, Viscount), Loftleidir (DC4), LOT (Polskie Linie Lotnicze) (Convair 240), Lufthansa (Convair 340 and 440, L1049G Super Constellation, L1649A Starliner), Olympic (Greece) (DC4, DC6/B), Sabena (Convair 240/440, DC3/C47, DC4, DC6/B/C, DC7C), SAS (Scandinavian Airlines System-Denmark-Norway-Sweden)(Convair 440, DC3, DC4, DC6/6B, DC7C, Saab Scandia), Swissair (Convair 240 and 440, DC3, DC4, DC6A/B, DC7C), TAE (Greece) (DC4), TAP (Transportes Aereos Portugueses) (DC4, L1049G Super Constellation), THY (Turkish Airlines) (Viscount).

African and Middle Eastern airlines included Arkia (Israel) (C47/DC3), Central African Airways (Viking, Viscount), East African Airways (DC4M Argonaut), El Al (Britannia, Curtiss C46 Commando, L049 Constellation), Iraqi Airways (Viscount), Lebanese International (DC6), MEA (Middle East Airlines) (Viscount), South African Airways (DC7B, L749A Constellation), Trans Mediterranean Airways (York).

North and South American airlines included Aerolineas Argentinas (Comet 4, DC6), American Overseas Airlines (Stratocruiser), Canadian Pacific (Britannia), Flying Tiger Line (DC4, L1049H Super Constellation), Marchitime Central Airways (Canada) (DC4), Overseas National Airways (DC4, DC6A), Panair do Brasil (DC7C, L049 Constellation), Pan Am (Pan American Airways) (DC4, DC6A/B, DC7C, Stratocruiser), Seaboard and western (DC4, L1049D/E/H Super Constellation), TCA (Trans Canada Airlines)(DC4M north Star, L1049G Super Constellation), TWA (Trans World Airlines (DC4, L749A Constellation, L1049G Super Constellation, L1649A Starliner).

Asian/Far Eastern airlines included Air Ceylon (L1049G Super Constellation), Air India (L749A Constellation, L1049C/E/G Super Constellation), PIA (Pakistan International Airlines) (L1049C Super Constellation), Qantas (L1049C/E/H Super Constellation).

D3. Airlines to Heathrow 1960s

British airlines operating from Heathrow included BEA (Argosy, BAC 111, Comet 4B, Dakota, Herald, Trident, Vanguard, Viscount), BKS/British Air Services (Ambassador, Avro/HS748, Viscount), BOAC (Boeing 707, Boeing 747, Britannia, Comet 4, DC7C, VC10,), British Westpoint (C47/DC3), Cambrian Airways (C47/DC3, Viscount), Eagle Airways/Cunard Eagle/British Eagle (Boeing 707, BAC111, DC6A, Viscount), Skyways Hermes, L749A Constellation), Starways (DC3, Viscount).

European airlines operating into Heathrow included Aer Lingus (BAC 111, Boeing 720/707 (Irish International/Aer Linte Eireann), Boeing 737, Carvair, DC3/C47, F27 Friendship, Viscount,), Aeroflot (Il-18, Tu-104A/B), Air France (Boeing 707, Boeing 727, Breguet Deux Ponts/Universel, Caravelle, DC3, DC4, L749 Constellation, L1049C/E/G Super Constellation, L1649A Starliner, Viscount,), Air Inter (Caravelle, Viscount), Airnautic (Viking), Alitalia (Caravelle, DC6B, DC7C/F, DC8, DC9,Viscount), Austrian Airlines (Caravelle, DC3, Viscount,), Balair (DC4F, DC6B, F27 Friendship), Braathens SAFE Air Transport (DC6B, F27 Friendship, F28 Fellowship), CSA (Czechoslovakian Airlines) (Avia 14, Britannia, Il-18, Tu-104A, Tu-124, Tu-134), Finnair (Caravelle, Convair 340/440), Iberia (Caravelle, Convair 440, DC4, DC8/F, DC9, L1049E/G Super Constellation,), Icelandair (Boeing 727, DC3, DC4, DC6B, F27 Friendship, Viscount), JAT (Jugoslovenski Aerotransport) (Caravelle Convair 340/440, DC6B), KLM (Convair 340/440, DC3, DC4, DC6/A/B, DC7C/F, DC8/F, DC9, Electra, F27 Friendship, L749A Constellation, L1049E/G/H Super Constellation, Viscount), Loftleidir (Cl-44,DC4, DC6B), LOT (Polskie Linie Lotnicze) (Convair 240, Il-14, Il-18, Tu-134, Viscount), Lufthansa (Boeing 707/720, Boeing 727, Boeing 737, Convair 340/440, Curtis C46 Commando (lease from Capitol), L1049G Super Constellation, L1649A Starliner, Viscount,), Luxair (F27 Friendship, L1649A Starliner, Viscount), Malev (Hungary) (Il-18), Martins Air Charter/Martinair (DC3, DC6A, DC7C, DC8, DC9), Olympic Airways (Boeing 707, Boeing 727, Comet 4B, DC6/B, DC8,), Sabena

(Boeing 707, Boeing 727, Caravelle, Convair 440, DC3/C47, DC4, DC6/A/B, DC7C), Scanair (Denmark), SAS (Scandinavian Airlines System inc. Denmark, Norway and Sweden) (Caravelle, Convair 440, Convair 990, DC4, DC6B, DC7C/F, DC8, DC9), Spantax (Convair 990), Sudflug (DC7C, DC8, DC9), Swissair (Caravelle, Convair 440, Convair 990, DC3, DC6A/B, DC7C, DC8, DC9), TABSO/Balkan Bulgarian Airlines (Il-18, Tu-134, Viscount), TAP (Transportes Aereos Portugueses) (Boeing 707, Boeing 727, Caravelle, DC4, L1049G Super Constellation,), Tarom (Romania) (BAC111, Il-18), THY (Turkish Airlines) (DC9, Viscount,).

African and Middle Eastern airlines included Air Algérie (Caravelle), Alia Royal Jordanian Airlines (Caravelle), Central African Airways (Viscount), East African Airways (Argonaut, Comet 4, VC10), El Al (Boeing 707/720, Britannia, L049 Constellation,), Ghana Airways (Britannia, Il-18, VC10), Iran Air (Boeing 727), Iraqi Airways (Boeing 720, Trident Viscount), Kingdom of Libya Airlines (Caravelle), Kuwait Airways (Comet 4C, DC6B, Trident), MEA (Middle East Airlines/Air Liban) (Caravelle, Comet 4C, DC4, Viscount, VC10), Nigerian Airways/BOAC (Britannia), Persian Air Services (DC7C), Royal Air Marchoc (Caravelle), Saudi Arabian Airlines (Boeing 707/720, DC6B, DC9), South African Airways (Boeing 707, DC7B), Sudan Airways (Comet 4C, Viscount), Syrian Arab Airlines (Caravelle, DC6B), Trans Mediterranean Airways (DC4, DC6A/B), Tunis Air (DC4, Caravelle), United Arab Airlines/Misrair (Comet 4C, Viscount).

North and South American airlines included Aerolineas Argentinas (Boeing 707, Comet 4), Aeronaves de Mexico (DC8), Air Canada/Trans Canada (DC8/F, L1049C/E/H Super Constellation), Canadian Pacific (Britannia, DC6A/B, DC8), Continental Airlines (Boeing 707), Flying Tiger Line (L1049H Super Constellation), Interocean (USA) (DC4), Marchitime Central Airways (Canada) (DC4), Nordair (Canada) (L1049H Super Constellation), Panair do Brasil (DC6C, DC7C, DC8), Pan Am (Pan American World Airways) (Boeing 707, DC4, DC6A/B,DC7C/F, DC8), Saturn Airways (DC7C, DC8F), Seaboard and western/Seaboard World Airlines (Cl-44, Curtiss C46 Commando, R4D5/DC3, DC4, DC8F, L1049D/E/H Super Constellation), TWA (Trans World Airlines) (Boeing 707, DC4, L1049H Super Constellation, L1649A Starliner), Varig (Boeing 707, Convair 990, DC8), Viasa (DC8), Wardair (Canada) (Boeing707), World Airways (Boeing 707).

Asian/Far Eastern airlines included Air Ceylon (L1049G Super Constellation), Air Ceylon/BOAC (Comet 4), Air India (Boeing 707, L1049E/G Super Constellation), Ariana Afghan (DC6), JAL (Japan Airlines) (Convair 880, DC8/F), Pakistan International Airlines (L1049C/H Super Constellation, Boeing 707/720), Qantas (Boeing 707, L1049C/E/G/H Super Constellation).

D4. *Airlines to Heathrow 1970s*

British Airways was formed in 1972, but BOAC and BEA were not dissolved until 1974, so it would be several years before the old colours vanished. BOAC flew the VC10, Boeing 747 and Concorde while BEA flew the Comet 4B, Viscount, Vanguard, BAC111, Trident and Tristar. British Airways would take over the BEA and BOAC fleets as the main British airline at Heathrow. Cambrian flew BAC111s and Viscounts, while Northeast and BKS flew Viscounts and Tridents until British Airways took them all over. Charter airlines were based at Gatwick and Luton. British Midland Viscounts and DC9s operated at Heathrow, while other British airlines seen occasionally included Air Anglia (F27 Friendship), Air UK (F27 Friendship), and BIA (British Island Airways) (Herald).

European airlines included Aer Lingus (BAC 111, Boeing 720/707(Irish International/Aer Linte Eireann), Boeing 737, Boeing 747, Viscount), Aeroflot (Il-18, Il-62, Tu-104A/B, Tu-134, Tu154), Air Charter International (France) (Caravelle), Air France (A300, Boeing 707, Boeing 727, Boeing 747, Breguet Universel, Caravelle, Concorde, Fokker Friendship, Viscount), Air

France/Air Alsace (Fokker F28 Fellowship), Air Inter (A300, Caravelle, F27 Friendship, Viscount), Alitalia (Boeing 727, Boeing 747, Caravelle, DC8, DC9, DC10), Austrian Airlines (Boeing 707, Caravelle, DC9, Viscount), Balair (DC8, DC9, F27 Friendship), Balkan Bulgarian Airlines (Il-18, Tu-134, Tu-154), Braathens SAFE Air Transport (DC6B, F27 Friendship, F28 Fellowship), CSA (Czechoslovakian Airlines) (Il-18, Il-62, Tu-104A, Tu-124, Tu-134), Finnair (Caravelle, DC8, DC9), Iberia (Boeing 727, Caravelle, DC8/F, DC9, DC10), Icelandair (Boeing 727, DC6B, F27 Friendship), Interflug (East Germany) (Il-62, Tu-134), JAT (Jugoslovenski Aerotransport) (Boeing 707, Boeing 727, Caravelle, DC9, DC10), Kar Air (Finland) (DC6), KLM (Boeing 747, DC8/F, DC9, DC10), KLM Cityhopper (Fokker F28 Fellowship), Loftleidir (Cl-44, DC6B, DC8), LOT (Polskie Linie Lotnicze) (Il-18, Il-62, Tu-134), Lufthansa (A300, Boeing 707, Boeing 727, Boeing 737, Boeing 747, DC10), Luxair (Boeing 707, Boeing 737, Caravelle, F27 Friendship, Viscount,), Malev (Hungary) (Il-18, Il-62, Tu-154), Martinair (DC6A, DC8, DC9, DC10), NLM Cityhopper (Fokker F28 Fellowship), Olympic Airways (A300, Boeing 707/720, Boeing 727, Boeing 747), Panair Ostend (DC8), Rousseau Aviation (HS748), Sabena (Boeing 707, Boeing 727, Boeing 737, Boeing 747, Caravelle, DC6B, DC7C, DC10), SAS (Scandinavian Airlines System inc. Denmark, Norway and Sweden) (Boeing 747, Caravelle, DC8, DC9, DC10), Swissair (Caravelle, Convair 990, DC8, DC9, DC10), TAP (Transportes Aereos Portugueses) (Boeing 707, Boeing 727, Boeing 747, Caravelle), Tarom (Romania) (BAC111, Boeing 707, Il-18, Il-62, Tu-154), TAT (Touraine Air Transport) (France) (F27 Friendship, Fairchild FH227), THY (Turkish Airlines) (Boeing 707, Boeing 727, DC9, DC10, Viscount), Transavia (Holland) (Caravelle), Trans Europa (Spain) (DC4).

African and Middle Eastern airlines included Air Algérie (Boeing 727, Boeing 737, Caravelle), Air Malawi (VC10), Air Malta (Boeing 720), Air Mauritius (Boeing 707), Air Zaire (DC10), Alia Royal Jordanian Airlines (Boeing 707, Boeing 727, Boeing 747, Caravelle), Cyprus Airways (BAC 111, DC8, DC9, Trident), East African Airways (Comet 4, VC10), Egyptair (Boeing 707, Il-62, Tu-154), El Al (Boeing 707/720, Boeing 747), Ethiopian Airlines (Boeing 707/720), Ghana Airways (VC10), Gulf Air (Tristar, VC10), Iran Air (Boeing 707, Boeing 727, Boeing 747/SP), Iraqi Airways (Boeing 707, Boeing 747, Trident), Kenya Airways (Boeing 707), Kuwait Airways (Boeing 707, Boeing 747, Comet 4C, Trident), Libyan Arab Airlines (Boeing 727, Caravelle), MEA (Middle East Airlines/Air Liban) (Boeing 707/720, Boeing 747, Comet 4C, Convair 990), Nigeria Airways (Boeing 707, DC10), Royal Air Marchoc (Boeing 727, Boeing 747, Caravelle, L749 Constellation,), Saudi Arabian Airlines/Saudia (Boeing 707/720, Boeing 747, DC8, Tristar), South African Airways (Boeing 707, Boeing 747SP), Sudan Airways (Boeing 707, Comet 4C), Syrian Arab Airlines (Boeing 727, Boeing 747SP, Caravelle), Syrianair (Boeing 747), Trans Mediterranean Airways (Boeing 707, Boeing 747, CL44, DC6B), Tunis Air (Boeing 727, Caravelle, DC4), United Arab Airlines (Boeing 707, Comet 4C, Il-18, Il-62), Zambia Airways (Boeing 707, DC8).

North and South American airlines included Aerolineas Argentinas (Boeing 707, Boeing 747), Air Canada (Boeing 747, DC8/F, Tristar), Air Jamaica (DC8), BWIA (British West Indies) (Boeing 707), Canadian Pacific Air (Boeing 747, DC8,), Delta Airlines (Boeing 747, DC8), National Airlines (USA) (Boeing 747, DC8, DC10), Pan Am (Pan American World Airways) (Boeing 707, Boeing 727, Boeing 747/SP, DC8), Saturn Airways (DC8F), Seaboard World Airlines (Boeing 747, C46 Commando, DC8F, DC10), TWA (Trans World Airlines) (Boeing 707, Boeing 747, Tristar), United Airlines (Boeing 747), Varig (Boeing 707, Boeing 747, DC10), Viasa (DC8, DC10), World Airways (Boeing 707).

Asian/Far Eastern airlines included Air Ceylon (DC8), Air India (Boeing 707, Boeing 747), Air New Zealand (DC10), Ariana Afghan Airlines (DC10), Bangladesh Biman (Boeing 707), Garuda Indonesian Airlines (DC8, DC10), JAL (Japan Airlines) (Boeing 747, DC8/F), Malaysian Airline System (Boeing 707, DC10), PIA (Pakistan International Airlines) (Boeing

707/720, Boeing 747, DC10), Philippine Airlines (DC8), Qantas (Boeing 707, Boeing 747), Singapore Airlines (Boeing 707, Boeing 747), Thai Airways International (DC8, DC10).

D5. Airlines to Heathrow 1980s

British airlines at Heathrow were Air UK (BAe 146, F27 Friendship, Herald), British Airways (Boeing 737, Boeing 747, Boeing 757, Concorde, Trident, Tristar, VC10), British Midland (BAe ATP, Boeing 737, DC9, Viscount), Brymon (DHC6 Twin Otter, DHC7, Herald), Dan Air (BAC111), Manx Airlines (BAC111, BAe ATP, F27 Friendship, Saab 340, Viscount), Paramount Airlines (DC9), TNT (BAe 146).

European airlines included Aer Lingus (BAC111, Boeing 707, Boeing 737, Boeing 747 (Aer Linte)), Aeroflot (Il-62, Il-76, Il-86, Tu-134, Tu154), Air France (A300, A310, A320, Boeing 707, Boeing 727, Boeing 737, Boeing 747, Caravelle, Concorde), Air France/Air Alsace (Fokker F28 Fellowship), Air France/Air Littoral (ATR42, Embraer 120 Brasilia), Air France/Brit Air (Saab 340), Air Inter (A300, Caravelle, Mercure), Alitalia (A300, Boeing 727, Boeing 747, DC9, DC10, MD82), Austrian Airlines (A310, Boeing 707, DC9, MD81/82/87), Aviaco (DC8), Balair (DC8), Balkan Bulgarian Airlines (Il-18, Tu-134, Tu-154), BHT (Boqazici Airlines) (Turkey) (DC10), Birgenair (Turkey) (DC8), Cargolux (Boeing 747), Cargosur (Spain) (DC8), Cimber Air (ATR42), Corse Air International (France) (Caravelle), CSA (Czechoslovakian Airlines) (Il-62, Tu-134, Tu-154), DAT (Delta Air Transport) (Belgium) (Fairchild FH227, Fokker F28 Fellowship), DHL (A300), Euroair (HS/BAe 748), Europe Air Service (France) (Caravelle), Finnair (Caravelle, DC8, DC9, DC10, MD82), Iberia (A300, Boeing 727, Boeing 747, DC8, DC9, DC10), Icelandair (Boeing 727, Boeing 737, DC8), Interflug (East Germany) (A310, Il-18, Il-62, Tu-134, Tu-154), JAT (Jugoslovenski Aerotransport) (Boeing 707, Boeing 727, Boeing 737, DC9, DC10), Kar Air (Finland) (A300, DC6), KLM (A310, Boeing 747, DC8/F, DC9, DC10), Loftleidir (DC8), KLM Cityhopper (Fokker F28 Fellowship), KTHY (Turkish Cyprus) (A310), LOT (Polskie Linie Lotnicze) (Il-18, Il-62, Tu-134, Tu-154), LTU (Tristar), Lufthansa (A300, A310, A320, Boeing 707, Boeing 727, Boeing 737, Boeing 747, DC10), Luxair (A300, Boeing 737, Boeing 747, F27 Friendship), Malev (Hungary) (Boeing 737, Il-62, Tu-134, Tu-154), NLM Cityhopper (Fokker F28 Fellowship), Olympic Airways (A300, Boeing 707/720, Boeing 727, Boeing 737, Boeing 747), Sabena (A310, Boeing 707, Boeing 737, Boeing 747, DC10), SAS (Scandinavian Airlines System inc. Denmark, Norway and Sweden) (A300, Boeing 747, Boeing 767, DC8, DC9, DC10, MD81/82/87), Spantax (DC9), Swissair (A310, Boeing 747, DC8, DC9, DC10, MD11, MD80, Fokker 100), TAP (Transportes Aereos Portugueses) (A310, Boeing 707, Boeing 727, Boeing 737, Tristar), Tarom (Romania) (BAC111, Boeing 707, Il-18, Il-62, Tu-154), THY (Turkish Airlines) (A310, Boeing 707, Boeing 727, DC10, DC9), Trans Europa Airways (A300), White Airways (Portugal) (A310).

African and Middle Eastern airlines included Air Afrique (Boeing 727, DC10), Air Algérie (A310, Boeing 727, Boeing 737), Air Malawi (Boeing 747SP), Air Malta (Boeing 720, Boeing 737), Air Mauritius (Boeing 707, Boeing 747SP, Boeing 767), Air Seychelles (Boeing 707, Boeing 767), Air Zaire (DC8, DC10), Alia Royal Jordanian Airlines (A310, Boeing 707, Boeing 747, Tristar), Cyprus Airways (A300, A310, A320, BAC 111, Boeing 707), Dubai Air Wing (Boeing 747), Egyptair (A300, Boeing 707, Boeing 747, Boeing 767), El Al (Boeing 707/720, Boeing 747, Boeing 757, Boeing 767), Emirates Airlines (A310), Ethiopian Airlines (Boeing 707/720, Boeing 767), Ghana Airways (DC10, VC10), Gulf Air (Boeing 747, Boeing 767, Tristar, VC10), Iran Air (Boeing 707, Boeing 747/SP), Iraqi Airways (Boeing 707, Boeing 727, Boeing 747, Il-76), Kenya Airlines (A310, Boeing 707/720, DC8), Kuwait Airways (A300, A310, Boeing 707, Boeing 727, Boeing 747, Boeing 767), Libyan Arab Airlines (Boeing 707, Boeing 727), MEA (Middle East Airlines) (Boeing 707/720, Boeing 747), Nigeria Airways (A310, Boeing 707, Boeing 747, DC10), Royal Air Marchoc (Boeing

707, Boeing 727, Boeing 737, Boeing 747, Boeing 757), Saudia (Saudi Arabian Airlines) (A300, Boeing 747, DC8, Tristar), South African Airways (Boeing 747SP), Sudan Airways (Boeing 707), Syrian Arab Airlines (Boeing 727, Boeing 747SP, Il-76, Tu-134, Tu-154), Trans Mediterranean Airways (Boeing 707), Tunis Air (A300, Boeing 727, Boeing 737), Uganda Airlines (Boeing 707), Yemenia (Boeing 727), Zambia Airways (Boeing 707, DC10).

North and South American airlines included ACS Canada (DC8), Aerolineas Argentinas (Boeing 707, Boeing 747), Air Canada (Boeing 747, Boeing 767, DC8/F, Tristar), Air Jamaica (Boeing 747, DC8), Air Transat (Canada) (A310), BWIA (British West Indies) (Boeing 707, Tristar), CP Air/Canadian Airlines International (Boeing 747, DC8, DC10), Cubana (Il-62), Federal Express (Boeing 747, DC10), Flying Tiger Line (Boeing 747, DC8), Nationair (Canada) (DC8), National Airlines (USA) (DC10), Pan Am (Pan American World Airways) (A310, Boeing 707, Boeing 727, Boeing 737, Boeing 747/SP, DC10, Tristar), Seaboard World Airlines (Boeing 747, DC8), Trans Internatioanal (USA) (DC8), TWA (Trans World Airlines) (Boeing 707, Boeing 747SP, Boeing 767, Tristar), United Airlines (Boeing 747/SP), UPS (DC8), Varig (Boeing 707, Boeing 747, DC10), Viasa (DC10).

Asian/Far Eastern airlines included Air India (A310, Boeing 707, Boeing 747, DC8), Air Lanka (Boeing 707, Tristar), Air New Zealand (Boeing 747, DC10), Ariana Afghan Airlines (DC10), Biman Bangladesh (Boeing 707, DC10, Tristar), CAAC (Formosa) (Boeing 707, Boeing 747), Cathay Pacific (Boeing 747,), China Airlines (Boeing 747), Garuda Indonesian Airways (Boeing 747, DC10), JAL (Japan Airlines) (Boeing 747, DC8/F, DC10), Korean Air (Boeing 707, Boeing 747, DC10), Malaysian Airline System (Boeing 747, DC10), PIA (Pakistan International Airlines) (Boeing 707/720, Boeing 747, DC10), Qantas (Boeing 747), Royal Brunei Airlines (Boeing 757), Singapore Airlines (Boeing 747), Surinam Airways/KLM (DC8), Thai Airways International (Boeing 747, DC10), Tower Air (USA) (Boeing 747).

D6. Airlines to Heathrow 1990s
British airlines included Air UK (BAe 146, Fokker 50), Ambassador Airways (Boeing 757), British Airways (A320, BAe 146, Boeing 737, Boeing 747, Boeing 757, Boeing 767, Boeing 777, Concorde, DC10), British Airways/Base Airlines (Netherlands) (Embraer 120 Brasilia), British Airways Express/Brymon (DHC7, Bombardier/DHC8), British Airways/British Mediterranean (A320), British Midland (A320, A321, Boeing 737, BAe ATP, DHC7, DC9, Fokker 100, Saab 340), British World Airlines (Viscount), Brymon (DHC7), Caledonian Airways (DC10), EAL (European AviationLtd) (BAC111), GB Airways (Boeing 737), JEA (BAe 146), Manx Airlines (BAe ATP, BAe 146), Titan Airways (Boeing 737), Virgin Atlantic (Boeing 747, A340).

European airlines included Adria Airways (A320, DC9, MD81/82), Aer Lingus (A321, A330, Boeing 737, Boeing 747, Boeing 767), Aeroflot (A310, Boeing 737, Boeing 767, Boeing 777, Il-62, Il-86, Il-96, Tu-134, Tu-154), Air Baltic (BAe 146), Air Exel (Netherlands) (ATR42), Air France (A300, A310, A320, A321, Boeing 737), Air France /TAT (Fokker 100), Air Holland (Boeing 737), Air Inter (A320, Fokker 70/100), Air Liberté (France) (MD83), Air Plus Comet (Spain) (A310), Air Ukraine (Tu-134), Alitalia (A300, A320, A321, Boeing 747, Boeing 767, DC9, MD11, MD82), Austrian Airlines (A310, A321, Fokker 70, MD81/82/87), Aviaco (MD88), Azerbaijan Airlines (Tu-154), Balkan Bulgarian Airlines (A320, Boeing 737, Boeing 767, Il-18, Tu-154), BHT (Boqazici Airlincs) ((Turkey) (DC10), Blue Scandinavia (Sweden) (Tristar), Braathens (Boeing 737), Brit Air (ATR42), Condor (Boeing 737), Bulgaria Air (A320), Croatia Airlines (A319, A320, Boeing 737), Crossair (Bae 146, MD81/82/83, Saab 2000), CSA (Czechoslovakian Airlines) (Boeing 737, Il-62, Tu-134, Tu-154), DAT (Delta Air Transport) (BAe 146, Fokker F28 Fellowship), Denim Air (Fokker 50), DHL (Boeing 727), Diamond Sakha (France) (A310), Eurofly (Italy) (DC9), Finnair (A300, A321, Boeing

737, DC9, MD82), Georgian Airlines (Tu-154), Iberia (A300, A319, A320, A340, Boeing 727, Boeing 737, Boeing 757, Boeing 767, DC10, MD87/88), Icelandair (Boeing 737, Boeing 757), Interflug (East Germany) (Il-62, Tu-154), Istanbul Airlines (Boeing 737, Caravelle), JAT (Jugoslovenski Aerotransport) (Boeing 727, Boeing 737, DC9, DC10), Kazakhstan Airlines (Tu-154), KLM (A310, Boeing 737, Boeing 767), KLM Cityhopper (Fokker F28 Fellowship, Fokker 50, Saab 340), KTHY (Turkish Cyprus) (A310), Lithuanian Airlines (Boeing 737, Tu-134), LOT (Polskie Linie Lotnicze) (Boeing 737, Boeing 767, Tu-154), LTE International Airways (Spain) (Boeing 757), Lufthansa (A300, A310, A319, A320, A321, Boeing 737), Lufthansa Cityline (BAe 146), Luxair (Boeing 737, F27 Friendship, Fokker 50), Macedonian Airlines (Boeing 737), Malev (Hungary) (Boeing 737, Boeing 767, Tu-134, Tu-154), Martinair/ KLM (DC10), Meridiana (BAe 146), Moscow Airways (Il-62), Nordic east (Sweden) (Tristar), Olympic Airways (A300, A340, Boeing 737), Privatair (Swiss) (Boeing 757), Pulkovo Aviation Enterprise (Tu-134, Tu154), Russian State Transport Co (Il-62), Sabena (Boeing 737), SAS (Scandinavian Airlines System inc. Denmark, Norway and Sweden) (Boeing 737, Boeing 767, DC9, MD81/82/87, MD90), Swissair (A310, A320, A321, A330, MD11), Tajikistan Airways (Tristar, Tu-154), TAP (Transportes Aereos Portugueses) (A310, A319, A340, Boeing 727, Boeing 737), Tarom (Romania) (A310, Boeing 737, Il-62, Tu154),THY (Turkish Airlines) (A310, A340, Boeing 727), Transaero (Boeing 737, Boeing 757), Turkmenistan Airways (Boeing 757), Uzbekistan Airways (A310, Boeing 767, Il-62), Venus Airlines (Greece) (Boeing 757), Viva Air (Boeing 737, DC9).

African and Middle Eastern airlines included Affretair (Zimbabwe) (DC8), Air Algérie (A310, Boeing 727, Boeing 737, Boeing 767), Air Malta (A320, Boeing 727, Boeing 737), Air Mauritius (A340, Boeing 747SP, Boeing 767), Air Namibia (Boeing 747SP), Air Tanzania (Boeing 767), Alyemen (A310), Bellview Airlines (Nigeria) (A300), Cyprus Airways (A310), Dubai Air Wing (Boeing 747SP), Egyptair (A300, A320, A321, A340, Boeing 747, Boeing 767, Boeing 777), El Al (Boeing 747, Boeing 757, Boeing 767), Emirates Airlines (A300, A310, Boeing 777), Ethiopian Airlines (Boeing 757, Boeing 767), Ghana Airways (DC10), Gulf Air (A330, A340, Boeing 767, Tristar), Iran Air (Boeing 747SP), Iraqi Airways (Boeing 727), Kenya Airlines (A310, Boeing 757, DC8), Kuwait Airways (A300, A310, A340, Boeing 767, Boeing 777, DC8), MEA (Middle East Airlines) (A310, Boeing 747), Midwest Airlines (Egypt) (A310), MK Airlines (Ghana) (DC8), Nigeria Airways (A310, Boeing 747, DC10), Qatar Airways (A300, A340), Royal Air Marchoc (Boeing 737, Boeing 747, Boeing 757), Royal Jordanian Airlines (Boeing 707, A310, Tristar), Saudia (Saudi Arabian Airlines) (A300, Boeing 727, Boeing 747, Boeing 777, MD11, Tristar), South African Airways (Boeing 747SP, Boeing 767), Sudan Airways (A310), Syrianair (Boeing 727, Boeing 747SP, Tu-134), Trans Mediterranean Airways (Boeing 707), Tunis Air (A320, Boeing 737, Tristar), Yemenia (Boeing 727), Zambia Airways (Boeing 757, DC8, DC10).

North and South American airlines included Aerolineas Argentinas (Boeing 747), Air Canada (A340, Boeing 747, Boeing 767), Air Jamaica (A310), Air Transat (Canada) (Boeing 757, Tristar), Air Transport International (USA) (DC8), American Airlines (A300, Boeing 747SP, Boeing 767, Boeing 777, DC10, MD11), ATA (American Transair) (Boeing 727, Tristar), Avianca (Boeing 767), BWIA (British West Indies) (Tristar), Canadian Airlines International (Boeing 767, DC10), Caribjet (Antigua) (Tristar), DHL (DC8), Evergreen (Boeing 747), Federal Express (DC10), Pan Am (Pan American World Airways) (Boeing 727, Boeing 747), Skyjet (Antigua) (DC10), Tower Air (USA) (Boeing 747), TWA (Trans World Airlines) (Boeing 747, Boeing 767), United Airlines (Boeing 747/SP, Boeing 767, Boeing 777), Varig (Boeing 747, Boeing 767, DC10, MD11), Viasa (DC10).

Asian/Far Eastern airlines included Air China (Boeing 747SP), Air Hong Kong (Boeing 747), Air India (A310, Boeing 747, Tristar), Air Lanka (A340, Tristar), Air New Zealand (Boeing 747), All Nippon Airways (Boeing 747), Biman Bangladesh (DC10), Cathay Pacific

(Boeing 747), Eva Air (Boeing 747, MD11), JAL (Japan Airlines) (Boeing 747, MD11), Korean Air (Boeing 747), Malaysian Airline System (Boeing 747), Philippine Airlines (DC10), PIA (Pakistan International Airlines) (Boeing 747), Qantas (Boeing 747), Royal Brunei Airlines (Boeing 767), Singapore Airlines (Boeing 747), Thai Airways International (Boeing 747), Vietnam Airlines (Boeing 767).

D7. Airlines to Heathrow 2000s
British airlines include Air 2000 (A320), Astraeus (Boeing 757), British Airways (A318, A319, A320, BAe 146, Boeing 737, Boeing 747, Boeing 757, Boeing 767, Boeing 777, Concorde), British Airways/Base Airlines (Netherlands) (Embraer 120 Brasilia), British Airways/British Mediterranean (A320, A321), British Airways/GB Airways (A320, A321), British Midland (A319, A320, A321, A330, Boeing 737, Boeing 757, Boeing 767, EMB145, Fokker 100), Eastern Airways (Jetstream 31/41), Flyglobespan (Boeing 767), JEA (Jersey European)/Flybe/British European (BAe 146), Manx Airlines (BAe 146), Titan Airways (BAe 146, Boeing 737, Boeing 757, Boeing 767), TNT (BAe 146, Boeing 737), Virgin Atlantic (Boeing 747, Boeing 777, A340).

European airlines include Adria Airways (A320), Aegean Airlines (A320, A321), Aer Lingus (A320, A321, A330, BAe 146, Boeing 737), Aeroflot (A310, A319, A320, A321, A330, Boeing 737, Boeing 767, Boeing 777, Il-86, Il-96), Air Atlanta Icelandis (Boeing 747), Air Baltic (Boeing 737), Air Exel (Netherlands) (ATR42), Air France (A318, A319, A320, A321, A380, Boeing 737), Air France/Airlinair (ATR72), Air France/Brit Air (CRJ), Air France/Cityjet (BAe 146), Air France/Flybe-British European (BAe 146), Air France Regional (ERJ190), Air France /TAT (Fokker 100), Air Liberté (France) (MD83), Air Luxor (Portugal) (A320, Tristar), Air One (A320), Air Plus Comet (Spain) (A310), Air Via Bulgarian Airlines (A320), Airzena Georgian Airlines (Il-62), Alitalia (A319, A320, A321, MD82), Austrian Airlines (A319, A320, A321, Boeing 737, Fokker 70, MD81/82/87), Austrian Arrows/Tyrolean Airways (Fokker 70/100), Azerbaijan Airlines (A319, Boeing 757), Azzura Air (Italy) (BAe 146), Balkan Bulgarian Airlines (Boeing 737, Tu-154), Blue One (Finland) (MD90), Braathens (Boeing 737), Brit Air (ATR42), Brussels Airlines (A319, BAe 146, Boeing 737), Bulgaria Air (A319, A320, Boeing 737), Cimber Air (CRJ), Citybird (Belgium) (Boeing 767), Click Air (Spain) (A320), Contactair/Lufthansa Regional (Fokker 100), Croatia Airlines (A319, A320), Crossair (Bae 146, MD81/82/83, Saab 2000), Croatia Airlines (BAe 146), CSA (Czechoslovakian Airlines) (A310, A319, A320, Boeing 737), DAT (Delta Air Transport) (BAe 146), Denim Air (Fokker 50), Deutsche BA (Boeing 737), DHL (A300, Boeing 727, Boeing 757), Euro Atlantic Airways (Portugal) (Boeing 757, Boeing 767, Boeing 777, Tristar), Eurocypria (Boeing 737), Eurowings (BAe 146), Farnair (Swiss) (ATR42), Finnair (A319, A320, A321, A340, MD80), Gainjet Aviation (Greece) (Boeing 757), Gir Jet (Spain) (Boeing 757), Hellas Jet (Greece) (A320), Hemus Air (BAe 146, Boeing 737), Iberia (A300, A319, A320, A321, A340, Boeing 757, MD87/88), Icelandair (Boeing 757), Istanbul Airways (Boeing 737), JAT (Jugoslovenski Aerotransport) (Boeing 727, Boeing 737), Khalifa Air (France) (A310), KLM (A330, Boeing 737, Boeing 767, MD11), KLM Cityhopper (ERJ195, Fokker 50, Fokker 70/100), KLM Exel (ATR42, ATR72), KTHY (Turkish Cyprus) (A310, A320, A321, Boeing 737), Lauda Air (Boeing 737, Boeing 767, CRJ), Loftleidir Icelandic (Boeing 757), LOT (Polskie Linie Lotnicze) (Boeing 737, Boeing 767, ERJ170, ERJ195), Lufthansa (A300, A310, A319, A320, A321, Boeing 737, Fokker 100), Lufthansa Cityline (BAe 146, CRJ), Lufthansa Regional /Eurowings (ATR42, CRJ), Lufthansa Regional/Augustsburg Airways (ERJ195), Luxair (Boeing 737, Bombardier/DHC8EMB135, EMB145), Malev (Hungary) (Boeing 737, Boeing 767, Fokker 100), Novair (Sweden) (A330), Olympic Airways (A300, A320, A340, Boeing 737), Portugalia (Fokker 100), Privatair (Swiss) (Boeing 757, Boeing 767), Pulkovo Airways (Boeing 737, Il-86, Tu-134, Tu-154), Pullmantur Air (Spain) (Boeing 747), Rossiya

Russian Airlines (A319, Boeing 737, Tu-154), Russian State Transport Co (Il-62, Il-96), SAS (Scandinavian Airlines System inc. Denmark, Norway and Sweden) (A319, A321, A330, A340, Boeing 737, MD81/82/87, MD90), Snowflake/SAS (MD82), Sobelair (Boeing 737), Swissair (A319, A320, A321, MD11), Swiss European (BAe 146), Swiss International Airlines (A319, A320, A321, A330, A340, BAe 146, MD83, MD11), TAP (Transportes Aereos Portugueses) (A310, A319, A320, A321, A330, A340), Tarom (Romania) (A310, A318, Boeing 737), THY (Turkish Airlines) (A310, A320, A321, A330, A340, Boeing 737, Boeing 777), Transaero (Boeing 737, Boeing 747, Boeing 767, Boeing 777), Turkmenistan Airways (Boeing 757), Tyrolean Airlines (CRJ, Bombardier/DHC8, Fokker 70), Ukraine Air Enterprise (Il-62), Ukraine International Airlines (Boeing 737), Uzbekistan Airways (A310, Boeing 757, Boeing 767), Vueling Airlines (Spain) (A319, A320), White Airways (Portugal) (A310, A319,), Yes-Linha Aereas Charter (Portugal) (Tristar).

African and Middle East airlines include Afriqiyah Airways (Tunisia) (A320), Air Algérie (A310, A330, Boeing 737, Boeing 767), Air Malta (A319, A320, Boeing 737), Air Mauritius (A340), Air Namibia (Boeing 747), Air Seychelles (Boeing 767), AMC Airlines (Egypt) (A300, A310), Arik Air (A330, A340, Boeing 737), Arkia (Boeing 757), Bellview Airlines (Nigeria) (Boeing 767), Comlux Malta (A319), Cyprus Airways (A310, A319, A320, A330), DAS Air Cargo (DC10), Dubai Air Wing (Boeing 747), east African Airlines (Boeing 767), Egyptair (A300, A320, A330, A340, Boeing 737, Boeing 777), El Al (Boeing 747, Boeing 767, Boeing 777), Emirates Airlines (A330, A380, Boeing 777), Ethiopian Airlines (Boeing 737, Boeing 757, Boeing 767), Etihad Airways (A330, A340, Boeing 777), Eurocypria Airlines (A320), Euro Mediterranean (Egypt) (Boeing 757), Ghana Airways (DC10), Gulf Air (A330, A340, Boeing 767, Boeing 777), Iran Air (A300, A310, Boeing 747), Kenya Airways (A310, Boeing 767, Boeing 777), Kuwait Airways (A300, A310, A340, Boeing 747, Boeing 777), Libyan Arab Airlines (A300, A320, Boeing 727, CRJ), Lotus Air (Egypt) (A319), MEA (Middle East Airlines) (A300, A310, A320, A321, A330), Midwest Airlines (Egypt) (A310), Nigeria Airways (Boeing 747, Boeing 767), Nouvelair (Tunis) (A320), Oman Air (A310, A330), Qatar Airways (A300, A310, A320, A330, A340, Boeing 777), Royal Air Marchoc (A321, Boeing 737, Boeing 757, Boeing 767), Royal Jordanian Airlines (A310, A320, A321, A330, A340), Saudi Arabian Airlines (A320, Boeing 747, Boeing 777, MD90), Skywings Airlines (Egypt) (Boeing 757), South African Airways (A330, A340, Boeing 747), Starair (Sierra Leone) (Tristar), Sudan Airways (A300, A310), Sun d'Or Airlines (Israel) (Boeing 757), Syrian Arab Airlines (A320), Syrionair (Boeing 747SP), Tunis Air (A300, A319, A320, Boeing 737), Yemenia (A310, A330, Boeing 737, Boeing 747SP).

North and south American airlines include Air Astana (Aruba) (Boeing 757, Boeing 767), Air Canada (A319, A330, A340, Boeing 747, Boeing 767, Boeing 777), Air Jamaica (A340), Air Transat (Canada) (A310), American Airlines (A300, Boeing 757, Boeing 767, Boeing 777), ATA (American Transair) (Tristar), BWIA (British West Indies) (A340, Tristar), Canadian Airlines International (Boeing 767), Caribbean Airlines (A340), Continental Airlines (Boeing 757, Boeing 767, Boeing 777), Delta Airlines (A330, Boeing 757, Boeing 767, Boeing 777), Kalitta Air (USA) (Boeing 747), Northwest Orient (A330), TAM Linha Aereas (Brasil) (A330, Boeing 777), United Airlines (Boeing 747/SP, Boeing 757, Boeing 767, Boeing 777), US Airways (A330, Boeing 757, Boeing 767), Varig (Boeing 767, Boeing 777, DC10, MD11), World Airways (DC10, MD11).

Asian/Far Eastern airlines include Air China (A330, A340, Boeing 747, Boeing 767), Air India (A330, Boeing 747, Boeing 767, Boeing 777), Air Lanka (A340), Air New Zealand (Boeing 747, Boeing 777), Air Sahara (India) (Boeing 767), All Nippon Airways (Boeing 747, Boeing 777), Asiana Airlines (Korea) (Boeing 747, Boeing 777), Biman Bangladesh (A310, Boeing 777, DC10), Cathay Pacific (A340, Boeing 747, Boeing 777), China Airlines (A330, A340), China Eastern Airlines (A330, A340), Eva Air (Boeing 747, Boeing 777,

MD11), JAL (Japan Air Lines) (Boeing 747, Boeing 777, MD11), Jet Airways (India) (A330, A340, Boeing 777), Kingfisher Airlines (India) (A330), Korean Air (Boeing 747, Boeing 777), Malaysian Airline System (Boeing 747), PIA (Pakistan International Airlines) (A310, Boeing 747, Boeing 777), Qantas (A380, Boeing 747), Royal Brunei Airlines (Boeing 767, Boeing 777), Singapore Airlines (A380, Boeing 747, Boeing 777), Sri Lankan Airlines (A330, A340), Thai Airways (A340, Boeing 747), Vietnam Airlines (Boeing 777).